I try to unknow my person every day. I can give what I never received. I don't try to get over it. I can do things differently. I rest. I find the beginnings in endings. I reject anything that tells me to fear myself. I trust my body. I tell myself better stories.

We Can Do Hard Things

The Dial Press
An imprint of Random House
A division of Penguin Random House LLC
1745 Broadway, New York, NY 10019
randomhousebooks.com
penguinrandomhouse.com

Much of the dialogue in this book is based on conversations, which have been edited for clarity, context, and concision. The approaches discussed in this book reflect the authors' and contributors' experiences and opinions only; they are not intended as professional recommendations and should not be construed as a substitute for professional advice. Please consult your doctor or other qualified healthcare provider with any questions or concerns you may have regarding any medical or mental health conditions or treatment.

Hardback ISBN 978-0-593-97764-4 | Ebook ISBN 978-0-593-97766-8

Printed in the United States of America on acid-free paper.

1st Printing

FIRST EDITION

The authorized representative in the EU for product safety and compliance is Penguin Random House Ireland, Morrison Chambers, 32 Nassau Street, Dublin D02 YH68, Ireland. https://eu-contact.penguin.ie

BOOK DESIGN
Art direction, cover design, illustration, and interior design
by Valerie Gnaedig and Annie Lenon
Word illustrations by Glennon Doyle

For our children,

Alice Amma Bobby Chase Cosmo
Elliott Frieda Senna Theodore Tish:

We Can Do Hard Things

ANSWERS TO LIFE'S 20 QUESTIONS

Glennon   Abby   Amanda
Doyle   Wambach   Doyle

AND 118 WAYFINDERS

LIFE'S 20 QUESTIONS

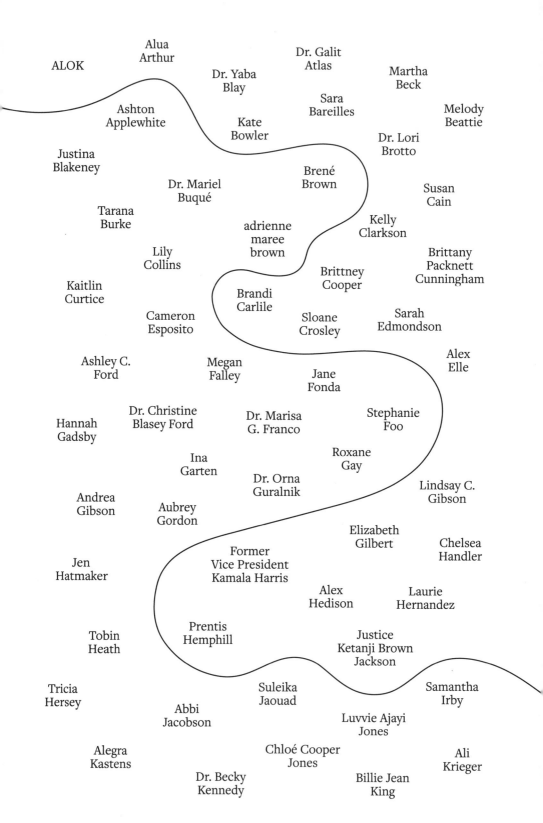

ALOK

Alua
Arthur

Dr. Galit
Atlas

Dr. Yaba
Blay

Martha
Beck

Sara
Bareilles

Ashton
Applewhite

Melody
Beattie

Kate
Bowler

Dr. Lori
Brotto

Justina
Blakeney

Brené
Brown

Dr. Mariel
Buqué

Susan
Cain

Tarana
Burke

Kelly
Clarkson

adrienne
maree
brown

Lily
Collins

Brittany
Packnett
Cunningham

Brittney
Cooper

Kaitlin
Curtice

Brandi
Carlile

Cameron
Esposito

Sloane
Crosley

Sarah
Edmondson

Ashley C.
Ford

Megan
Falley

Jane
Fonda

Alex
Elle

Hannah
Gadsby

Dr. Christine
Blasey Ford

Dr. Marisa
G. Franco

Stephanie
Foo

Ina
Garten

Roxane
Gay

Andrea
Gibson

Dr. Orna
Guralnik

Lindsay C.
Gibson

Aubrey
Gordon

Elizabeth
Gilbert

Chelsea
Handler

Jen
Hatmaker

Former
Vice President
Kamala Harris

Alex
Hedison

Laurie
Hernandez

Tobin
Heath

Prentis
Hemphill

Justice
Ketanji Brown
Jackson

Tricia
Hersey

Suleika
Jaouad

Samantha
Irby

Abbi
Jacobson

Luvvie Ajayi
Jones

Alegra
Kastens

Chloé Cooper
Jones

Ali
Krieger

Dr. Becky
Kennedy

Billie Jean
King

x

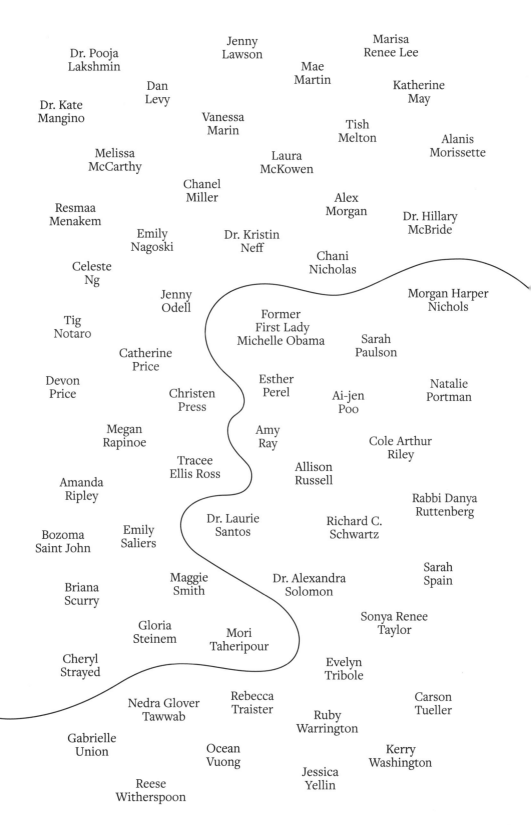

Dr. Pooja Lakshmin

Jenny Lawson

Marisa Renee Lee

Mae Martin

Dan Levy

Katherine May

Dr. Kate Mangino

Vanessa Marin

Tish Melton

Melissa McCarthy

Laura McKowen

Alanis Morissette

Chanel Miller

Alex Morgan

Resmaa Menakem

Dr. Hillary McBride

Emily Nagoski

Dr. Kristin Neff

Chani Nicholas

Celeste Ng

Jenny Odell

Morgan Harper Nichols

Tig Notaro

Former First Lady Michelle Obama

Sarah Paulson

Catherine Price

Devon Price

Christen Press

Esther Perel

Ai-jen Poo

Natalie Portman

Megan Rapinoe

Amy Ray

Cole Arthur Riley

Tracee Ellis Ross

Allison Russell

Amanda Ripley

Rabbi Danya Ruttenberg

Bozoma Saint John

Emily Saliers

Dr. Laurie Santos

Richard C. Schwartz

Briana Scurry

Maggie Smith

Dr. Alexandra Solomon

Sarah Spain

Gloria Steinem

Mori Taheripour

Sonya Renee Taylor

Cheryl Strayed

Evelyn Tribole

Nedra Glover Tawwab

Rebecca Traister

Carson Tueller

Ruby Warrington

Gabrielle Union

Ocean Vuong

Kerry Washington

Jessica Yellin

Reese Witherspoon

Every day I spiral around the same questions: *Why am I like this? How do I figure out what I want? How do I know what to do? Why can't I be happy? Am I doing this right?*

Each morning, I've somehow forgotten all the freaking answers. Another day arrives along with the inevitable, entirely predictable questions of being human and I swirl around them like I'm brand new here. I blink and think: *Wait. Hold on. I feel like I knew that one. Didn't I learn that answer at some point?*

Yes, I did. I've been a human among humans at this earth school for almost a half century. I survived childhood and adolescence, for God's sake. I've recovered from addiction after addiction. I've built a marriage, dismantled it, and built a new one. I've raised three entire people who have grown up and left me, which I'm told is the best-case scenario (even though it feels like a stupid heart-shattering system to me). I've lost friends and animals and versions of myself I couldn't live without. I've written four whole books that people swear to me helped *them* find their way. Like you—like everyone who has survived as much as we've survived—*I have certainly learned stuff.* So why do I wake up every morning having forgotten everything I know?

My sister, Amanda, and my wife, Abby, are the people I call first when I'm drowning, because they are my life preservers. Recently, all within a year, I was diagnosed with anorexia, Amanda was diagnosed with breast cancer, and Abby lost her beloved brother. We felt so alone and so lost. Our spiraling questions became: *What is the point? How do we go on? How do we feel better right now?* At first, our conversations fell strangely silent. For the first time, we were all drowning at the same time. So, we started turning outward for life rafts, toward the only thing that's ever saved us: deep, honest conversations with wise, kind, brave people.

On our podcast, on phone calls, on long early morning emails and late-night frantic texts with each other and our friends, we asked: *Do you spiral around these questions all day, too? Do you have any answers?*

Two things became thrillingly clear:

1. We are not alone: It seems that everyone swirls around the same 20 human questions.
2. We do not have to stay lost: There are answers.

As we wrote down every life-saving answer we discovered during those conversations, we realized we were creating our own personal survival guide. Now we had a place to turn to when we woke up, yet again, feeling clueless, alone, and afraid. A place to go when we needed language for how we felt. A place of clarity in the chaos. A place not to learn—but to remember—what we already knew. A place to save ourselves. Together, we built one huge locker of life preservers. Eventually, one of us said: *Wait, why are we keeping this to ourselves? What better thing could we give to the world than this?* That's how this book was born.

Halfway through this book's creation, I decided to stop the presses. Abby was still deep in grief, I was in a new level of anorexia recovery hell, and Amanda was facing a double mastectomy. I told my colleague, Valerie: *I know we can do hard things, but this is just too hard. We have to stop.*

A few hours later, Valerie's reply arrived: *I understand. If you ever want to begin again, know this: This book is it. This is the life guide I want to hand to my daughter. To help her make sense of her life, her people, and her world. To remind her that she already has all the wisdom she needs inside of her. To help make this hard, beautiful life just a little bit easier for her. This book is the life preserver I want to leave her with so she remembers she can always save herself. Because that is what this book does for me.*

We began again, even though life was hard. We began again *because* life is hard. Our hope is that this book makes yours just a little bit easier.

We Can Do Hard Things.

glennon — Abby Amanda

One

Why am I like this?

I am a great mystery to me. Understanding why I do the things I do is important to me because the things I do affect the people I love. So I don't want to live on autopilot. I want to choose carefully which patterns to pass on. I want to break cycles. I want to live with freedom and agency and intentionality. This means I have to look under my own hood and tinker with and examine my programming.

Responsible adulthood is being both the engine and the mechanic.

I'm the mystery and the detective.

Tricky.

GLENNON

As soon as we're born, we enter into cultural and familial systems that say: *You cannot trust your appetite. You cannot trust your desire. You cannot trust yourself. Since you cannot trust yourself, here's a list of rules for you to follow instead.*

So we lost vital parts of ourselves. We *had* to lose those parts of ourselves to survive in families, institutions, and societies that denied us access to our history, power, and innate wisdom.

We've been losing and losing and losing parts of ourselves for our entire lives. So of course we are not fully present now. Of course we are not able to be present in an authentic, whole way. The very path that we've taken to survive leaves us here, fractured.

AMANDA

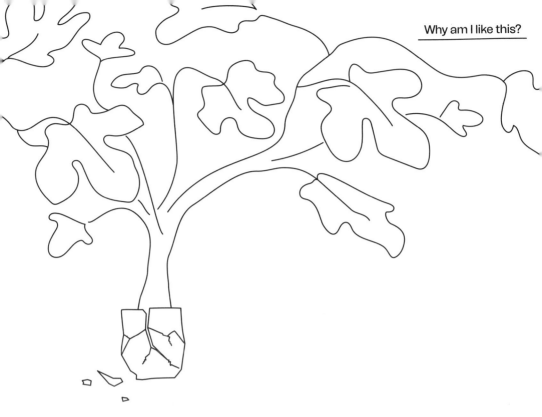

I am aware now, more than ever, of the boxes I've placed myself into—the ones that were introduced to me by my family and by my culture. I consciously stepped into them and closed the lid in order to stay safe, in order to be liked, in order to fit in. Now I'm pushing the boundaries I've set for myself so that I can settle into a new acceptance of who I am. It's almost like I'm stuck in a flowerpot and I'm expanding while it's breaking. It's breaking. But in order to do that, in order to break out of my molds, I need to understand what they are and why they were made in the first place.

ALEX HEDISON

I'm like this because

I carry the patterns of my family of origin.

The moment we're born, we look up at our caretakers. We notice—before we even have language—what makes them smile and come close, what makes them frown and turn away. We notice—and we keep noticing—and then we adapt to survive. We magnify the parts of ourselves that earn us love and protection, and we hide what doesn't. We know instinctively that we need our caretakers to survive—so we become what we believe they want us to be.

And then we grow up and one day we look in the mirror and wonder: *Why am I still hiding so much of myself? Have I ever even met my real self?*

GLENNON

I became an athlete to get my mother's love.
All I really wanted was love, full acceptance, and attention from my mom. But because I had this deep knowing about my gayness, I felt like my mom would never accept this part of me. So I developed an athlete persona to make up for my gayness. It worked! I was celebrated. But that kind of affirmation was something I could never really latch on to. I'd come home from soccer and my family would be so amazed at all my goals. But I always felt like: What if I stop scoring goals? Will they be able to love what's left?

ABBY

I became more attuned to others' emotions than my own.
In my family, there was one person whose emotional fluctuations dictated everyone's experience. This dynamic teaches a child to be highly attuned and vigilant to others' emotions to keep the peace. I did that my entire life and only recently learned that it's an actual thing. It's called emotional monitoring, and it involves living your life as a fixer in hyperactive awareness of everyone else's experience. You're so busy keeping everyone comfortable that you completely lose any boundary between everybody else's experience of a situation and your own. And because of that, you actually do not have your own experience. Their experience *is* your experience.

AMANDA

I became extreme to be seen.
I used to speak in extremes. I didn't just dislike someone, I hated them. I wasn't just a little bit bored, I was going to die of boredom. It's interesting to consider what kind of people feel the need to express themselves so dramatically. Maybe some of us learn early that our needs won't be met unless we become extreme about them.

GLENNON

I'm like this because
I learned what earned me love and what didn't.

I became a reflection of my dad's values.

Growing up, my dad was making films like *Grapes of Wrath* and *Twelve Angry Men*, with strong, brave characters who stuck up for the underdogs. And I always knew those were the roles that he loved, representing the values that he respected. I wasn't conscious of it then, but I think seeing the roles he loved was like fertilizer that was being sprinkled on my soul. When I learned the truth of the Vietnam War, that fertilizer allowed the sprouts of my activism to start growing.

JANE FONDA

I became a comedian to make my mom laugh.

It's so hard to tell what part of our personality is a coping mechanism that was formed years ago and what's our actual personality. Like, who would I have been if I'd grown up on a beach alone? I don't know that I would've done comedy. I'm pretty introverted. I think we're all just trying to cheer up our moms.

MAE MARTIN

Attachment Styles

WITH DR. ALEXANDRA SOLOMON

The way we show up in our relationships today is a reflection of the way our caregivers showed up for us. Their ability to meet, or failure to meet, our earliest needs—to feel safe and secure, to be seen and validated—leads us to form an "attachment style." Our attachment style is formed in early childhood—before we are two years old!—and follows us into adulthood. Learning about attachment helps us understand why we are the way we are, heal from insecurities, end painful relationship patterns, and move toward more trusting bonds. Although attachment has a pretty profound effect on how we *do* relationships, our attachment style is not our destiny; we can move from insecure to secure attachment.

① Secure Attachment

Secure attachment is what we're all working toward: feeling safe, confident, and trusting in our relationships. I might have a secure attachment style if I have high self-esteem and can communicate my needs. I feel comfortable being emotionally close to my partner. I'm confident doing my thing out in the world because I trust that there's someone at home who gets me and believes in me.

If I have a secure attachment style, my caregivers were attuned to my emotional and physical needs and responded with care. They encouraged me to explore the world and gave me room to grow. Their words and actions said: *You are worthy. You are safe. You matter.* Even if I didn't form a secure attachment in childhood, I can have secure attachment later in life by cultivating healthy and trusting relationships.

② Anxious Attachment

I have a hard time trusting my partner, even if they've proven themself to be trustworthy. I need constant reassurance that they won't leave me, and I am terrified of rejection or abandonment. I feel like my worth depends on my partner's validation. My anxious attachment formed because my caregivers were inconsistent in meeting my physical and emotional needs, which made me constantly question our connection. My caregivers also may have turned to me to satisfy their emotional cravings, rather than providing me with the consistent love and support I needed to grow.

My healing involves learning to soothe myself, affirm my worth, and give myself the affirmation I am craving so that my relationships feel more reciprocal and less frantic.

*I'm like this because **I learned what earned me love and what didn't.***

ABBY: Glennon and I could not be more opposite in our attachment styles. I'm anxious, she's avoidant. So when we get in an argument, I always jump to: *Am I loved? Don't leave me!* I'm desperate for comfort.

GLENNON: And I immediately turn to ice. The second there's a disconnect between us, I can actually feel my walls go up. Then Abby's trapped outside my wall. I'm trapped inside my wall. And we're both alone.

③ Avoidant Attachment

I might have an avoidant attachment style if people say I'm self-sufficient. Even though I may have high self-esteem, I struggle to emotionally connect with partners. I tend to push people away when they get too close. I often think: *I don't need them. I don't need anyone.* I developed an avoidant attachment style because my caregivers were emotionally distant. When I reached out for emotional connection, I may have been neglected, shamed, or punished. To cope with my caregivers' distance, I learned not to depend on anyone but myself.

My healing involves letting myself get close to people, trusting that I won't be smothered by them, and knowing that someone's desire to be near me does not mean they want to, or will be able to, control me.

④ Disorganized Attachment

If I have a disorganized attachment style, I feel conflicted about loving relationships. I desperately want them, but I'm terrified of letting people in. Instead of clinging to partners or pushing them away, I do both. I seek out emotional closeness and then lash out or push people away because I'm intensely afraid of being hurt. Disorganized attachment often stems from childhood abuse. As a child, I craved my caregivers' love and nourishment, but they were also a source of fear.

My healing involves recognizing that my strong emotional reactions, like anger, reflect that I feel scared or confused and then taking steps to calm myself. My ability to practice self-awareness and self-compassion will help me feel sturdier on the inside and create more consistency in my relationships.

Attraction in adulthood is an activation of our earliest attachment patterns. That's all attraction is. Our body is saying: *I know how to be the corresponding puzzle piece to this person.*

Think about that. Going back to the years before age three, how many times do you think a kid had to work hard to get attention, had to perform, had to be a certain way? I don't know, a million? A million moments. Well, that's a very practiced circuit. So as an adult when the body is like: *Wait, I think I see this pattern again,* it makes sense why the body would be attracted to that.

DR. BECKY KENNEDY

*I'm like this because **I learned what earned me love and what didn't.***

In large families like mine, it's hard for each kid to get the attention they need from their parents. I learned that I had to chase love to get it. So when I sought out relationships as an adult, I was attracted to people who were a little aloof and even a little bit mean. I recognized the feeling of the chase as love.

I thought: *That relationship feels like home to me.*

When I met Glennon, she was the polar opposite. She was all there, all open, all love already. When I felt that, I didn't get it, because it was new. There was probably a little grief inside of me about it, actually. My whole life, I was trying to win over people's affection to somehow prove that I was worthy and good enough. It was so tiring and scary. When Glennon loved me and wanted me as I was, I had to give up on the chase of winning her over. I've had to rewire my brain to say: *Oh, this is real love. Her love for me is done, and I have to just trust it instead of chasing or forcing or controlling it.*

It's scary in a different way. But this is the way I want to be.

ABBY

In a perfect world, my family would have embraced and nurtured my full self. But all families face stress. To adapt to that stress, we become rigid and one-dimensional. We learn to play characters to restore status quo to the family dynamic. But playing our roles comes at a cost. We aren't able to develop into our full, real selves. Now I'm waking up and realizing that my family role isn't my actual personality; it's just the script I was given. The good news is that every role has a particular hero's journey, and if we embark upon it, we learn to break character, become fully human, and begin to bring our full self to our relationships, work, and world.

GLENNON

I'm like this because

I played a role in my family to keep the peace.

I performed to prove everything was okay.

By performing, accomplishing, and excelling while growing up, I was trying to be the "easy one." I was trying to say: *Don't worry about me. I'm fine. Everything's fine over here. Our family is fine!* I was doing the work of proving that as a family, we were okay, we could be proud, even. And along the line, I internalized that the way to prove to the world and to myself that I am okay is by performing, accomplishing, and excelling. But I don't want to have to excel to be okay anymore. I want to be a fully human person. I don't want to have to perform to receive love and acceptance, and I don't want the people I love to have to perform to receive my love and acceptance.

AMANDA

I became the hero.

My athleticism allowed me to become, in some ways, the hero of my family—the shiny, powerful, exciting one. But I despised that part of myself, because I knew it wasn't real enough. I was idolized but never known. One of my deepest wounds is the fear of not being known. And I wasn't.

ABBY

I thought I had to stay sick.

The story I've had about myself forever is: *I am the sick one.* My role was to stay sick, to stay damaged. My job was to embody inside me the unhealth of the family. It didn't matter how that damage was manifesting; it could be anxiety, depression, bulimia, alcoholism. The important thing was that if I stayed sick, everyone else understood their roles and all was balanced in the family. That kept all of our family damage contained and easily explained away. I've spent my life saying that I was "born broken." How can that be true? No one is born broken. I was not born broken. I got sick from breathing in all of the toxins of the family unit. So now I'm entertaining this idea: What if I'm not broken at all? What if I never was? How would I live differently? How would my life story change if I adjusted my understanding of the main character?

GLENNON

Family Roles

WITH DR. ALEXANDRA SOLOMON

① Hero/Perfect One

I'm the responsible one. I got good grades and believed that if I was perfect enough, my family's problems would go away. I'm high performing and competent. Because I expect a lot from myself and others, I find it difficult to embrace imperfection in myself and others. I'm self-critical and never satisfied with my effort. *Now, my healing work is to be less controlling and more patient, especially in stressful moments.*

② Scapegoat/Rebel

I often said what no one else would say. I called people out to try to help the family function better, which created distance between me and the people I love. Now I'm a gifted leader—ferocious and fearless. But sometimes I feel misunderstood. I struggle with hypervigilance because I'm used to standing outside the family system and criticizing it. *Now, my healing work is to find comfort in connection and belonging.*

③ Parentified Child

I felt a deep responsibility to empathize with and provide comfort to the adults in my family. I often acted as a "little adult" for others to confide in and was expected to tend to their emotional experiences. I'm compassionate and collaborative. But I often seek out relationships with people who need to be "fixed" and try to solve their problems for them. *Now, my healing work is to set clear boundaries and tune in to my own desires.*

④ Peacemaker/Mascot

I learned to defuse family conflict with humor, mediation skills, and diplomacy. As the "middleman," I drew attention away from conflict. I kept calm under pressure and brought laughter as a form of distraction. Now I can be an entertainer or mediator during times of intensity. But because I was so attuned to others, I have trouble accessing my own feelings. *Now, my healing work is to explore suppressed emotions.*

⑤ Lost Child/Easy One

I was easygoing in an attempt to reduce the stress on the grown-ups. I went with the flow and withdrew to avoid being a burden. But all I wanted was to be seen and loved. My gifts include my flexibility, adaptability, and independence. But I have a hard time letting myself be seen or asking for support. *Now, my healing work is to express my needs and take up space.*

⑥ Identified Patient

I was my family's "reason" for having problems or for coming to therapy, the common cause my family organized themselves around. Allowing others to focus on my challenges served as a distraction from deeper issues and let others off the hook. Now my strengths include self-advocacy, self-awareness, and resilience. *Now, my healing work is to consider that I'm not broken at all.*

*I'm like this because **I played a role in my family to keep the peace.***

We can heal from the roles we played, but I think it starts with grieving. If you were the scapegoat and you were outcast and vilified by your family; if you were the one who could never be a kid because you were mediating between people; if you were the invisible one who was never seen and so you think you're not worthy of being seen; if you had to take care of your family by making everyone laugh even when someone else should have been taking care of you; if you were told you were broken when really your family was broken—there's a lot to grieve there. It's sad.

But it's also liberating to know that family roles are a scam, because it means you can put down your script.

I no longer want to be a hero. No one can love a hero, because heroes aren't real. Stepping out of a role takes time. It's a million little choices that feel excruciatingly uncomfortable before they feel like freedom. It's saying out loud, "I can't get everything perfect right now." "I can't do all of this." "Too much depends on me." Or "I'm not going to pretend to be sick anymore. I'm not going to act helpless anymore." Or "I'm resisting the urge to defuse this tension with a joke, because your behavior is not funny." Slowly, we can put down the script and learn to become our full, complicated selves.

AMANDA

AMANDA: Every cell in our body has DNA. And DNA is covered in molecules, markers that tell that particular DNA how it should be expressed, which is how we end up with one cell that's an eye cell and another cell that's an ear cell and another that's a liver cell. When we go through trauma, the trauma changes us on a molecular level; it pushes on those markers, which results in different genetic expression, literally changing the way our DNA works. The study of how our environment changes the way our DNA works is the science of epigenetics. And epigenetics shows that our trauma is passed down genetically from generation to generation. There was a study done in the Netherlands which found that the DNA in descendants of famine survivors reflected the trauma of famine even though that trauma *never even happened to them*. They inherited the trauma from their ancestors; it lived in them through their DNA expression. Their body remembered something they never experienced.

DR. GALIT ATLAS: Exactly right. Trauma doesn't change the genes; it changes the expression of the genes, which some people like to call the memory. The genes have memory. But what we find in our clinical work is that we don't only inherit the anxiety or biological response to the trauma; our minds also know something about the actual content of the trauma. We inherit things that sometimes seem amazing and incredible about different times in our ancestors' lives, like dates or specific memories. For example, my mother's brother drowned when she was ten years old. He was fourteen. And, even before hearing this story, the children in the next generation were afraid of water. That happens often if you have been explicitly told about the trauma, but many times even if you have not.

—

I'm like this because

I carry the trauma and triumphs of my ancestors.

I was severely beaten if I got a B+, and I know lots of other kids who were, too. Our parents went through a lot of really tough stuff, and when they came here, they were like: *The way that you're going to survive is you're going to get good grades and make money and become a doctor, and then you'll be safe in this world.* The physical abuse was driven by fear and trauma. San Jose has the biggest concentration of Vietnamese people outside of Vietnam, and there are a lot of Vietnamese refugees in my community. There are a lot of Korean War survivors. There are a lot of Chinese survivors of the Cultural Revolution. There's a big Cambodian population who are survivors of the Khmer Rouge genocide. Over time, I realized they were terrified. I have come to understand that I was part of a community of trauma. Coming to terms with that helped take some of my self-loathing away, that critical part that kept saying: *I'm a freak. I'm the worst.* I realized I'm a product of war and capitalism and big global socioeconomic factors that are a lot larger than me.

STEPHANIE FOO

Every single person has some element of trauma that is generational. And the pain of generational trauma will have some form of rage. That's *righteous rage.* It's rage that has to be honored.

DR. MARIEL BUQUÉ

Understanding why we are the way we are isn't just about learning what happened *to* us and how we survived it; it's also about learning what happened *before* us and how they survived it.

GLENNON

I draw so much inspiration from my ancestors, from the freedom makers of my past. There was no way out, but they made a way. They had a trickster energy. They existed in two different worlds; they were able to build community within a culture that was so toxic and violent. My grandmother was working two jobs, raising eight children, and healing from post-traumatic stress because she left Mississippi after seeing a lynching during Jim Crow terrorism. I say that my ancestors floated on a spaceship that they built out of uncertainty and hope. They floated up north, away from the South, hoping for a new world. And they built new worlds within a world that didn't want them free, that didn't see them as human beings. *That's* the resistance I'm pulled to. No one can tell me that something is impossible. I don't believe it.

TRICIA HERSEY

*I'm like this because **I carry the trauma and triumphs of my ancestors.***

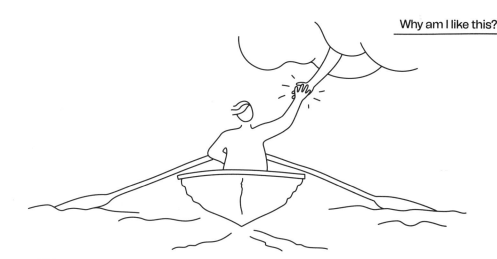

GLENNON: I've had many moments in this healing journey when I think: *Thanks a lot, ancestors. Why did I end up with all of this work to do? What the hell were you doing?* My sister and I actually started looking back at our ancestors and discovered that it was only a few generations ago that my great-great-grandfather was separated from his parents—ripped from his family, home, and country—and put on a boat to cross the ocean and escape starvation in Ireland. Sometimes I can almost hear my ancestors saying: *Okay, this assignment you have—healing this bit of generational trauma—this is your ocean. You are the one in our lineage who transforms this so that it stops with you. We weren't able to because we didn't have the time or the resources. We had different oceans to cross. Now, lucky one, this is the ocean you cross for us.*

ABBY: The blessing and the curse.

PRENTIS HEMPHILL: That's right. It's a beautiful thing to honor where we've come from. It's a remembering. And they are us. Like you said, this is your part in it. You're the edge of your lineage, and there's something for you to attend to. There's something for you to transform.

—

There's an intergenerational unconscious, which means that one generation lives inside the other and they share unconsciousness and then communicate with each other bidirectionally. They communicate with each other things that they're not aware of and often that they don't intend to communicate.

DR. GALIT ATLAS

Seeking to understand where our loved one's pain comes from may be the thesis of all of my work. Where *does* pain come from? When you ask that question and start to find answers, you realize that the complexity of the various violences we experience with our mothers or otherwise come from them being hurt by systems that began way before they were even born. They were up against so much. It doesn't erase the harm that we've experienced, but it throws it into context and amplifies them as people who tried their best. It's actually really beautiful to see that every mother had their limit, which actually renders them human.

I can't speak for others, but for me, I saw that the violence in my mother was an expression of her powerlessness. She had no agency as a person, as a woman, in her relationships with men, in her relationship with the world, with society, at her job. And so it just exploded out of that frustration. Her frustration was always a desire to make me better, to protect me. It sounds so antithetical, but that's what trauma is. Trauma doesn't make sense. It should never make sense. ⁓

⁓ When we think about PTSD, we're talking about people who are displaced in memory. They are acting as if the danger is around the corner, even when they're in relative safety. This is true with survivors of domestic violence; it's true with refugees and veterans. If you think about veterans' hypervigilance and paranoia, they're thinking in the war zone.

A lot of Holocaust scholars are trying to reorient what we think about epigenetic trauma as something akin to epigenetic strength. It wasn't just the passing of trauma or baggage or suffering; it was the passing of strength, vigilance, or even paranoia, this desire to control. My mother would, before she went to the DMV, for example, prepare days in advance: the paper, the files, the money, cash to slip. She prepared to go to the DMV like she was preparing for war. On one hand, it's really sad to see. But on the other hand, that was a skill. There's innovation there, there's survival.

Nobody survives by accident. Survival is a creative act.

OCEAN VUONG

I'm like this because

What happened to me shaped me.

Trauma is not conscious. It's your body saying: *This particular thing that happened is too much, too fast, too soon, or too long without enough repair.* When trauma activates, your sense of self in the world drifts and gets stuck. But pervasive trauma that happens over long periods of time—in the world or in a person's body—can begin to be perceived as personality traits. Trauma in family systems can look like family traits. Trauma in a people can look like culture. Trauma in a culture can look natural and/or standard. Someone who's endured trauma might seem "crazy." They're not crazy. They're keeping themselves alive. Untended trauma responses are not defective; they are protective.

RESMAA MENAKEM

I survived ongoing sexual abuse as a child. This happened during a time when kids are supposed to be learning how to move in their bodies, the age that they're learning how to be free and have agency in their bodies—that they can jump from here to there. And I was learning how to leave my body to survive. I'm certainly no expert, but we know that's a very common and necessary trauma response. Dissociation gets a bad name, but in the immediacy of trauma, it's actually a mercy. Unfortunately, that disembodiment can extend into our later life even when the threat is no longer there and we no longer need it for survival.

COLE ARTHUR RILEY

If you get in a car accident—let's say you're getting doughnuts—your brain encodes all of the details around you. Maybe the guy who hit you was wearing a blue sweater and you're in front of this doughnut place. So it encodes all of these details as potential threats because you're going through a traumatic incident. In the future, your brain isn't trying to be sensible; it's trying to save your life. So you might see a doughnut and you might feel panicky. That doesn't make any sense, of course, but that's how your brain works. This is the adaptation that our brilliant bodies have come up with to try to keep us alive.

STEPHANIE FOO

It's an odd thing to be a Black child raised in a white supremacist abusive family. There was physical abuse, and your body eventually heals from that abuse generally; but it's always the psychological abuse that's more insidious. It's the colonization of our minds. I think we're all decolonizing our minds all the time because we've been raised in these toxic systems of hierarchy.

ALLISON RUSSELL

There was this abuse that was happening during one season of my childhood. Something was happening to me at night from a child that was an acquaintance of the family. I knew something was happening, but I didn't know what it was. I had a sense that the reality was different from the performance that we were all engaged in. But I was told that sense was wrong or that sense was to be ignored or that sense made me crazy. And so I learned very early on to not trust myself.

KERRY WASHINGTON

Glennon: Okay, Sam, did you have a happy childhood, or are you funny?

Samantha Irby: I'm funny. No, no. Let's say I'm *very* funny. Whenever you meet anyone you think is funny, you just get to the point where you're like: *Okay, what's your damage? How did you get here?*

I'm like this because

What happened to me shaped me.

—

GLENNON: You said, "Somewhere around the same time that my internal shame alarm started going off, I started leading a double life. I joked instead of crying. I shoved my pain way down and put a joke on top, getting funnier and funnier by the minute." You say, "Eleven was the age my self-hatred became sentient."

As I read, I wrote down in my notes, "At eleven years old: Glennon became bulimic, Abby became a soccer star, Cameron became funny." We know that from age eight to twelve we begin to split—we hide our real self, and we become something else to present to the world.

CAMERON ESPOSITO: Yes. I didn't realize this until just a few years ago, but I think I was pretty badly bullied as a child. I thought that's how everybody was treated. I had glasses and braces and a bowl cut and something weird was going on with my gender and I was gay and I had crossed eyes. So I tried to make the joke first, like: *I know what you're going to say. Well, here's an even funnier spin.* I also did this to have value. I wasn't able to play the game of being a girl that might be valuable for some other stuff that women are valued for. So I got super funny.

—

I'm like this because

I have many selves inside of me.

Is the self a fixed, understandable entity? Probably not. I feel more like a community than a singular self. I feel like I'm made up of many competing, conflicting parts that developed in response to the trauma and magic of living. As Whitman said, we each contain multitudes.

GLENNON

The core idea of Internal Family Systems is that we are all made up of many autonomous little parts. They are little minds inside of us, and they are what we usually call "thinking." They argue or talk or try to give us advice all the time. Like kids in a family, parts start out innocent and pure and open—eager inner children. But traumas force them out of their natural roles into extreme roles. These are the most sensitive parts of us, so they get hurt the most by the traumas and the rejections and the betrayals. They take on the burdens of emotional pain, terror, and worthlessness. They get scared the most by whatever trauma happened. And they get stuck at the age of that trauma—frozen at that scene and terrified. We don't want to feel that pain all the time, so we lock these parts of ourselves away. We exile them to inner basements. And we do that without realizing that we're actually distancing ourselves from our most precious qualities. But through Internal Family Systems therapy, we can learn to heal and gain access to these exiled parts again. What we often find is that as people gain access to their exiled parts, they want to start to paint, they want to start to play. They get access to these things that they had locked away.

RICHARD SCHWARTZ

Our parts develop to protect us. They try to keep us from feeling too much—to keep us a little dissociated from our bodies. When our parts experience injuries or trauma, they take on what Richard Schwartz calls "burdens." And then their job becomes controlling the outside world so those burdens don't get triggered. Our parts started to protect us when we were just children; they think we are still children, and they protect us the way they did back then. And these behaviors, which protected us when we were little, often become something that hurts us later on like an eating disorder or an addiction. The world tells us: *That part of you is bad. It is creating pain for you and everyone around you. Tell that part to go away. Focus on these other parts of you.* But when we try to drown out any part of ourselves, it just gets stronger, defending itself; it flails around wildly, taking over until it can get our attention. Because every part is equally valuable and beneficial to us. Our parts served their purpose at the time of the trauma. That's why we have to look deeper and say, "I trust that you are trying to help. What are you trying to protect? What are you trying to say?"

AMANDA

There are certain voices inside my head that will never quiet down until they first feel fully heard, acknowledged, and understood. I find myself wondering: *What is this part's problem? Why on earth is it telling me not to eat? Why? Why? Why? Turn it down, turn it down, turn it down.* No. Turn it all the way up. It needs to be heard. It's saying: *Glennon, your house wasn't a safe place to indulge your appetite. So I protected you by keeping us small and safe. That's what I'm still trying to do. I'm trying to keep you small and safe so we can survive. I'm just trying to protect you.* We have these parts that have worked so hard for so long and have done a really good job helping us survive. They just have old information. They just don't know that we're safe now and all the rules are different. They just need an update.

GLENNON

I created a little avatar, a little fighter in the video game of life who wears a motorcycle jacket and holds a microphone to go out into the world in front of me. It's a dissociative protection of the real me, my little self, and it's actually very sweet. Thinking about taking care of myself like that, especially at a young age and also still now, I like thinking that there's someone saying: "I got you. You hang out back there, I got this one." And then that high-haired stand-up comic goes out into the world and takes care of my more tender self.

CAMERON ESPOSITO

I'm like this because

I have many selves inside of me.

I had a client who cut herself in addition to having bulimia. I got curious and asked, "Why do you do this to her?" The part proceeded to tell me the whole history of how when she was being abused as a child, it had to step in and distract her from that. And it turned out that it was a heroic story. I could actually shift and have a huge appreciation for how it basically saved her life. As I did that, the part broke into tears because everyone had demonized it and tried to get rid of it. And finally somebody was understanding and appreciating it. Our parts think they are helping us survive.

RICHARD SCHWARTZ

How old were you when you looked around and thought: *I have to take control of this.* Elementary school? You were just a little kid, and you took on the responsibility, probably for your family, for the rest of the world, because you wanted the best for everyone. So you put your own happiness into the furnace. And you were just a little kid. So how do you feel toward this little one who was trying to help their parents be happy, help keep the world on its axis? How do you feel toward that person now?

MARTHA BECK

I'm like this because

I am shaped by my culture.

There are two kinds of suffering in the world.

There's a kind of suffering that is inevitable, that's a part of the human experience, like we are all going to have our hearts broken. We're all going to have loss and grief. We're all going to have to work hard at some point.

I believe—and this is an idea adapted from wisdom originally shared by john powell—that there's another kind of suffering that is actually avoidable. That has to do with the systems we live within and what they tell us about who we are and how much power we have.

AI-JEN POO

The label is not a finite container; it's a project; it's a field of knowledge. When I say I'm Asian American, I'm talking about a journey, I'm not talking about a checkbox. People try to put me into a checkbox, but how can we be finished with anything: masculinity, femininity, anything? I don't know what this is yet. How could you know? How could any of us know?

OCEAN VUONG

I'm like this because

I am shaped by the boxes culture put me in.

When we go out to eat, I look at the menu and I'm like: *Okay, so here are my options.* I order from the menu. Then the waiter turns to Abby, and she's like "Can you please do that but add that, and then can you take away that?" Then she gets her dish, and it's always so much better than mine. Every time I secretly feel jealous because it's like she's broken the rules and been rewarded for it. I thought we were supposed to stay on the menu to be polite.

That is how women feel when another woman goes off the menu and she seems to have this delicious, creative life in front of her. We look at her, and we think: *Well, it's too late for me, because I already ordered.* So instead of admitting we feel cheated—we get angry at her.

The world gives us a menu about sexuality, gender, work, motherhood. There are specific reasons why we have limited options. It's because the menu doesn't serve the person ordering; it serves the order of things. Somebody made that menu, and it wasn't us.

GLENNON

Isn't it so weird that we only have two categories that we're *allowed* to be?

ABBY

We view gender as inherent and inborn—something that just exists. But in reality, we make gender exist by giving it meaning.

We create gender by telling a child who they are a thousand times a day, even before the child is born—through our overt and implied expectations, reactions, fears, and goals for them. What is appropriate for them? What is taboo for them? What do they get shunned for? What do they get praised for?

Kids have different experiences of the world based on our gender-specific expectations, reactions, fears, and goals for them. This difference becomes embedded in their identity, in their sense of self-worth, creating different people. Then we say, "Look! These people are different! Gender must be why!"—instead of seeing that our constant construction, policing, and reinforcement of gender is the reason for that difference.

People believe that biology is destiny. But actually, *culture* is destiny. Because cultural rules become infused into who we are. And then we point to who we are as evidence of inborn biology. And the self-fulfilling prophecy continues.

But the good news is that culture is always changing—and so too is our destiny.

AMANDA

I'm like this because

I've been shaped by my culture's gender rules.

It's so funny to me that people accuse trans and nonbinary people of imposing this gender conversation on them, when the real imposition was dividing billions of complex, divine, nuanced souls into two categories: men and women. They tell you that there are only two genders, and they get away with it because they kill, disappear, erase, discredit, and delegitimize all of us who, for hundreds of years, have lived alongside you.

ALOK

When I watch men play sports or see them in the stands, I'm amazed by how they hug and kiss each other, become giddy together, lie on the field and cry together, express unbridled sorrow, vulnerable enthusiasm, passion, tears. I always wonder: *Is this why men love sports? Because it's a place where they can let go of the boy rules: don't touch each other, don't show vulnerability, don't care too much, don't show joy or connection? Is sports the place where they're allowed to be free from all of that and finally be fully human?* And women and girls in sports, they seem so free, too: free to abandon the girl rules and be fierce, animalistic, mighty, competitive. In a realm that is so deeply gendered, it's fascinating to see people free from gender rules.

GLENNON

As a teacher, I observed up close how we train little girls and boys. Every time a boy had an issue with another boy, the boys would be instructed to deal with each other in an honest, direct way. But when little girls had conflicts with each other, the adults would become extremely uncomfortable. The imperative was always "Just be nicer. Be nice. Get along." It was very, very important that all the girls made peace, even if it was a false peace maintained by swallowing their feelings and never even addressing the original rift. The girls didn't have the right to have a rift. Girls are always being trained to choose their own inner conflict instead of daring to create outer conflict.

So it's not shocking that women might struggle to handle conflict with each other plainly and directly. We were taught to swallow conflict, to ignore when people hurt us, to fake it when we don't like people—to act like we *do* like them. But the truth always comes out. If you can't tell the truth directly, it comes out sideways—which is where the trope of "cattiness" comes from. I think that women would stab each other in the back less if, when we were young, we were allowed to stab each other in the front and then get on with things.

GLENNON

*I'm like this because **I've been shaped by my culture's gender rules.***

I struggle with masculinity as a disabled man. I still have a pull to want to fit a traditional masculine role, feeling like I'm not a "real man" because I've assimilated those arbitrary values of manhood. I remember very clearly, within the first year of my injury, sitting in the passenger seat of my mom's van. She was going into the grocery store to pick something up and I didn't want her to have to get my wheelchair out for me, so I told her I could stay in the car. As she walked across the parking lot, thoughts and fears crept in. I thought: *What if something happens to her? I hope she's safe. It's dark.* I realized if something happened, there was nothing I could do.

I thought to myself: *What does it mean for me to be a man if I can't help or protect the people closest to me?*

So much of masculinity is about ability and what your body can do, and I can't do a whole lot. I feel shame for even wanting to conform to this idea of "masculinity," but I try to remind myself: *Carson, it's not your fault. You internalized these expectations from someone else.* And now I get to choose who to be. I get to choose how to define manhood or masculinity for myself.

CARSON TUELLER

There was a study conducted in Fiji soon after the introduction of television. After a while, almost 50 percent of the girls had developed disordered eating. What's fascinating is this: They asked the girls, "Why are you dieting and purging?" The girls essentially said, "Because the women on TV who are thinner are more powerful." It wasn't about beauty for beauty's sake; it was about beauty for power's sake.

My anorexia recovery requires me to look hard at the body hierarchy ladder—at what power and benefits I'm getting from controlling myself, from staying thin, from adhering to beauty standards. There is power in thinness. There is power in not allowing wrinkles on our foreheads, not having gray roots, in adhering to beauty standards. It's all about power. Beauty is all about power.

GLENNON

I'm like this because

I've been shaped by my culture's ideas about which bodies are valuable.

—

GLENNON: As you say, Sonya, we are *all* on the ladder of body hierarchy. We are both victims of it and complicit in it.

SONYA RENEE TAYLOR: Yes. The goal of the body hierarchy is to ascend as high as possible while recognizing that most of us live in bodies that will never exist at the top. But as long as there are people below us, then we know we're better than somebody—even if that's not conscious. *At least I'm not down there. So I'm going to close my eyes and hold on and pray nobody shakes me off.*

But I believe that ladder is only real because we keep trying to ascend it. It's only as real as our investment in it. If you step off it, you'll absolutely lose something. But what you get in exchange—radical self-love—is beyond anything you can imagine. Because you can hear about a really stunning sunset, but you really can't *know* it until you're in it, until you're standing there watching that giant orb of flame and fire and heat and gas descend over the horizon and you're like: *Oh, my God, this is so much greater than anything I could have ever imagined.*

—

Being in a woman's body on this misogynistic deadly planet and developing disordered eating or other coping mechanisms is not some kind of anomaly. This is not about "Do my thighs look fat in this?" It's not about vanity. It's about safety and agency and lack of both. It's about desexualizing yourself in order to survive. It's about trying to find a way to feel safe. If you live in a house that's likely to get broken into, it might feel quite wise to make it less enticing to home invaders. To anyone who has developed maladaptive coping mechanisms as a result of living on this planet crawling with predators: I get it. You've been gaslighted. You are not crazy. It's not us, it's them.

GLENNON

Girls are riddled with rules and protocols. I've seen little girls who are fully dressed be told, "Go put some clothes on"—because a man is there. I'll never forget going to visit my uncle in jail when I was a preteen. I must've been nine or ten. When we got to the prison, they made my grandfather turn around. I couldn't go in. I'm a kid, a little kid, but because I had a spaghetti strap tank top on, they said it would be a distraction to the other prisoners. Girls get these messages that if somebody's attracted to us, it's our fault because we didn't do enough to protect ourselves.

TARANA BURKE

Isn't it weird that we've collectively decided that half the population's faces are good to go? Why on earth are men's faces deemed perfectly fit for public consumption as is but the other half of faces—women's faces—are so inadequate or jacked up that we have to cover and plaster ourselves every morning with correctors and contours and colors. There's Chad over there, hanging out with his face hanging out, and we're good with it. But when I don't wear concealer, I'm told I look tired. I truly feel like I'm breaking some law when I don't wear makeup, like I actually owe the world smooth skin and weirdly thick eyelashes. Isn't that weird? Isn't that just insanely weird?

GLENNON

*I'm like this because **I've been shaped by my culture's ideas about which bodies are valuable.***

If you're a fat person, the world demands a disordered relationship to food and to your body. Deb Burgard says, "We prescribe for fat people what we diagnose as disordered in thin people." So we're requiring disordered eating behaviors of fat people. We expect them to eat as little as possible. We expect them to hurt themselves in order to become thin, and anything short of that is unacceptable. So me "loving my body" doesn't really change how all those other people act. That's still an external world that I can't just manifest away. That's not a possibility for me.

AUBREY GORDON

Something that has followed me around as a very visually disabled woman is that people have a lot of ideas and assumptions about who I am or who I could possibly be or how my life could unfold or what things I do or don't have access to. Being dehumanized or reduced through the eyes of other people, whether they be strangers or the people who love you, I think that's the most painful experience—the feeling that your interiority is impossible for anyone to see. Maybe our most profound pain comes from that disconnect.

CHLOÉ COOPER JONES

GLENNON: We tend to attribute racial violence to white men and ignore the role of white women, but all whiteness is about power. When white women are challenged about race, we often become so stunned and defensive that we cry. We evoke sympathy to avoid accountability. If you're thinking to yourself, *Well, that's not me, I don't cry,* that's defensiveness. When white women go straight to defensiveness, we're proving the very fragility that we're denying. Our white lady fragility is not fragile like a flower, it's—as Frida Kahlo said— "fragile like a bomb." When we white women wield our power as weakness, people die.

DR. YABA BLAY: We find all these ways to let White folks off the hook. We absolve them of whatever decisions they made at the time or things they did. But these people *made decisions.* We want to believe that they didn't see Africans as human beings, but yes, they did, they just decided it didn't matter.

The same thing is true of fragility. White people can't position themselves as the center of existence, exacting diabolical harm to the entire world for generations, and be fragile at the same time.

There was a social media challenge where all these White girls get in front of the camera to show how quickly they can cry and how quickly they can turn it off. ⌒

I'm like this because

I am shaped by my culture's racial hierarchy.

DR. BLAY: So I'm unmoved by White tears. Most of us are unmoved by White tears because we don't actually think they're real. It's a performance. It's a switch that White people turn on because they know that we have been socialized to see them as more human and of more value, so whatever it is they think and feel, we are supposed to respond to it.

And no one responds to Black women crying the same way. Nobody does. Nobody does. The minute a White woman cries, the world has to stop. *Oh my God, what's wrong with you, baby?* Black women cry, we could be rolling around on the ground screaming, and people aren't moved because they've been socialized to not see us as human beings.

How do I hold White people accountable if they're all up in their feelings? How come I don't get to be in *my* feelings? I'm sitting here telling them about generations of their people, ancestors, killing mine. How come I don't get to turn tears on and move them? Sounds like I should be the one crying, no? Sounds like those tears should be mine. Sounds like the fragility might be mine, but no, I got to be strong. Look at me. I got to sit here.

And this is the thing that really pisses me off: In your tears you now expect me to hold your hand and rub your back and make you feel better because you're crying. Again, your experiences are more important than mine. That is diabolical. I'm not here for it. You're not fragile.

As an Asian American, you have to earn your way toward value and worth. We start in the negative. We're in a mode of having to work to get to the starting line of human worth.

OCEAN VUONG

Growing up, I was one of very few Black people in my environment. And I experienced microaggressions and microracism all the time. So I developed an armor in the way I presented myself, in the kinds of clothes I wore. I decided to play the role of somebody who couldn't be messed with.

TRACEE ELLIS ROSS

Wendell Berry, a white poet and artist, talks about how white people have not had the opportunity to heal from the wound—or even to understand that there *is* a wound—from white supremacy. When you hear "white supremacy" and "racism" and "slavery," you think: *Wow, what was done to Black people is horrible.* But understand that it was actually *also* killing you. It is spiritually killing for a white person to believe that they're superior in some way to another divine human being. That is a spiritual deficiency; that is a disconnection to your power and to who you are. That has robbed you of your own humanity as well. That's why this work is global. It's not just for Black people; it's for anyone who needs to disrupt and push back and heal.

TRICIA HERSEY

I'm like this because **I am shaped by my culture's racial hierarchy.**

I knew I was dark-skinned before I knew anything else about myself. It was always a measure of my value. In knowing that I was dark-skinned, I knew that I wasn't beautiful; the potential didn't even exist for me. Colorism is a system of hierarchical perceptions of value based upon our proximity to Whiteness—with Whiteness at the top, Blackness at the bottom, and a range of colors in between. Looking at bodies this way takes it back to the historical moment of an auction block and the idea that you could know something about a person's value based on what their body communicates: The darker your skin was, there was an assumption you were fresh off the boat, closer to Africa, closer to barbaric. Often, the darkest bodies garnered the highest prices because of how you could work them. There's a particular masculinization of dark skin for that reason. There's a feminization of light skin for the opposite reason. What does it mean to be feminine and demure? White, fragile—the lighter a woman's skin is, the more delicate she is considered, the more feminine she is considered, the more beautiful she is considered.

DR. YABA BLAY

Our culture feeds us a lie about laziness. It tells us: *You have a character flaw if you are failing to hustle nonstop to meet these unattainable standards of productivity set for you.* When our bodies break down, when our bodies tell us to stop, we often think we need to do the opposite: to berate ourselves into persevering. We think the problem is our laziness, our failure to manage our time, our inability to push through. But no. The problem is hustle culture. And when our body feels exhausted, it's not a deficiency, it's a message we should pay attention to.

AMANDA

I'm like this because

I am shaped by my culture's insistence that my value is in my productivity.

A lot of people don't know that capitalism was created on plantations, right out of the chattel slave system. Even the people who say, "Down with capitalism," don't trace the roots back to the history of this idea of looking at a body as a machine, looking at a human body as not being divine, seeing us all as tools for the production of wealth, for profit.

When you bring that back and you start to really study the history, you see that grind culture has the same energy, the same ideology that was on those plantations: Work all the time, have four or five jobs plus a side hustle. Have your hobbies as a way to make money. Never rest, never.

It's the same energy that looked at human beings, my ancestors, as human machines who worked twenty hours a day. It's still happening in our corporations and in our world right now.

White supremacy has used bodies for centuries as tools of evil—devaluing our divinity so we do not see each other as the divine miracles that we are. Being under a system like white supremacy has caused a true brainwashing and spiritual deficiency in all of us. So you blend those things together and you beget grind culture. You get this idea of a body not being able to be owned by ourselves.

I say a lot, "I don't belong to capitalism. I don't belong to grind culture. And I don't belong to white supremacy. You can't have me, I'm not the one you're going to get." And because of that, I'm resting. I'm using rest as a vehicle to disrupt it, to disturb that idea, to push back.

TRICIA HERSEY

I want to belong.

Fitting in is about assessing a situation and becoming who you need to be to be accepted. Belonging, on the other hand, doesn't require us to *change* who we are; it requires us to *be* who we are.

BRENÉ BROWN

The need to belong—to be safe and protected by our people—is primal. Belonging kept us tucked safely inside the herd. The last thing we wanted was to stand out and get picked off.

What happens to seekers is that instead of wrestling with real belonging—which requires withstanding the tension of surrendering to community while maintaining individuality—we abandon our individuality and settle for the comfort of fake belonging. When we do that, we lose ourselves.

I've tried hard to make that fake belonging work. I tried with strict Christianity, anorexia, white lady culture, social media, even politics. At first, melting into the group and not having to think so hard was comforting. But as soon as I got uncomfortable again and started asking questions, the house of cards crumbled. I left or was kicked out. If you have to trade your integrity and abandon yourself for belonging, it's not belonging. If there is no room in your community for questions, for dissent, for you to be you, you're not in a community, you're in a cult. There is no certainty. Whoever says differently is amassing power by selling you fake belonging.

Sometimes I feel like I belong only to myself, and that can feel lonely. But the thing about being a seeker is that I must forever be seeking. If I think I'm found, I know I'm in trouble. I'm a seagull who never gets to land. But flying's nice, too. Better views.

GLENNON

My first memories of church are actually very beautiful. I remember loving to sing. My feet would be planted on the church floor while I was holding the back of the pew in front of me and I'd just belt out the songs. I really do remember a moment then of feeling completely free and held in that community. But quickly came the overwhelming understanding that who I was on the inside and who the church expected me to be on the outside didn't match. I understood that I had a choice to make, that I could choose to be myself and be free or I could choose to hide and be accepted. I chose myself, and I really believed, for a long time, that accepting myself meant choosing God's rejection.

ABBY

The church became my safe space, but also my space of assimilation and pain and severing the ties to the understanding of what it means to be Potawatomi in a family that didn't know how to talk about it. Colonization took those healthy conversations from us. The painful part of that church culture is that I was safe. I was loved by the people in my church. But in that process, it was still colonization. It was still assimilation. It left me with all the residual trauma and disembodiment that I now have to work to heal.

KAITLIN CURTICE

Social media is a little bit like all drugs: It started off really fun, and then we found out, oh, this algorithm wasn't really designed to help us connect with each other; it was designed to sell us something that looked like belonging—but really feeds on our sense of unworthiness. It's destroying women and girls. It's turned into this venomous-toothed monster. It's not a safe place anymore.

ELIZABETH GILBERT

I'm like this because

I want to belong.

—

SARAH EDMONDSON: Many high-control groups, like the cult I was in, use a ranking system to rank members. In that structure, the person above you in the system knows better than you do and has immediate power over you. Now that's one of the red flags I pay attention to: when I'm asked to subjugate my own beliefs and understanding to what someone else sees and knows.

GLENNON: The easiest way to control people is to convince them to mistrust their intuition and bodily knowing. That's what happened to me in fundamentalist Christianity. If I had a gut feeling, I was told my body would lead me astray. If my heart broke over a bigoted teaching, I was told my heart was wicked. If I had an intellectually challenging question, I was told not to lean on my understanding. I ended up completely lost, disembodied, separated from my mind, body, and spirit—which is the point. They told me not to trust myself, to trust "God" instead—but what they meant was *Don't trust yourself, trust us instead.*

—

Life is chaos. We grab on to religion, wellness plans, busyness, and productivity because, bless our hearts, we just want a little control. We're just trying to feel okay. It's like life is the sinking *Titanic* and everybody's scrambling to stay at the tippy top, to stay in our minds and our dogmas because we know if we let go of these structures, we'll sink, too—and land in our bodies. Our bodies are where all of our memories, trauma, wildness, and messiness are. But our bodies are also where healing is.

Healing doesn't happen by replacing our failed dogma with another dogma—by finding another religion, another diet, another discipline, another whatever. But there is a magical moment of possibility that arises if we allow our false certainty to be replaced with nothingness and do the impossible work of sitting there—clueless and surrendered—long enough.

It's like we're sitting on the couch with a puzzle in front of us and we're hunched over and our brows are furrowed and we're trying, trying to solve it. We have to stop trying. We have to abandon the puzzle in front of us and sit there on the couch empty-handed and still.

This feels panicky and terrifying at first, because with our hands and minds no longer busy, all we're left with is who we are and what we have to heal from. Our childhood stuff comes up; it all comes up. We start to struggle with whatever we've been avoiding our entire life. But if we stay with ourselves and don't grab for somebody else's false certainty, a healing journey becomes possible. On that journey we slowly learn how to be real adults—responsible, whole people who can regulate ourselves and withstand the uncertainty of life without grabbing for and using people or false certainty to make ourselves feel okay.

We finally learn that our problem was never that we couldn't solve the puzzle of life; the problem was that life was never a puzzle at all. Life is a dance. There is no solving life, there is just letting ourselves feel and move to the music.

GLENNON

Two

Who am I really?

When I was a kid, my family gave me the label *athlete*. It made me feel important and safe; I wore it as both a superhero cape and a cozy blanket. But I always had another part of me whispering: *That is not all you are.* I think I knew it wasn't safe to define myself in that one way, because it was something I could easily lose.

Feeling safe inside labels and still yearning to break free from them is so frustrating. It has caused me so much suffering.

After I retired from soccer, I jumped into parenting with both feet. I felt relieved. I remember thinking: *Perfect, now I'll know who I am for at least the next ten years.*

Here I am, two years from our youngest leaving the house. I've kicked the can down the road as far as I could. I have to finally figure out who I really am in here.

ABBY

GLENNON: We're obsessed with figuring ourselves out. I mean, the online quizzes: "What character would you be? What dog breed are you?" We had a bunch of kids over the other day, they're making tea and one said, "Okay, everybody say what kind of tea you'd be." One kid was chamomile, another chai. Someone even wrote an article about our podcast asking "Are you a Glennon, an Abby, or an Amanda?" We're all trying to solve the mystery of ourselves.

ABBY: We never will. It's so annoying. I have always been a seeker, trying to figure out more about not just the world but about myself. If I can understand myself, maybe I'll understand the world and other people better. I think there's some kind of false safety in all of these tests. Putting ourselves into categories makes us feel as if we have sorted it all out, brought some order to ourselves and our place in the world.

AMANDA: We take all those ridiculous quizzes and surveys because there is some nugget in there that allows us to say, "*This* is me." We have such an insatiable craving to be seen and understood, but it's impossible—we don't have language to translate the fullness of who we are. So when we say, "Look, this one thing, this is me"—even if it's as ridiculous as a flavor of tea or a dog breed—it satisfies part of our existential need to express who we are and to have someone else say, "Oh, I get it. I see you."

I had set out to reinvent myself, but it turned out that I didn't have to start from scratch. I just had to dust myself off because the best parts were already there.

TARANA BURKE

AMANDA: In a world where everyone's trying to figure out what self-care is, and we're all being sold endless products to improve ourselves, you have such a hopeful message. You're saying that it is not about us acquiring skills or taking steps to get somewhere new. Rather, it's about us excavating back to our original intelligence, back to our innate possibility.

SONYA RENEE TAYLOR: Exactly. The acorn doesn't have to be told to become an oak tree. It doesn't have to *do* anything to become an oak tree. It simply needs to exist as itself inside the conditions that are fertile for oak trees. We are all acorns with all of the wiring and encoding necessary to become oak trees.

Societies have created a world that is incompatible with our ability to grow into what we authentically and inherently are. So what I'm always asking us to do is realize: Who you are is already in you.

We do not have to figure out how to radically love ourselves. We have to figure out what conditions have paved over the fertile ground that allows that thing that is naturally in us to sprout, to grow. And it's not that we were an acorn and then we fell on some concrete and now we're never going to grow. It's not that. ⁓

I am already everything
I need to be.

SONYA: It's that we were already a growing plant and then somebody was like "You'd be better as a parking lot." And then enough people said, "You'd be better as a parking lot." And we were like: *You know what? Maybe they're right. Maybe whatever it was that I thought I was, maybe that's a lie. Maybe that's not true at all.*

I think about it in the relationship with my Blackness, for example. Even if nobody ever came up to me—although people have—and flat out said, "Sonya, your Blackness is wrong," they would be showing me the same message again and again by making me invisible in the external world, by offering me skin-lightening cream, by making jokes about dark-skinned people, or by creating entire media landscapes in which I am absent.

So the work that I am proposing is: What if we remember that these messages are lies? That's it. What if we remember that there is no beautiful vibrant verdant place in the world that should be a parking lot? Nobody thinks this except for the person who benefits and profits off of parking lots. So the only person who would say that you are somehow deficient, not good enough, or not inherently valuable enough in the beingness that you are today is someone who profits from you not believing that—someone who profits from your failure to see your own magnificence.

I am always trying to figure out: *Am I crazy or sane? Am I good or bad?*

Internal Family Systems has helped me figure out that I'm not crazy or sane. I'm not good or bad. I have all of these parts inside me. I am more of a community than an individual. I have a part who wants to control, a part who wants to let go, a part who wants to hide, a part who wants to be seen.

And then I have a capital-S Self, who is my wisest, original intelligence. Not an alter ego, but a consciousness I can always tap into. The real me.

Now when I'm making a decision or choosing a reaction, I feel like I'm sitting at a long conference table with all of my sweet little frantic parts and they are all trying to lead—trying to get control, trying to hide, trying to be seen. My capital-S Self is seated regally and calmly at the head of the table. She's the wisest one, so she's listening to all the other parts, taking it all in, understanding and empathizing with each part's fear and motive. This capital-S Self is the part of me that is not traumatized, not needy—the part of me that is whole. She will gather information and make the best decision, because she knows a little bit more than everybody else at that table. She makes our final decisions. All my parts are allowed to weigh in, but she's the only one who is allowed to decide.

GLENNON

I am someone I can trust.

The Self is who you are at your essence. This part of you knows how to relate to the other parts of you in a healing way and knows how to relate to other people in a healing way. This Self in you has wonderful qualities. I call those qualities the Eight C's:

Calm
Curiosity
Compassion
Connectedness
Confidence
Creativity
Courage
Clarity

It turns out that virtually every spiritual tradition knows about this Self, whereas almost no other psychologies do. It's inherent in you. You always possess all of these qualities, and you can always tap into them.

RICHARD SCHWARTZ

A truth that every person needs to understand and let sink into their body is: You are not your thoughts. And since you are not your thoughts, you cannot necessarily trust your thoughts to tell you who you are. We have to figure out: Who is the me beyond my thoughts that I can really trust? The more we can move toward who we are beyond our thoughts, the more free we will be from the shame and the self-hate that is keeping us half-dead.

AMANDA

People will say, "Just trust your gut. Just trust your feelings. Trust your inner knowing." Well, that often can't happen for someone with OCD whose brain is misfiring and they're getting all of these false-alarm feelings in their gut. It's so important for all of us, with OCD and without, to remember we aren't our thoughts. We're a lot more than that. We're our values, we're our character, we're our actions. Society places such a large emphasis on the idea that we are our thoughts, and our thoughts create things. Thoughts are important to a certain extent, but regardless of your thoughts you can still go out and be an amazing person and live a very values-based life.

ALEGRA KASTENS

If you are noticing a tree, you know you're not the tree. If you are noticing a thought, you know you're not the thought. The noticer is your soul, your spirit, your consciousness. You can't be the subject and the object at the same time.

GLENNON

I've done so much healing, but I still struggle a lot with vigilance—feeling like bad things can happen all the time and trying to prevent those things from happening. I wonder who I would be if I didn't have to be so vigilant all the time. I really want to meet that person and want her to succeed. That curiosity of really knowing her keeps me going.

CHANEL MILLER

I am not my thoughts.

How do I talk to myself on a daily basis? Most of that runs on default. It's the outside voice that we believe is the inside voice. We've been listening to it for so long that we think it's our own. But beneath that, we find radical self-love: our inherent sense of enoughness. That can't be externally changed. The same thing that decided that there should be daisies and butterflies and the River Nile and sunrises also decided that there should be a me, there should be a you, and that's divine. The most stunning sunset I've ever seen is made of the same material reality as my own beingness. That's miraculous.

SONYA RENEE TAYLOR

At my center, there's a place where safety lives. There's a place inside of me that can trust my belonging. There is a place inside of me that is wise, where all the lessons of my life have been learned. I can live from that place. I can settle into that place.

PRENTIS HEMPHILL

I think my inner voice is pretty cool. She is mostly loving and kind and respectful to me and others. I think she has high expectations, which is where other voices have to come in and tell her: *It's okay to relax, it's okay to rest, and it's okay to disappoint people.* But overall, I think the chorus of all of my inner voices is a beautiful one.

JUSTINA BLAKENEY

I am worthy of kindness.

"The splendor of recognition" is an ancient idea that came out of the Himalayas. It's the idea that God is omniscient and it's boring for God to be omniscient: What do you do once you can create anything and once you know everything?

So God's like: *I'm going to play this incredible game of hide-and-seek with myself. I'm going to see if I can hide myself so thoroughly from myself that I forget that I am myself.* And where better to do it than in the mind of a human being, which is the most chaotic arcade game of consciousness?

So God decides to hide God's consciousness in the last place anybody would ever look for it: inside a crazy human mind. God's like: *I'm going to see whether the me that is in the human mind can find me, because it's so unlikely that I ever will. But if we do, it will be miraculous. Like "Oh my God, I forgot. I forgot that I'm divine again!"*

That's the splendor of recognition: *Oh, my God, there you were the whole time. The whole time. That was such a good game!* Okay, now I'm going to forget about divine consciousness again. I'm going to go back to being this compressed, angry, anxious, controlling ego. And I'm going to hate myself so much and be so lost, and I'm going to reach for all these things for relief, and I'm going to get so broken.

You're always on your own heels. You're always on your own heels to almost remember what you really are.

There's always this little tiny moment where you remember. And God's like: *I was right here the whole time! LOL!*

ELIZABETH GILBERT

I am connected to everything and everyone.

I feel like every soul—everyone's true self—is a bucket of ocean. Like when we're born, somebody scoops a bucket full of big ocean and pours it into our little body. That's why our souls are all exactly the same, because they're made up of the same God stuff. We're all ocean at our core—all God at our core. When I can tap into my truest, highest self—my soul—I know everything and I love everyone. Because everyone is me. This ocean/God part in me is the same ocean/God part that's in Abby and in Amanda and in every single person on the planet. We are all just buckets from the same ocean. That's why we feel the ache of separation so acutely inside these human bodies. Maybe when we die, we just get poured back into the big ocean we came from. No more bucket. No more separation. We all just dissolve into each other again. No more ache. **GLENNON**

Some people think dressing up is weird. I love it. When I am having a bad day, one of my favorite things to do is go in the closet and play dress-up. I bought a new sweater and I woke up this morning at 6:30 and literally looked in the mirror and was like: *Yeah, you got it. That's what I'm talking about, Tracee!* I have no idea where I'm going to wear that outfit; I never leave the house. But it's one of the ways I wear my insides on my outside. All these different parts of me that seem to match or don't match or whatever, I let my clothing be that. Sometimes I want to feel really sexy, and then sometimes I don't want to feel sexy. It just depends on what I'm covering up and what I'm wanting to share. Beauty is something that blossoms. I really wish everyone would adopt that understanding of beauty.

TRACEE ELLIS ROSS

When I was on the field, I wasn't thinking about gender. I was out there just being free, powerful, fast, talented, competitive, creative, skillful. In retrospect I can see that on the field I was free from a lot of gender rules. But I was just going out there and playing. I was *playing.* Maybe that's what's so contagious and magnetic about watching our women's national team: We're watching women not just break free from the social norms we were handed at birth but we're also watching women be free—free to play and to use their bodies for their own goals and their own joy.

ABBY

As women, we are so programmed to play the supporting character—the wife, the mother. And we have to make the choice to have moments where we put on the supporting character hat, but we also have to cultivate the idea that we are the lead character in *our* story. It's my life. I can choose to be supportive in the life that belongs to my children, because they deserve to be the lead characters in their lives, too. But there have to be times when I'm the lead character in my life. My husband is the lead character of his life, and I love that I get to be a supporting character in his story. Also, he should be a supporting character in mine.

KERRY WASHINGTON

I am unique.

I was nearing the end of my thirties, and I was driving to the optician one day. This woman came on the radio, and she started talking about what it was like to be autistic. At the time, I would've considered myself to be someone that understood autism pretty well. Half my degree was in psychology. I had worked in school settings, I had worked in special educational needs settings. I thought I knew it. But for the first time, I heard it described from the inside. And I immediately recognized myself. After a lifetime of searching, trying to figure out why I didn't fit in with the pattern of living everyone else seemed so comfortable in, I saw myself. It was just immediate recognition, like we were the same person.

KATHERINE MAY

In preparation for my sixtieth birthday, I made a little video about myself. I spent a year researching myself, and one of the things that I discovered was that I'm brave. I've always been brave. I hadn't realized that. I'm a brave, strong, persistent, curious woman who wants to make things better. That's who I am.

JANE FONDA

—

JUSTINA BLAKENEY: As an artist and a collector and someone who likes to surround myself with inspiration, I love beautiful things. I love finding treasures. It's a real joy for me. Why? I enjoy having my home be an extension of myself in some way. It feels good to be known. I want to express myself. I want people to be able to experience it and feel it.

GLENNON: You describe your decorating as music for your eyes. When you have music on in the house, it makes you feel a certain way. And what your eyes fall upon around you makes you feel a certain way. Beauty is so important and so personal. The beauty I offer and the beauty I create can only come from me.

—

I'm
fighting for beauty. A
lot of people get confused by
that because the only definition of
beauty that they've inherited is so basic
and flat that they just associate beauty with
that commodity that we're told grants people
power. That is not what I'm saying.
What I'm saying is:

Beauty is your soul's fingerprint on the earth, and no one else in the world can have your beauty.

Beauty is when I'm speaking to someone and
I'm like: *I could talk to you for the rest of my life
because finally I can breathe again.* The world
for me is a series of drowning and then
having conversations with people
where I can finally breathe
again. ⌒

〜 And
the reason I can
breathe is because it's you, it's
not that imprint of what you've been
told—the cookie-cutter sheet that says:
Hi, I only know myself from my identities. So
beauty work for me is actually deep healing
work to say: *Who am I outside of what I've been told
I should be?* Beauty is about that attitude of
showing up and saying:

I'm worthy of being here.

ALOK

—

GLENNON: Our daughter just had her seventeenth birthday, and she said, "I can't believe I'm never going to be sixteen again." I said, "Honey, you're going to be sixteen for the rest of your life. You don't just become seventeen and let go of all the other yous. Now you get to be seventeen and sixteen and fifteen and fourteen and thirteen." Kaitlin, you know how when people get quite old, they sometimes regress to their childhood selves? It makes me wonder if our child self is our truest self.

KAITLIN CURTICE: We still are those things, even as adults. It's so important to have care for who we were, to know inside, at the core, at the root, we're still who we've always been. "Coming home to ourselves"—that phrase that a lot of writers have written, that just resonates so much with me. If we can't be safe with ourselves, then what? It makes the world a much scarier place if we can't at least love ourselves well.

—

I am home.

Think about yourself as a seven-year-old.

Not as a different being, but the *you* inside you that's looking out into the world right now. That's the same you that was looking out at the world through your little eyeballs when you were seven. That's the same you that will be looking out into the room on your deathbed. You have always been in there peeking out. Since your first day on earth and until your last day.

What is the *you* that is peeking out, taking in the world, noticing all of these outer events and inner thoughts and emotions?

It's not a body, it's a consciousness. This is why in scripture it says the *you* in there—the soul, the spirit, whatever language people use when they're talking about consciousness—is beyond race, beyond gender, beyond age, beyond class. The spirit/soul is not touched by any labels or trauma. At our core we are pure, unpolluted consciousness that is somehow divinity, peace, vision, and order.

GLENNON

The joy of
returning
to our
bodies—
and
accepting
all of
the pain
and the
scars
and the
history
written
there—
is beautiful.
Who
fooled
us into
thinking
that the
unmarked
page was
more beautiful?
Who did that?

ALLISON RUSSELL

Three

How do I know when I've lost myself?

The way I notice I'm not fine is: When someone asks me how I am, I hear myself repeating, "I'm fine. I'm fine. I'm fine!"

Every time a kid hurts themselves or cries, what do we say? "You're fine. You're fine!" Even when they clearly feel something other than fine, we get scared. We train them to convince themselves that they're fine. Then we wonder why as adults—every time we definitely feel not fine—we are constantly saying, "I'm fine!"

GLENNON

When life became one flat gray relentless to-do list, I was officially gone.

When there was no difference between the things that I should be looking forward to and the obligations I had to meet. When catching up with friends and getting the work project finished were both just things that needed to be done.

You know you're lost when it's all the same never-ending Groundhog Day gray. When every moment requires something of you and there are more requirements than there are moments and there's no way you're ever going to catch up, so you just keep trying to meet that moment's requirement. But there's no finish line. It's a pie-eating contest, and the prize is more pie.

When you can't think of anything that makes you happy other than knocking things off your to-do list. When relief is your joy. When it's easier to be at work than it is to be at home because it's just as demanding, but at least you know what you're doing there.

When your robot power eclipses your life force. When you tell yourself you can always dig deep. You'll find it. But you don't find it. You steal it from somewhere else. From your spirit, from your sleep, your marriage, your peace, your dreams. But you don't admit that. You say: *I'm a person who digs deep.* You never say: *I'm a person who steals soil from where it rightfully belongs.*

When you are doing well but you are not well.

When folks ask you, kindly and casually, what you do to "earn a living," you don't think of how it says everything. You earn your right to live. Earn your right to exist. Earn it by producing, making money, being useful—being used.

When you internalize that so deeply that every time you spend even thirteen seconds in a group of your neighbors, you all compete furiously in the Busyness Olympics: "Oh, my God, I have been to four practices today and have two tournaments tomorrow and work is crazy and . . ."

When what you're really saying is: *I'm worthy of this life because look how hard I'm hustling for it. And don't be mad at me for having all this stuff I know I don't deserve because, Look! I'm as miserable as you are!*

Because have you ever seen anything as offensive as a carefree woman?

AMANDA

I was talking to my daughter about my need to control people. I said, "Wait, is it possible that it is not normal to spend all day thinking about your people and exactly what they should and should not do?"

She said, "Yeah. I've wondered how it could be possible for somebody who is as smart as you to not even realize she was anorexic for so many years. I think you must've spent a lot of time and energy using other people's problems to avoid looking at your own. Right?"

GLENNON

I know I've lost myself when

I'm trying to fix other people.

I didn't think I needed therapy this year, because the times I'd gone to therapy in the past, I was struggling with something obvious: an addiction or a terrible heartbreak. But this year was different. Everything seemed fine—not only on the outside but the inside. It was fine. I was doing everything I needed to do. Bills were paid, kids were off to school at the right time. It was okay.

And then we had a conversation with Suzanne Stabile, and she said something that sunk my stomach. She said, "Abby, you need to really work on acknowledging your shadow side. Otherwise you're only living half a life." It was the truest thing that anybody has ever said to me. Because I've known it all along. Deep down, I knew I'd been avoiding the painful part of life at all costs. I called this *staying positive*.

My shadow side is my anger. When I was growing up, we were not allowed to scream or cry. We had to assimilate to the emotional energy of the adults in the room. And then I went off into countless locker rooms.

The unspoken rule was: *Suck it up. Don't have needs, and don't be the one who rocks the boat.* So I buried all of my anger, and I think that has made me half a person.

I've felt split. I've never really lived into the fullness of my emotional experience. I'm working on that now.

ABBY

I know I've lost myself when

I'm hiding parts of myself.

The dissociation that helped make me a great soccer player hasn't served me in my personal life. There's Megan Rapinoe, and then there's *me*. I think so much of the dissociation has been to avoid my inner life and just keep going. I'm a joyful person. I didn't even really realize how much I was not listening, not understanding myself, and not feeling the feelings that I have. I want to feel those things now. I don't want to be floating above what is my real life.

MEGAN RAPINOE

I always have a moment of dissociation before my disordered eating behavior kicks in. I didn't even know that for the last thirty years. I just thought: *I do these weird things, and I don't know why.* But when I slow it down completely, I can see that there's a moment that arrives in front of me that feels scary or triggering. A moment when I abandon my power to respond and take care of myself. A moment when I forget I'm an adult with agency. And then: Bam. I come to, and I'm in the bathroom throwing up. And I don't even know what happened. I'm so disconnected from my body that I don't even know how I got there. When we find ourselves hurting ourselves—it's always after some sort of break, a moment of dissociation when we lost our agency. This is why embodiment work is so life changing. It's how we practice staying with ourselves, not abandoning ourselves, so we can make conscious decisions.

GLENNON

I used to be morbidly fascinated with how I looked on social media. What's wild is, a phone is not very big. It's a tiny fraction of your visual field. You're just in this little rectangle, and it somehow takes over and becomes massively important to your brain. When looking at myself on social media, I would often find that I was not breathing very deeply, and I'd forget that I had a body. I would just become this pure cognitive force of likes and not likes and nothing else. In those moments, I didn't have a body, I didn't have an appetite, I didn't have a history, I didn't have a future.

JENNY ODELL

I know I've lost myself when

I'm ignoring my human needs.

I've started to tell myself: *Cole, if you're not in your body, someone else is.* So who is it? Who's at the helm? It's not you. You're not leaving behind an empty vessel. And I think that someone is probably different for different people, whether it's capitalism or the patriarchy or white supremacy. If we leave our place, if we leave our bodies, if we lose our connection to the sensory, it might seem like survival, but really it's a death. And it's very dangerous.

COLE ARTHUR RILEY

Many of us are so burdened by what we do that we feel a sense of loss of who we are. I think that at my core I am a playful, silly, funny, absurd person. Over the last several years, that playful, silly, funny person has been inaccessible to me—so much so that I started to resent when others were that way around me. I'm like: *Must be nice to be able to be playful and silly.* Because I know that is actually my true self and since I can't access it, I'll be damned if you're able to access it around me. Then we look back on who we were twenty years ago and wonder: *What happened?* Well, what happened is that we all took our responsibilities very seriously, and good on us for doing that. But it would be tragic if our whole lives were spent functioning and never *being*. I've been functioning really hard for a long time and not being. I only remember this when I have glimpses into my essential playful, silly self, and it feels good.

AMANDA

I had a complete meltdown at the end of last year. I was teaching online and taking care of all five kids while we were all at home. I would literally forget to eat. I would forget to drink water. I wouldn't even get out of bed sometimes because I was so tired. I was caretaking for my outside and inside community but not for myself, and I was really devastated by getting so out of touch with myself. So I found a new therapist, got on some meds that actually worked, came out of my fog, and realized: *Wow, girl, you have been deprioritizing yourself and you have been holding your breath.*

ALEX ELLE

Anger is the armor I put on to cover my fear. When I'm really fired up, Abby always asks me what I'm so afraid of.

GLENNON

When I'm dysregulated, I blame everyone for everything. Everyone is against me. Everyone's trying to ruin my life, and it's everybody else's fault. That's a good signal that I've gone away from myself.

CHANI NICHOLAS

Projection is something we all can identify with. Let's say there is something about myself that I really don't like. Maybe I'm afraid of my aggression. So I look at Abby, and I project the feeling that I'm afraid of onto her. I say, "Abby's such an aggressive person." I just need to get rid of this. I need to find a good target, and maybe Abby looks like a good target to me. I just take my aggression, and I put it on her. She becomes the aggressive person. That's what we all do to some degree.

DR. GALIT ATLAS

When we're off, we are misaligned. And we tend to invalidate our own natural, normal human responses to life. No one can gaslight us as well as we can gaslight ourselves; we tell ourselves our feelings don't matter, what we want doesn't matter, and that we're overreacting.

MELODY BEATTIE

I know I've lost myself when

I'm blaming others or shaming myself.

When my daughter gets knocked down on the soccer field, it's so upsetting to me that I used to make her flash a secret thumbs-up sign while she was lying there so I could breathe in the stands again.

But then I realized I was using her to quell my anxiety. It's not her job to regulate her mother's nervous system. It's her job to play soccer on the field. It's my job to regulate myself in the stands.

We are always using our kids and friends and partners to regulate ourselves, but that's *using* people. No good. Our regulation is our responsibility.

GLENNON

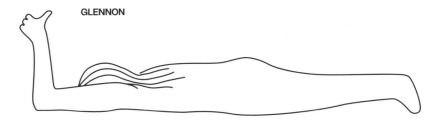

I know I've lost myself when

I'm using others to manage my own anxiety.

Hustle culture was serious in our family. If I was sitting on the couch and my dad was out, when I heard the car come up the gravel driveway, I would stand up and grab a dust rag. I'd just try to look busy. A part of me developed that said: *In order to stay connected, stay busy, Glennon. In order to stay safe, stay busy. In order to stay approved of, stay busy. Or at least look busy.* And so when I see Abby relaxing, I get irritated and think: *Oh, really? Another vampire movie at 2:00 p.m.?* I'm resentful. But the reason I'm resentful is not because she needs to stop resting. The reason I'm resentful is that I need to listen to the part of myself that wants to rest. Now when I get annoyed and think: *That must be nice,* I stop and think deeper: *Yeah, actually, that would be nice. Maybe I want that, too.* I think of resentment as a big flashing arrow pointing me toward what I want but learned I couldn't have.

GLENNON

I knew I had to make some serious changes in my life when I was deeply resentful of even my husband's gestures to connect with me. In the middle of a crazy workday when I hadn't peed in five hours, he would text me an article about, say, geopolitical developments in Asia. And he'd say something like "This is really interesting. We should discuss." Instead of receiving it as it was offered—a lovely gesture from my partner to deepen our intimacy by talking to me, hearing my thoughts, and respecting my intelligence—I would only think: *You have got to be kidding me. You're telling me you have the time to identify and digest soul-feeding and mind-edifying content, and then you have the audacity to suggest that we have the time to discuss it when I haven't taken a shower in three days and my mental checklist is five weeks long?* I actually received it as an insult to all that I was carrying as opposed to an outreach for connection. When bids to connect from people you love feel like burdens, it's time to pay attention.

AMANDA

I know I've lost myself when

I'm stewing in resentment.

It can be annoying—but hugely helpful—if a partner or some-body who knows you really well has a go-to phrase to use when they see you struggling to be human. Sometimes Abby will say to me, "Hey, honey, have you had any water today?" Or the kids will say, "So, Mom, how about some yoga?" They say it with love, not judgment. That's when I know. That's when I know I'm off.

GLENNON

If something happens where I get triggered and I start feeling something, my initial instinct is that I need to think about it to exhaustion before I can find the words to articulate it. It's like I'm so terrified of letting someone witness me in that state—probably because I've never felt comfortable enough to be in that state knowing that the other person might leave. But now when I'm in one of those moments, it is so clear to my husband, Charlie, who can read me like a book. He calls it out in the moment, like "That look. You're doing that deer-in-the-headlights thing. What's happening?" I've learned that it's so important to talk it out, even if I don't have the words.

LILY COLLINS

I know I've lost myself when

Someone I trust tells me I'm off.

We all self-soothe. I sucked my thumb until sixth grade, and I had a blankie that I brought to college with me. We all ritualize comfort practices in our lives. The problem arises when our self-soothing becomes maladaptive or turns into addiction. It's odd that thumb sucking is not acceptable for adults but getting lost in other people's drama or drinking every night is.

GLENNON

The best thing about drugs, alcohol, shopping, work addiction, love addiction is that it feels really, really good for the first twenty minutes. But then it kills you dead. Those twenty minutes were such relief that I didn't care about dying—until I became a parent. And then I was like: *Oh, I have to stick around.* I'd like to live to 127 now, whereas in the past I didn't even care. I would drink tequila so that I could be another temperament. And I miss her sometimes. I think: *She was fun.* But we'll find other ways to be fun. The definition of fun changes as we change anyway.

ALANIS MORISSETTE

Identifying when I'm dysregulated and moving through it is the crux of every good and healing therapy session. How do I recognize there's been an internal disturbance? I'll work on that until the day I die and probably when I'm a ghost. When I'm dysregulated, I could easily get high on my own anger, spiral out, and have a whole good time just raging in my head. Or I could ask myself: *What's going on?* If I can get ahold of what's going on, then I've got a window. Then I've got a little tiny avenue of space.

CHANI NICHOLAS

I know I've lost myself when

I'm distracting and numbing.

If you're pretending to be someone you aren't, if you're in a relationship that isn't authentic, you're going to tend to fill that empty space with something. For me it was food. It can be drugs, it can be shopping, or sex, gambling or workaholism. It can be all kinds of things. But that hole created by inauthenticity will want to be filled.

JANE FONDA

When our self-soothing mechanisms outlast their use or they become more harmful than useful, we have to find a way to let them go. The problem is, it's letting go of something you don't know how to live without, like letting go of air. With alcohol, I was just like: *No, cover it. Just cover the pain. More bandages, more gauze. Put a cast on it.* When you finally take off the cast, it burns so much you want to die. But there's possibility there—because the wound is finally exposed. When the wound is exposed, it can finally get air—it can breathe. And then there's actual healing that's possible and available to you. *That* is why you have to find a way to let go of your thing.

LAURA MCKOWEN

It's really important to get comfortable
with being uncomfortable.

BILLIE JEAN KING

The single sign that we've lost ourselves is suffering. It's so simple, and it's a gift. It's an ally.

If we stop and say, *Okay, this hurts so much, I'm going to go in my room by myself and figure out how to let go of what hurts me,* that usually is the only thing that starts the process of change for people, it's the thing that quiets the outer voices of consensus and starts to reveal your inner compass.

To break free from suffering requires a force that is intense. And the process is not fun. But I now really value suffering because I've come to understand that it's always telling me that I've lost myself.

MARTHA BECK

I know I've lost myself when

I'm suffering.

My body tells me what I need.
One day, I cleaned up the apartment. I took everything to the laundromat. It was hot outside. I thought to myself: *Oh, I really wish I could just sit down in the cool and rest for ten minutes.*

I deny myself what I need.
I denied my need to rest. I thought: *No, when the going gets tough, the tough get going. I've got to keep working.* Instead of giving my body ten minutes to rest, I pushed through, because never stopping is one of my internalized cultural values.

My self-abandonment leads to self-sabotage.
Then I went off the rails. Even though I don't eat eggs because they make me sick, I ended up at a diner, thinking: *Screw you, world, I'm going to break the rules. I'm going to hoover a huge plate of eggs right now even though eggs make me feel terrible. Watch me eat these eggs. That'll show you.*

My self-sabotage leads to suffering.
Because I hadn't let my body rest when it asked for it, my self-denial created self-sabotage, which literally made me sick. Self-sabotage is how we rebel against a culture that wants us to deny our needs. It's the same reason we all scroll for fourteen hours a night, even though we desperately need to go to sleep—because we're not giving ourselves the rest in another way. Your true nature is trying to trick the system into letting you be free. Self-sabotage is the truth trying to get you out of the cultural matrix to which you ceded your freedom.

MARTHA BECK

I thought my twenties and thirties were for losing myself through grinding, family building, assimilating and that in my forties I'd return to myself and be done with it. That's not how it's worked for me. I am forty-eight, and I'm still lost and found—back and forth between fear and love—all day long. One moment I'm gone and panicked and stressed, and the next minute it's a deep breath and: *Ah, there she is.*

I guess the difference is that now I know how to get back to love and peace. For me, it's by remembering I'm just a person. A human being. I just need rest and love and food and breath and comfort. It's so simple, after all—the returning.

GLENNON

Four

How do I return to myself?

I feel lost a hundred times a day—lost to stress, lost to regret, lost to social media, lost to anxiety, lost to scarcity. I heard a wilderness guide on TV say that when you're lost in the woods, the goal is to get found, and to get found you have to stay in the same place, but to survive while you're waiting you have to wander out to find food. So he recommended finding a Touch Tree: a tree that's so big and recognizable that you can go out and forage and then easily return to the same spot again and again.

I don't know how to stay found; I'm going to get lost every single day, maybe every hour. So I need Touch Trees. I need practices and truths, big and strong and rooted enough that whenever I return to them, I feel found.

GLENNON

We are free now.
This is now.
We don't have
to wait for anyone
to tell us that,
to give us that.

TRICIA HERSEY

There's this really cruel rhetoric out there that says: *If you don't believe that you're beautiful, no one else will.*

Instead, I think we can have a mysterious framework for existence that says: *Your beauty is actually not predicated on your belief.* You don't have to believe it when you wake up in the morning. *You just are.* You can choose to believe in the air or not believe in the air, but the air is there. It's there.

It's more of an awareness than anything else, and that's been so healing to me. Instead of trying to contrive this really triumphant form of dignity that says, *I deserve to be honored,* I now say: *I possess honor.* I possess dignity. I'm not waiting. I'm not waiting for anyone to give me the honor that I need. It's in me. And that changes how I'm able to survive in a world that doesn't love my body, that doesn't love Black women's bodies. It changes things.

COLE ARTHUR RILEY

TRACEE ELLIS ROSS: I have abandoned myself way too many times. But each time, in the aftermath of the hurt, I ask myself the question: *How do I not end up here again?* And what I have discovered is: *I will end up here again.*

ABBY: Oh, God. It's true. Why do we have to keep learning those same lessons over and over?

TRACEE: That's it, though. It's funny, I have been nursing another deep disappointment, and my little inner child was just crying so hard. And for the first time, I was able to sit with her and I was like: *Here's the thing, my love, I'm not going anywhere. I'm not going anywhere.*

I don't know how to be anybody else. I just don't. But what I know how to do is to be me and to just hold that space with as much compassion and curiosity and gentleness as possible. And to find all the things, even if it's a bag of fricking Funyuns. What is it that we need today to just try and hold that space of love?

I think that's the thing we're sold that's wrong. I don't think that life is supposed to be a thing that just feels good all the time.

So how can we hold the spaces and the days and the periods when it just doesn't feel good? And when I just feel so unlovable? And how can I have the hurt without deciding it means I'm unlovable? How do you not give meaning to it? And that's where the work is, in that little space.

—

I return to myself when

I'm gentle with all of my selves.

There's a lot about our child selves that we blame. We blame them for these things that they went through. But now there's just a softness I want to hold for her because *she didn't know.* She didn't know a lot. She didn't know that she had grief and trauma. She didn't know how to communicate the things she needed. I need to be softer toward her and toward myself.

KAITLIN CURTICE

Go easy on you. The younger you, the you from twenty years ago, the you from fifty years ago, the you from yesterday. Every single version of yourself was using exactly what you had in the moment, to do the best you could with what you knew. So forgive all of your old selves—no, do more than forgive; embrace and celebrate every single version of yourself who worked so hard to survive. And *did.*

GLENNON

When I was trying to get sober, I knew I had to start letting myself feel. I was so scared of feeling. I'd forgotten how because I'd been numbing for so long. So I practiced through mini–feeling sessions. I'd make myself lie on my bed and listen to one Indigo Girls song at a time. Just four-minute sessions. For the first couple months of sobriety, I'd promise myself: *You don't have to feel any other time, just these four minutes.* Music slowly helped me learn how to feel again—how to survive feeling.

GLENNON

I return to myself when

I let myself feel it all.

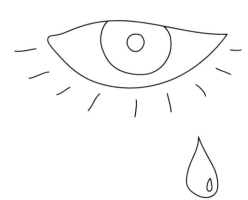

It makes me cringe when anybody says, "Don't cry." It's so weird. It's like saying, "Don't sneeze! Don't pee!" Why on earth not? Crying is how we submerge, feel it all, and begin again. Crying is organic baptism.

GLENNON

Laughter is crucial because laughter turns out to be the one emotion that can't be compelled. It's a proof of freedom. You can make somebody afraid. You can even make someone feel they're in love if they're kept isolated and dependent for long enough. But you can't make them laugh. And laughing together is such a communal experience. I think we should be wary of churches and temples that keep us from laughing.

GLORIA STEINEM

—

AMANDA: Your dad says to you, "Do me a favor, Ashley? When you write about you and me? Just tell the truth. Your truth. Don't worry about nobody's feelings, especially not mine. You gotta be tough to tell your truth, but it's the only thing worth doing next to loving somebody."

A little bit later you say, "Inside of myself I let go. For half a minute, I was flying. For half a minute, I knew I had it in me to tell the truth and be loved anyway."

ASHLEY C. FORD: That's all it takes. Half a minute of *Maybe*. Half a minute of *That might work out. That might be okay. It could be okay.* I had to allow that for myself because my dad could've offered that gift and I still could've rejected it. I still could've come up with a million and five reasons why he was wrong.

I just pushed away all of the reasons that I could've come up with to deny that help in that moment, and I let myself have hope. I let myself have it for half a minute.

—

I return to myself when

I say the thing I'm scared to say.

I think we all know this feeling of a thing that we're holding. It could be anything, but the thing we're holding, we think if we articulate it, it makes it true. And we're more scared of that thing being true out in the world than we are of keeping it inside.

My thing had balled up inside of my body, it was in the pit of my stomach for so long that I was scared of it. It would come up, and I could think it, but I couldn't say it out loud. And I think some part of me thought: *If I say this out loud, I'll die. It's over. This is it.* I forced myself to say it, to look at myself while I said it. And I was like: *Oh, look at me. I'm still here.*

TARANA BURKE

I was on a call with my family recently, and for the first time, I said the truth of how I was feeling. I said, "I have to be really honest, I feel . . ." and then I said the truest, hardest thing—the thing no one in my family is "allowed" to say. It just came out. Three days later, I found myself on another call with my family, dealing with the truth of things for the first time. It was all because I'd said, "I have to be honest." What a beautiful guide to start this process if you find yourself really struggling to express the way you feel. "I have to be honest." Don't we all just have to be honest?

ABBY

Nothing is wasted. None of that old pain is wasted. We use every bit of it to create the next version of ourselves. Sometimes when we're feeling really tender, really porous, really sensitive, we decide we're in a weak state, but I think tenderness is actually a transformative state in which we are becoming the next thing. When I'm feeling super tender and vulnerable, I think of myself as a crab. When crabs outgrow their shells there is a slice of time between shedding the old and finding the new when they have to hide—because they are extra soft, extra vulnerable. We get soft and have to hide sometimes, too. I think that means we're growing. We're just between shells.

GLENNON

I return to myself when

I take care of the softest version of me.

—

BRENÉ BROWN: I remember when I first started seeing my therapist. I said, "I'm like a turtle in a briar patch, and you took away my beer, and you took away my cigarettes, and now you've taken away the apple fritter, and now you've taken away the seventy hours of work a week. I'm a turtle without a shell in a briar patch. Everywhere I turn, it hurts. I'm going to need something." And she goes, "Have you thought about getting out of the briar patch?"

ABBY: Oh, my gosh.

BRENÉ: Yeah. And I was like "But is that the world?" And she said, "It can partly be the world, but it's also your relationships, the family stuff, the worlds you create."

GLENNON: It's such permission. We don't always need the next strategy to cope with our life. Sometimes we need to create a life that requires less coping.

—

If the whole world is waging a relentless effort to separate us from our humanity, then our whole life needs to be a relentless fight to stay human.

AMANDA

Twenty-five years ago, I woke up in the middle of the night. I can't remember the exact moment of inspiration, but I decided to take out a notebook and write a letter to myself. I said the things I've always wanted someone to say to me.

There was this presence that said: *I am right here. I have always been right here. There is nothing that you can do to lose me. There is nothing you can fail at so much that it will cost you my love. You can't earn my love. You can't lose my love. It is innate. It's yours. I am never going to leave you. I was here at the moment of your birth. I'll be here at the moment of your death. Whatever you need to do, I'll be with you.*

Over the years I just kept reaching out to it, and then I just started calling it Love. And it's what it is. It's this unconditional loving voice.

There are a few things that Love constantly says.

One is: "I'm right here."
Another is: "You can't lose me."
The third is: "You haven't done anything wrong."

ELIZABETH GILBERT

I return to myself when

I'm on my own side.

There are two faces of self-compassion. There's tender self-compassion, which you can feel by putting your hands over your heart and just being with yourself. Accept that you're a flawed human being. No one's perfect. That's just the human condition. We can unconditionally love ourselves. This is a real healing power of self-compassion.

Then there is what I call "mama bear self-compassion." That's the fierce self-compassion that says: *Hey, I love you uncon-ditionally, but this behavior has got to change. How can I help?* Or: *This relationship is not good for you.*

The two faces of self-compassion, the tender and the fierce, are yin and yang. We need both, and they need to be in balance constantly.

DR. KRISTIN NEFF

Healing is a love offering to the world. When we heal ourselves, we start to heal the world. When we see ourselves, we start to see other people.

ALEX ELLE

We are terrified, as humans, of a lot of things. I think we're really scared of our humility. I think we're scared of that. The power and the ego that don't allow us to sit under a tree and say, "You're really old and really wise. I bet you could teach me a few things." That scares a lot of people to imagine doing that, because what would it start to pull on? What would start to unravel? I told these women at this conference to talk to their houseplants, and they all giggled. You need to talk to your houseplants because they are beings that take care of us every day. They're sitting in our homes. They're bringing us joy. They're cleaning our air. What if we thanked them and watered them and said, "Oh, you're beautiful. Thank you." It's so funny and silly, but it would change something in us if we actively began to shift the way we think and examine our relationship to other beings. It really would.

KAITLIN CURTICE

I return to myself when

I return to nature.

I go out and walk along the ocean every morning, no matter what the weather is. Early in the morning, there is always junk washed up on the shore. It makes me sad, but I think of it like this: Together, the ocean and I spend the morning emptying ourselves of toxicity, clearing ourselves of all the junk that careless people and systems have littered into us. The ocean is getting it out through her waves, and I'm getting it out through this long walk I take every morning to allow the gentle inner rising of things. I think we keep ourselves so controlled and busy that what needs to rise and be acknowledged in us never rises. If it doesn't rise, we can't let it go. So in the morning, I let it all rise. Some mornings the ocean is angry and scary and nobody can go near her, but she's not apologizing for that. This is just the way she is today. Some mornings she's so gentle and there's no judgment attached to any of it. It's just the way the ocean is today.

GLENNON

GLENNON: Christen, you helped lead the charge for racial and gender justice in the National Women's Soccer League. People tend to assume that "spiritual" folks have their heads in the clouds—that they are not involved in the boots-on-the-ground level of justice work. But you said, "The revolution is not about what you say or post. It is about the inner work you do today and every day to fuel a lifetime of activism. The work starts within." How does racial justice start within?

CHRISTEN PRESS: I believe that the thing you can do to help the world is to help yourself and to cultivate peace and energy. I believe in that energy exchange. There is a place for anger and frustration. But there's also a place for cultivating your own sense of groundedness so that you can go and fight again. There's a lot of guilt that goes into activism: *I'm not doing enough. I'm not contributing. I should be doing this. Look what that person's doing.* And that's balanced by knowing yourself and your truth, being grounded, knowing that it can't all get solved in one day, and taking things one step at a time.

For me, that's looked like having really hard conversations with reporters about coaches that were treating people unfairly. That takes a strength that can only come from being well and being me. I just think that that balance is important. It's actually crazy to think that people think fighting for justice and spirituality are at odds, because for me, they're exactly the same. And it's like your belief in a greater good is *how* you get through the work. It's how you *do* the work. It's your *why* at the end.

—

I return to myself when

I accept that nothing will change until I do.

—

GLENNON: I've been in activism spaces where nobody's working on their own healing, and those spaces can be as dangerous as any other space. Tell us about when you were sharing your healing journey and an activist friend said to you, "Oh, you're going to be one of those 'feelings people' now?"

PRENTIS HEMPHILL: I'm a really unlikely person to be talking about healing. If you knew me twenty years ago, a lot of people from that era are like "How in the world did you get into this healing thing?" But I have to say: Doing my work helped me do my work. Healing myself helps me heal the world.

There is tremendous work to do to heal the world. So what would a society look like where an organizing principle was healing? How would we distribute resources? How would we structure our society? Who would have access to what? Orienting justice work around healing would have a major impact on everyone's well-being. If we're talking about healing, we can't just stop with our individual selves; we have to understand how our world creates trauma and how it limits people's abilities to heal from trauma.

We all embody a whole lot of things we have learned from our families and from the world. We embody all these things we don't really value or believe in, but they come out of us. And so before we try to heal the world, there's work to do in our interiors. There's work to do around realigning who we actually are and how we behave with what we believe. You can't heal the world without looking inward first.

—

For me, the bigger my problem, the smaller the solution. Every time I feel like I need a new town, a new home, a new friend group, a new religion, what I usually need is a glass of water. My breakdowns happen when I've been so frantically busy adulting that I've forgotten how to human. So I only trust healing that is simple, free, back to the basics of being human.

If I feel filled to the brim with stress or pain or confusion, I write it down. Pulling all the ick from my insides and exorcising it outside me where I can see it makes me feel emptied, clear again, ready to act. A good cry always helps, too. And focusing on my out-breath calms me. It's interesting that these practices are all about releasing, letting go. We think of healing as something that has to come from the outside and fix us on the inside. But writing, breathing, crying—that's all release. They are all different ways of not holding it all in.

Also, I never underestimate the healing power of a long walk. So many of the wisest people I know swear by their walking practice. I do, too. I have found that when I'm facing a mental or emotional block, there has to be a physical element to solving it. It's like my brain puzzles only get solved when I start moving my body. On my walks, I'm just with myself: no headphones, no other input. That's another form of release, actually. We have so much input in our lives, so many voices—when do we listen to our own voice? When do we let our own ideas, feelings, thoughts exist and be heard? Most of my creative breakthroughs about work, recovery, and relationships have come to me on one of my walks.

GLENNON

I return to myself when

I give my body what it needs.

I find meditation absolutely critical. Right now I don't know how to get through any day successfully without meditating. I live in a very natural, beautiful place. But it's not about where we live; it's about our home inside of ourselves and how that home feels to be in and if we're comfortable in that home. I can't control everything in my environment, but I can make choices that lead to an optimal environment in my home inside of myself.

MELODY BEATTIE

I step outside on my porch or put my feet on actual grass or go for a swim in the ocean and feel the capacity of my body to do anything. And I pay attention to the leaves. Leaves just fall off the trees. They just all go. And that's not insignificant. Whether I live my life well or don't live well, I'm going to fall off the tree. So I might as well be a bombastic leaf. I might as well be the greenest, the brightest orange, leaning in and trusting the sensation. The sensation leads you to the most bombastic wonderful life.

ADRIENNE MAREE BROWN

There is no rush to get it right, right now.

There's grace, there's mercy, there's imagination. There's taking a walk, there's having a cup of tea in the morning. There's taking a longer shower. All of these things are rest. All of these things are opportunities for us to connect with our body and mind.

We are going to have to reimagine rest. It's not just what you think it is: a full nap away from the kids with the pillow up, closed eyes, eye mask on, closed door. In this culture, that's not going to be possible for all people. It's going to have to be a reimagining—like my grandmother resting on a couch with her eyes closed for thirty minutes, centering her own body and her own self, while all of the world was still happening around her. She didn't care. She was going to sit on that couch and do that.

My dad would wake up early before his job to sit and pray and read the paper. And I asked him why he got up so early. He was like "I want to have a moment where I'm not on someone's clock and I can just be. I want to have a moment where I can be human."

TRICIA HERSEY

I return to myself when

I trust that there is enough time.

I was reading something the other day and it talked about how we never could see a baby grow, can we? We can't sit there all day and say, "Oh, she just grew."

I've never seen a plant grow. I've come out the next day and I've seen that it's grown, but I can never see it when it's growing. I can never catch it.

And the same holds true with us. I have found that the changes I make on the journey to self-love are quieter. And they're the kind of changes I can't see any more than I can see a plant or a baby grow. But, little by slowly, I can see the difference. And then in spring we go out and we go, "Oh, my garden's grown."

And we need to do that with ourselves too. We need to also tell ourselves about the progress we've made little by slowly.

MELODY BEATTIE

little by slowly

Healing is this constant unlearning to relearn. It's a cycle. It's a cycle because there are always going to be things that scare us in life. There are always going to be things that trigger us and make us go back to our old self. So how do we redirect? How do we learn that *I was not safe then, but I am safe now*? We can practice recognizing we are safe now by answering the questions "Why am I safe? Where am I safe? How am I safe? Who am I safe with?" That brings us back. That brings us back to the moment.

ALEX ELLE

I learned to strive and perform for love from my family and the world. I continued to chase that kind of transactional love until I was forty. It's wild to think back to being a kid and realizing that because of my fear of detachment and abandonment, I actually learned how to perform. I learned that. I love thinking of it that way because it's proof that I did it. I taught myself those things then, which means I have the capacity to teach myself new things now. I'm forty-five now, and I'm retraining myself to replace the idea that love is something to earn with the idea that love already exists between me and my closest people. It's already there. It's not like money I have to hustle to earn; it's more like air I just get to breathe.

ABBY

I return to myself when
I remember that I've overcome before and I'll overcome now.

—

JUSTICE KETANJI BROWN JACKSON: My mother and my father both grew up in Miami during a time of segregation, where Black people really were not allowed to swim in public pools or get ordinary swimming lessons in public facilities. So my parents weren't trained to swim. But they wanted me to do everything, so I took swimming lessons. I loved to float on my back. That was my big thing—with the sun on my face and just kind of calm and serene. And I was doing this at a pool party. I wanted to float, so I went over to the deep end, but I thought I'd be close to the edge in case I needed it. I started floating, and I got kind of out into the middle, and I looked and saw I was too far away from the edge, and I panicked. And I basically just flailed around and sunk to the bottom of the pool. I might have been under not too long when one of my mom's friends jumped in the water fully clothed and brought me up. It was very dramatic. But I was so disappointed in myself because I knew how to swim. And I don't know why I had given in to the doubts the way that I had. It was sort of a life lesson for me, that I really just felt like: *From now on I'm not going to allow my fears to get in the way of what it is I'm trying to accomplish.*

GLENNON: Yes. We can always handle the deep end if we remember that we know how to swim.

—

I can trust me to take care of me. I can trust me to love me through anything. I can trust me to see me to the other side of anything. When I am most clear, when I am most present, when I am most aware of who I am in a moment, that truth is undeniable. It is coursing through my veins. It is in my marrow. It is traveling from the top of my head to the tips of my toes, out to my fingers, and I feel like I am on fire. I feel like I could catch anything else on fire that I wanted to and we could burn it all down and rebuild something beautiful from the ashes.

That's how I feel when I am in the center of myself. And I am always trying to get back to that place. With everything I do, with everything I say, with everything I am, I am always trying to get back to that place, because that is true Ashley. That is core Ashley. That is the Ashley that was Ashley before Ashley knew her own name.

I'm not going to hate myself into being the version of the person I want to be. It's impossible. Only love is going to get me there. I've got to love myself into being that person. I've got to trust myself into being that person.

ASHLEY C. FORD

Five

How do I figure out what I want?

The other day I asked a struggling friend, "Do you want to stay in your marriage or leave?"

She looked at me with very tired eyes and answered, "I don't even know what I want for dinner."

Remember when we were kids and we knew what we wanted? Even if we couldn't do it, at least we knew what we wanted. What happened? Why don't we know how to know what we want anymore?

AMANDA

During the women's rights movements for voting and labor rights, the marching strikers chanted, "We want bread and roses, too. Bread for all, and roses, too." Their message was: Not only do we want decent working conditions and fair pay, but we want liberty over our own lives. We want pleasure. We want the delights of life. We want music and time.

And here's the complicated thing about life's delights: They require time, peace of mind, and a community that will hold our stuff for us so that we can step away for just a couple of minutes and stand in life's sunshine to get access to the roses. We need support to protect us through all the demands. We want bread—and roses, too.

So the question is not and never has been: *What do women want?*

It is: *How can we get free enough to learn what we want and then actually access life's delights?*

EMILY NAGOSKI

One thing I know can be trusted is that I have something inside of me guiding me. I experience this guide differently all the time, so I'm not even going to try to describe what it feels like. I just have something inside of me that always knows what to do next. Even so, following that knowing is so difficult. I often try everything else first—anything to avoid trusting it.

Every time I notice a cage around me—a job, an event, a relationship, something that just doesn't feel right—I can trace it back to a moment I felt a knowing on the inside and ignored or defied it. Every misstep starts with a knowing that I didn't turn into a doing. The flip side is also true: When I find myself inside of something miraculous, I can trace it back to a moment of alignment between my instinct and my action. The more we act on these tiny inner inklings, the more our outer life changes and becomes aligned with who we truly are and what we truly want. That's how we match our outsides to our insides.

GLENNON

To figure out what I want

I trust my intuition.

Intuition is not a *woo-woo* supernatural thing. It's real, for everyone. Intuition is the ability to process information you are not even conscious of, to know something without analytical reasoning. Science shows us that intuition operates through the entire right side of the brain and through our gut—that's why it's called *gut instinct*. So whether you acknowledge it or not, intuition is being processed inside your body. In our most desperate moments, when we literally have nothing else to turn to, our intuition is there. And we can practice finding it. For me, inner knowing feels like joy and freedom and anything that makes me feel alive. It shows up for about thirty seconds. It's never sustained, and it's not a static place of arrival. It's the flash of seeing another way for myself. It is how we know that something is for us, how we know that something is of our knowing and our choosing. We can practice learning what our intuition is by running toward anything that feels like a few seconds of being alive. Anything that feels like freedom to me is what I can trust.

AMANDA

—

GLENNON: You write about how wise we were when we were younger, before we learned all this crap that made us stop trusting ourselves. You wrote, "When my life was new I understood in my bones how little it mattered what anybody else was doing or what they thought about what I was doing. I believed my bones then." What does it mean to believe your bones? Do you believe your bones now? What does that feel like?

ASHLEY C. FORD: Yeah, you can call it intuition. You can call it self-trust. It's just trusting yourself. I tend to attribute so many things to either luck or circumstance, and that's real. But also, *I've kept me alive this whole time.* Any success I have, anything I hold on to within or outside of myself that makes me feel pride and makes me feel happy and makes me feel love—I sought those things out. I was smart enough to do that. I was smart enough to hold on to them when I found them. The things that weren't serving me, for the most part, I have been smart enough to either let them go or be in the practice of letting them go. I can trust myself to keep doing that.

—

If you want to know what intuition is, ask yourself: What does ten-year-old me need? Because ten-year-old you is not going to say that she needs a new business strategy. Ten-year-old you is going to say, "I need rest. I'm hungry. I want to feel safe. I need fresh air. I need to scream."

GLENNON

I've been traveling the planet for months on a wild pilgrimage-sojourn thing. I was supposed to be in Greece for ten days, but I ended up staying in Greece for thirty-four days at some stranger's house, just listening to my wild wildness. One day I was meditating, and I visited my little Sonya. I spent some time with her. I went up to her and asked her what she wanted.

And little Sonya said, "I want to go home." I was like "Oh, I'll be your home. We are our own home." It was really sweet and tender and beautiful. And little Sonya was like "No, chick. I want a plane trip to Pittsburgh, and I want a hoagie. Thanks for all your fluffy duffy therapized meaning, though." It was this phenomenal moment of awareness. That need didn't come from my head; it came from my soul, from the smallest parts of me.

Sometimes the work is to not be in our head at all. You have no answers there. The answer is in the center of you. It's in your gut, it's inside the deepest, quietest, usually most disavowed part of ourselves. And that part isn't thinking.

SONYA RENEE TAYLOR

I'd been working in Rwanda for a little less than a year. I was scheduled to return to the United States the next day but had taken a short trip by myself before leaving. That night I flew in from Egypt with a stopover in Ethiopia in order to catch the last flight to the United States.

I'm sitting at the airport in Addis Ababa having a drink with a bunch of other backpackers and passers-through. A few minutes before I have to board my flight, one of them says, "You should come with us to South Africa."

Suddenly I am frozen, staring at two paths. One is a path of extraordinary adventures and unknowns with who the hell knows. The other is a path of ordinary adventures with a man I love and the family that we would eventually have.

Both paths were so beautiful to me. Choosing either one meant forsaking the other. The cruel reality hit me for the first time that choosing one thing you love means losing another thing you love.

I'm frozen in that crucible for what felt like a long time. Over the airport intercom, I hear, "Amanda Doyle, your flight is departing."

I was forced to make a momentary, lifelong decision. The calculus happened. My body chose. I threw on my backpack and sprinted like hell to the gate.

I stepped on that path, and the other one disappeared.

AMANDA

Most people are lying when they say, "Oh yeah, this is who I am." It's performance art. Actually, they go home in the halo of their phone scrolling, being like: *Is this really what I want? Is this really who I am?* So if you're not sure of exactly who you are, you're not alone. You're just honest.

One of the joys of being a stage performer is that it's one of the few places in the world where experimentation is encouraged. When you're doing improv or when you're doing drag, you start to just try things. I didn't know my gender was possible, and then I started to dress up for the stage.

Then I was like, *Wait. This was really fun,* and I found out: *Oh, this is kind of who I am.* So what I've learned as an artist is that everyone needs experimentation. It's okay to get it wrong, because it's all going to take you closer to where you need to end up.

Authenticity is not a destination, it's an orientation, and what matters more is that you're showing up, not where you're going.

ALOK

To figure out what I want

I experiment.

When I sold my store, I had no idea what I was going to do next. I was around fifty years old. I actually thought my best career was behind me. I thought I would never figure out what to do next.

My husband, Jeffrey, said to me, "Well, you love the food business. Maybe you can do it in a different way." I thought to myself: *Well, people have asked me to do a cookbook. At least that will give me something to do.* I'd never written a cookbook before. But I just started doing it and tried to figure out how I could make it enjoyable and fun.

You don't always know exactly what it is you want to do, but just start. Just start doing something that would be interesting. And that will lead to something else that's interesting. And that leads to something else.

INA GARTEN

Desire Experiments

WITH GLENNON

My teenager and their friends were hanging out in our family room one weekend, and I popped in and asked, "Are you hungry?" The boys kept their eyes on the screen and yelled, "Yes!" while the girls paused and searched one another's faces. Finally one spokesgirl looked back at me, smiled, and said, "No, thank you, we're fine." In moments of uncertainty, boys are trained to look inward for their own desire; girls are trained to look outward for others' permission and consensus. We forget how to want when we learn how to please. Experimenting can help us remember.

① Flip a coin.

My friend couldn't decide whether she wanted to remain in her present career or quit and go to grad school. I held up a coin and said, "I'm about to toss this into the air. If it lands heads up, you're going to grad school. If it lands tails up, you're staying on the partner track at work. The results are final. Call it."

She watched the coin launch and then yelled, "HEADS! HEADS!" "Okay," I said. "Grad school it is. We're going to grad school."

② Try new language.

A new friend told me that even when she's cold, she can't seem to say, "I'm cold." Instead, she asks, "Is anybody else cold?" When she's hungry, she doesn't say, "I'm hungry." She asks, "Is anyone else hungry?" She doesn't believe she has the ability or the permission to know or express her individual wants or needs, so she asks around to find out what she *should* want.

We all seem pretty comfortable in the language of *should*. To get to know ourselves for the first time, we have to practice new language.

Instead of: *I should . . .*

Let's try: *I want . . . I need . . . I feel . . . I am . . .*

*To figure out what I want **I experiment.***

③ Decide based on who you are *now*.

We're putting the groceries away. Abby holds up the kale and asks, "Shall I toss this directly into the trash or put it in fridge purgatory, wait for it to rot, and *then* throw it away?"

I am not a kale person. I have never been a kale person. But when I'm at the grocery store, I am not shopping as the me I've always been, I'm shopping as some different, future version of me who *is* a kale person. I do this when packing for a trip, too. The real me has never worn anything but sweatpants and jeans, but I pack as some fabulous, imaginary future version of me who will *definitely* want to wear this sequin jumpsuit. I do this when deciding whether to accept or decline an invitation. In almost fifty years, I have *never wanted to go to a party*. Yet I do not RSVP as me; I RSVP as some future me who will become a social butterfly and would be delighted to attend! I RSVP: "YES! I'll bring a kale dish! I'll wear my sequin jumpsuit!"

After I RSVP, I curl up on my couch and begin dreading the party and dreaming up ways to cancel while my kale rots in the fridge and my sequin jumpsuit stays forever in my suitcase.

Now I grocery shop as *me*. I pack as *me*. When I receive an invitation, I ask myself: *Glennon, would you want to attend this event tonight? If you don't want to go* this *night, you're not going to want to go* that *night.* Then I curl up in my sweatpants with my Doritos, and I am happy.

④ Imagine your eighty-year-old self.

I have a very clear vision of myself as an eighty-year-old. It's actually my favorite vision of myself. I'm walking slowly on a beach, and I have the most beautiful gray hair. It's long and curly, pulled back in a ponytail. I'm wearing loose, flowy clothing, no shoes, a couple dogs gleefully running up ahead. I'm just doing my daily walk, heading back to my tiny purple cottage. I'm so full of peace and power and calm. I always think: *What do I have to do today to get closer to becoming that badass peaceful woman in the flowy robe walking barefoot on the beach? What would she tell me to do about this situation?* It's a cool exercise to imagine the truest, most beautiful older version of you. Then that image can become a lighthouse, guiding you to her. Instead of growing older being something to avoid, it becomes something incredible to become.

NATALIE PORTMAN: I've been working with an executive coach, Diana, who has been helping me learn how to recognize my desires and undo my people pleasing. She's taught me to pay attention to my body. She calls it a "full-body yes." Think about something that you have a full-body yes to. You feel it in your body. Now think about something that feels like a full-body no. Feel what that feels like in your body, name where it shows up. And then feel something that's in the middle. In your life, practice moving toward things that are full-body yeses. It's a physical experience, practicing: *What is the physical experience of yes?* Of: *Yes, I completely want this.* And of: *No, I completely do not want this,* and those moments in between.

GLENNON: When we try to decide what we want or don't want, we always go to our mind to try to figure it out. But what I have discovered again and again is that it's never there. I need to do the body thing to figure out what feels warm or cold—spacious or restrictive.

NATALIE: It's great to put it in any kind of physical terms, because also that's objective experience. Thoughts and feelings are so subjective and confusing, but physical experiences feel good and don't feel good. I have a friend who says she wants to be more like her dog. Where she's like: *Person's nice, I go toward. Person's not nice, I back away.* It really is relying on your instincts.

ABBY: The body knows.

—

To figure out what I want

I listen to my body.

I'm just trying to follow what makes me feel good inside, what makes me feel tingly. I can feel when my aliveness is being drained from me, and I can feel when it's being added to. And that is the measure by which I'm currently evaluating all of my business decisions: Is it giving life, or is it taking it away?

JUSTINA BLAKENEY

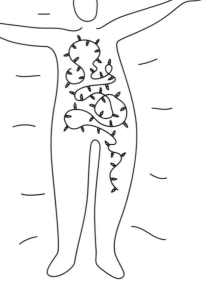

Sometimes it takes a moment of quiet, of stillness, to figure out what brings you joy and what sparks your curiosity—and then it takes a bit of initiative to make it happen for yourself. For example, there was a Saturday afternoon a few years ago when I was taking a break from screens—I was doing a Digital Sabbath—and found myself with a full hour completely to myself. It should have felt luxurious, but instead I had this real existential moment where I realized that I didn't know what I actually *wanted* to do. I had gotten so used to allowing my time to be filled by whatever presented itself on a screen that when that option was taken away, I was clueless.

I ended up asking myself a question I'd been asking *other* people: *What's something you say you want to do but you supposedly don't have time for?* I answered: *Well, I've always said that I want to play guitar.*

And so in that moment on the couch, in my existential hole, I was like: *Okay, the next time I'm online, I'm going to find a guitar class.* And I did. I signed up for a class and started spending my Wednesday evenings with a group of other adults, many of whom were parents of young kids, *playing.* And I mean that in both senses of the word: We were learning to play the guitar, but we were also just playing, because there was no broader point; none of us was trying to become a professional musician. I never would have predicted it, but before long, that class had become the highlight of my week. I was getting this sense of joy and buoyancy and energy that was deeply nourishing, that powered me through the rest of the week. It felt like this shining light in the exhausting darkness of early parenthood. It took me a while to put a word to my experience, and when I finally did, the word was *fun.* I was having fun.

CATHERINE PRICE

To figure out what I want

I get still enough to notice the tiniest nudge.

Wanting comes from somewhere inside of us. It connects with a little sense of impulse and sensation inside. When you start to know what this looks and feels and sounds like inside of you, then you can start to recognize it with bigger things. That wanting has a quality to it that we can start to actually build a relationship with.

Our body communicates what it needs with energy and temperature and impulse. It's really hard to listen to these sensations if we don't make space. We can be really quick to distract ourselves and move into what we might call our defenses, our ways of intellectualizing, ignoring, numbing out, or deferring responsibility to somebody else.

If we can start to slow down in our lives in general, then we're more likely to catch those sensations. And when we catch those sensations, then we can make space around them and lead with curiosity.

I often like to allow myself to take a breath and imagine that I'm breathing into a sensation. And then I ask the sensation: *Is there something you want me to know? What is it that's there? What needs to happen next? What do you want for me?*

DR. HILLARY MCBRIDE

The real work is paying attention when you are having uncomfortable feelings. That will reveal what your needs are. When I am feeling anxious, what is the thing? Is it that I have to interact with a person who doesn't allow me to ever speak about myself? If so, my need is to talk more about myself in this relationship. When we have the discomfort of anxiety, depression, resentment, those are all times to really think about why. *Why am I feeling this?* And the need will come up.

NEDRA GLOVER TAWWAB

Resentment and jealousy are in fact very helpful data points. When I'm feeling jealous and resentful, it may come out as "I don't like that person." But likely it isn't even about that person. I'm probably just super annoyed that they're always posting their #FriYAY Date Night pictures, and it makes me think I don't like them, when it actually means I just really need a #FriYAY Date Night.

AMANDA

Disgust and desire are really in deep relation with each other. I experienced this recently while watching the work of dancer and choreographer Matty Davis. I saw his work for about five seconds, and it was so physical, so visceral, and there were a really wide variety of bodies—and I slammed my computer screen shut. I was like: *I hate this.* Later, I realized that watching that video was the first time that, as a disabled woman, I could imagine a dance universe where my body would be valued. That was so threatening to me because it asked me the question *Do you want to do this?* and that terrified me. So desire and disgust live very close in relation to each other. When there's deep dismissal or profound judgment of something, maybe that's actually a voice that's telling you you want it and you're afraid of it.

CHLOÉ COOPER JONES

To figure out what I want

I pay attention when I feel bad.

When you ask a woman, "Why do you need that bottle of wine tonight?," she'll tell you, "I just need a break. I just need a moment of peace." Big alcohol took a very real human need and slapped a label on a product to fake solve it—commodifying celebration, joy, and rest because that's the role of marketing. The booze is just some crappy consolation prize, but the deeper desire beneath the need for that bottle of wine is what's real and interesting. That deep desire is *good*. It can be trusted. It's the human desire for some rest, some peace, the ability to check out of your mind for a minute. To stop being so damn *responsible.*

GLENNON

Coping mechanisms—like alcohol abuse, compulsive shopping, love addiction, and overwork—are pointed ways of finding relief in a sensitive body, when what we're really trying to access is joy. We're chasing dopamine. We're chasing oxytocin. We're chasing serotonin. We're chasing the feel-good because it is a birthright for us to have some semblance of joy in our bodies. If we realized that what we were truly looking for was joy, maybe we could find other ways to get that.

ALANIS MORISSETTE

Allow your longing.
I believe our
longing
is the
thing
that
has
already
happened
to us, but
we haven't
caught up to it
in time. It's loving
something before we
believe in it. It is right
to long. It is right to yearn.
It is our yearning that takes us
forward toward our soul's desire. ⌒

⁓ The only real map of our lives is in our yearning. If you can sit in it and say: *You know what, Yearning? I believe you. I believe you're meant to be fulfilled,* you will feel a piece of truth come into your heart. There will be freedom in believing your yearning can be fulfilled. **MARTHA BECK**

Conjure up the truest, most beautiful life, relationship, community, world you can imagine. Write it down. Put pen to paper. Think about an architect. Before imagination becomes three-dimensional, it usually needs to become two-dimensional. Now read what you've written and consider that your imaginings are not a pipe dream. Your imaginings are your marching orders. We must start accepting that what we can imagine, we can also create.

GLENNON

—

BRIANA SCURRY: When I was in my early teens, I made a sign with basic printer paper, and it said, "Olympics 1996, I have a dream." I made it very nice, very specific, very exact, with my ruler and my pencil. I put that sign on my wall, and I looked at it every morning when I woke up and every night before I went to bed. Sure enough, guess where I found myself in 1996?

ABBY: And women's soccer wasn't even an Olympic sport when you made this sign! So you imagined *that* into existence, too.

—

To figure out what I want

I let my imagination guide me.

We're in this hard period of trying to imagine a new space. But this is why I love fiction. Fiction, for me, is like a doorstop that wedges the door open. It holds open a space where new stuff can come in. It says: *Yes, things can be different. We don't know exactly what that looks like yet, but it could be different. The way things are now is not the way that things have to be.*

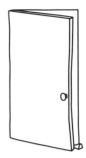

CELESTE NG

The whole philosophy of *Schitt's Creek* wrote itself when we decided that this town was going to be a safe haven. We thought: *What if this town was a better place than we could ever imagine? What if this town was a place that allowed our family to feel free and safe enough to understand ourselves?* Sometimes that's all it takes—just a desire to write something that is a sweeter world than the one we live in now and hope that people catch up.

DAN LEVY

It turns out that providing an energy—a kind of imaginative possibility—and the space for hope and optimism can bring us to a place where we can really surprise ourselves.

REBECCA TRAISTER

People think imagination is just frivolous. But to be able to imagine and wonder, that's where the ideas for liberation come. We can imagine ourselves free. The world that we live in now was imagined and thought up by people. Some folks, mostly white men, sat down and invented and created this. But we can imagine a new way—a new world and a new opportunity for us to be liberated.

TRICIA HERSEY

I believe this in my heart: I think that most people who write to me know what they need to do or they want to do—but they're really afraid to know it or want it.

I came upon this because I started to write the column and people sent in letters asking for advice. And I started to notice that very often there would be a sentence right at the core of the letter that would just say, "I know this relationship is wrong" or "I know what I really want to be is a teacher instead of a doctor," whatever it was. Then they would say, "But here are all the reasons I can't know that or want that . . . because it will cause trouble in my life, it will disappoint my family, it will somehow be against the story I've told myself so far—that I don't deserve this or I'm not allowed to want that."

I think my most important work is to show people what they already know but are afraid to know. It's okay to want what you want. You have permission to do the thing you want. Because wanting to is enough.

I'm simply telling you what you already know. I am saying you are allowed to know it. You are allowed to know the true thing about yourself, and you are allowed to act on it.

CHERYL STRAYED

Six

How do I know what to do?

When I was young, I loved those Choose Your Own Adventure books. As I read, I'd get to make decisions for the main character and the story and the ending would change based on what I chose.

It freaks me out that my life is a Choose Your Own Adventure book and every single decision I make determines my plot and my ending. It makes the stakes seem so high.

Do I go to college? Do I get married? Who do I marry? Do I have kids? How many? How do I raise them? What career do I choose? When relationships get hard, do I try harder or walk away? Where do I live? What friends do I choose? It's exhausting, man. How am I supposed to know what to do?

ABBY

One of the things I tend to do when I'm trying to make a decision is I ask everybody their opinion. I do all the research that I can to become an expert on the question. But that's having a monkey mind, where you go out into a tree filled with other monkeys and you ask all the other monkeys what those monkeys think you should do. That's called taking a monkey survey. And it is the farthest thing from wisdom that you could possibly get.

Instead of taking a monkey survey, give your brain permission to stand down and allow guidance from some other place. Even if it's just for five minutes, allow something else to speak. Your body knows what's true.

ELIZABETH GILBERT

This life is mine alone.
So I have stopped asking
people for directions to
places they've never been.

GLENNON

The word *right* can be a red flag. If you're looking to do what's *right,* then you know you're looking to somebody else's map instead of your own inner compass. That approach is never going to feel like knowing. Knowing doesn't speak in the language of being right; it speaks in the language of feeling alive, of feeling free. So we can just remove the right. Let's stop asking, "Is it right for me?," and start asking, "Is it for me?"

AMANDA

Women face an excruciating double bind. We can never make everybody happy—we're screwed either way. The mom who doesn't want to take a long leave after she's given birth because she really wants to go back to work, she's suddenly an irresponsible mother. Whereas the mom who wants to stay at home and take that leave, well, of course she does, because, "That's what women do." And then she's left out of promotions. You can't make everybody happy. The only person you can really focus on is yourself—build yourself up, find your truth, understand what you need, and give yourself the opportunity to choose the things that *you* want.

MORI TAHERIPOUR

I know what to do when
I live by my own compass.

136

—

GLENNON: I always made big decisions by polling—by asking everyone else what I should do. I would get a consensus, and that's how I would decide. When my marriage started to fall apart, my Christian friends were like "The right thing to do is to stay. A good woman would stay. A brave mother would stay." My feminist friends were like "The right thing to do is get yourself out of there. A brave mother would leave." And I realized: *Ah. Right and wrong, good and bad, strong and weak—these are not objective ideas. They are all contextual. They are words we use and conclusions we make to justify our specific dogmas.* These voices telling me what to do—they're the barking sheepdogs trying to keep me in that particular herd. I had a beautiful moment when I realized: *Oh, I see. I can't please everybody. I guess I can go ahead and please myself.*

MARTHA BECK: That actually is the way most people live. We look around at the pressures on us from other people, and then we come to consensus, we choose what makes us fit in best. The true knowledge of what to do next is not in the brain, but it's in all the senses. It's in every single bit of you once the clamor of consensus is gone. Don't live by coming to consensus. Live by coming to your senses.

—

I want to be the president of my life, the governor, the mayor of my town. I don't want to have to answer to anyone but me. I want to live honestly and make honest choices for me. I can't have the noise from other people, it's too much. I need to listen only to me.

SARAH PAULSON

Martha Beck: Drop into your body. What feels like calm, what feels warm and free? You'll always find the right answer there. Some impulses will feel chaotic. Your desire will feel peaceful. It's when your heart, your mind, your body, and your soul are all saying the same thing. It feels like puzzle pieces clicking or locks coming into alignment.

When you're trying to make a decision and you get to the right decision—if you really pay attention—you'll notice your body spontaneously relax and feel at peace. And you can do that one decision at a time.

Glennon: Yes. I have an inner guide that always knows what to do next. It never tells me the five-year plan, just the next right thing. It waits until I commit to that next right thing, and then it shows me the next thing. One step at a time, the path lights up in front of me like a yellow brick road. I can find my whole way home like that—just one step, one next right thing, at a time.

I know what to do when

I go toward what feels warm.

When I met Abby, I fell desperately in love for the first time. It was the best feeling I'd ever had in my life. I was full of warmth and joy. At the same time, I had all these reasons why I couldn't be with her. My mind was a constant loop of: *No, no, no, I can't.* I was so afraid. Martha listened to me rattle off all my fears, and she said to me, "I need you to get back into your body, and I need you to tell me what feels warm. It is okay for you to go toward what feels warm. It is okay to trust that." That moment changed my life. I started to go toward what felt warm, and it brought me to Abby.

GLENNON

I have this thing I say to myself when I'm tempted to make a decision that goes against my intuition: *Abby, don't get out of the hot tub.* I have a friend who knew she shouldn't be marrying her partner. An hour before the ceremony, she was still sitting in a hot tub at the hotel. Her sister kept telling her, worriedly, "Honey, you gotta get out of the hot tub." My friend kept resisting. Her resistance was her body saying: *This isn't right. Don't do it.* But she did get out of the hot tub, and she got dressed, and she got married. Because what was she going to do? All those people had come. The tuna tartare was ordered. Who cares if the tuna tartare is ordered? Who cares if it rocks the boat? It's never too late to say, "Turns out I'm not getting out of the hot tub after all. Enjoy the tuna tartare on me."

ABBY

If you're unsure about whether or not to do something, imagine standing on a high diving board over a pool on a very hot day. Is the water sparkling and blue but you're scared because it's a really long way down? Or is it a pool of stinky toxic sludge and you're just revolted by the idea of going down? If it stinks, don't do it. If the water is calling to you but you're scared to jump because it's a long way down, then you're having a conflict between the longing for the water and the fear of the fall.

If your fear and your longing conflict, choose your longing no matter what anybody else says.

If you're deciding about whether or not to have kids and you long for a life of travel, free from children, where you can do anything you want, go with that no matter what pressures are placed on you. But if you long to have children and then something comes up and says: *But I can't do it well enough, I'm not good enough,* those are social voices coming in and conflicting with your heart. Always go with your longing no matter how frightened you are, and you'll always find the right path.

MARTHA BECK

I know what to do when

I let my longing be louder than my fear.

A man wrote to me and said, "I'm approaching forty. Do I want a kid or not? Do I want to be a father or not? I don't know. I really don't know."

I said, "Get out some big pieces of paper and make a list of the life you imagine without kids and make a list of the life you imagine with kids. What won't you be able to do if you have kids, and what won't you be able to do if you don't? And have the good things in your life happened because of ease or hardship?"

When I was turning forty, my husband and I were talking about having a third child, and we made two lists. One of them was all the reasons not to have a third child, and one of them was all the reasons to have a third child. There was one thing on the reasons to have a child, and there were like three hundred things on the reasons not to, but that didn't necessarily matter. There might be only one thing on one side of the list, but that might be more important than all the other things.

You make the list to get your unexpressed feelings and thoughts out on the page, so you can look at them analytically. Then you rank the list, circle the truest things on those lists, and see where that puts you, see where that lands you.

I think of it as self-therapy. You just draw out from deep within yourself everything that you can imagine that's true. Then you get to look at it. You get to let it be a map of where to go next. Instead of a to-do list, this is a to-know list.

CHERYL STRAYED

Making big decisions was already a big no. It was like: *I'm going to need my agent, my mom, my sister, whoever, to do that for me. I will not make a decision.* And God forbid if it's wrong. I couldn't handle that. It would make me crumble and disintegrate.

And so my practice just became making small decisions, literally like going to the store and picking out a candle or a shirt, picking out what outfit I was going to wear for the day. At the time, those things would take me hours because the idea of making a decision and trusting myself was so hard and heavy.

Then I started learning how to trust my gut and I could speed up the decision-making process. It became "Oh, I actually don't like the idea of going to this thing" or "This day doesn't work for me." Being able to say those things took years, but what kick-started it all was learning how to make small decisions.

LAURIE HERNANDEZ

I know what to do when

I practice trusting myself with small decisions.

Overthinking is a sign that I'm frozen because I don't trust myself. I can rebuild self-trust by trying anything, one thing at a time. Just one little decision at a time. That's how I slowly unfreeze. Life is improv.

GLENNON

In improv, I'm forced to be present and to trust the decisions I'm making in real time instead of overthinking. I would imagine it's like an athlete where you work out and you train and the team is so used to working together, so that when you go out into the field, you're not thinking; you're just doing and trusting each other. And to get in your head while you're playing would be the worst thing.

It's the commitment to letting unfold what should unfold while also putting your own energy and spin into it. I think we can all take that into our daily lives, the spontaneity and trust we learn from sport or improv. With improv you have to trust that your choices will work or they'll fail or they'll just be what they are.

ABBI JACOBSON

People are always saying that they do this or that to "take the edge off." The edge they're talking about is the stress, the discontent, the daily suffering of being human. I get it. But when I stopped taking the edge off, when I stopped numbing daily and started just sitting with and living with the edge, my life changed. I've come to believe that we deeply need the edge. The edge is the discomfort that propels us to change the job, make the move, say the hard thing, quit the habit, end or begin the relationship. The edge is the catalyst. Numbing the edge every day makes folks live half a life.

GLENNON

The instructions are there. They're there inside the rage. They're there inside the dejection and the limpness and the suffering. The suffering is teaching you the instructions for your life. And here's the cool thing: Nobody else has them. The only way you're going to ever find them is if you go in and get them from inside yourself. Your instructions are nowhere else but inside you.

MARTHA BECK

I know what to do when

I don't take the edge off.

Directions for Rock Bottom

WITH MARTHA BECK

(1) You've pushed yourself to the point where you can't do it anymore.

(2) Go in your room, get out a piece of paper, and say, "Here is what I am sick of. I hate this. I hate it." Write it all down. I call it liberation through pain and rage. The rage inside you is the wild animal saying "No." When you get to the place where you hate life and you want to die and you actually let that part of you die, there's still something left and it comes to its senses. It's often a place where no social pressure can reach, and it raises its head out of the crowd of the world and says: *Oh, come here.*

(3) Next, as Mary Oliver says, you let the soft animal of your body come out and let it love what it loves. You express everything it loves and write it down. Write it *all* down. The most forbidden things, because the forbidden things you're thinking are the things that consensus told you never to think. When you realize you're still alive, you come out of it as I did when I said, "Well, now I don't really care what anybody thinks of me. And I'm gay."

The knowledge of what to do next is there. It's not in the brain, it's in all the senses. It's in every single bit of you once the clamor of consensus is gone. The Buddha used to say, "Wherever you find water, you can know if it's the ocean because the ocean always tastes of salt." Enlightenment can take many different forms and look different for everyone, but you always know it's enlightenment because it always tastes of freedom. Always.

It may hurt. It may make your family hate you. It may terrify the crap out of you. But it will always feel like freedom.

Glennon: Someone asked me, "How do we know when we're quitting because it's wrong for us or just because it's hard for us?"

Amanda: I'm trying to understand the question. Are they trying to figure out, "Do I just want to become free of this thing because it's hard for me?" Or, "Do I want to be free of this thing because it's not *for* me?"

Glennon: Well, I think you just answered the question. I often want to quit hard things that I do not quit. I mean, writing a book is hard, raising kids is hard, staying sober is hard. There are things that I continue to do every day, even when I want to quit. So I think the answer is what you just said, Sister: You don't quit just because it's hard for you; you quit because it's just not *for* you.

I know what to do when

I quit what is no longer for me.

*I'm quitting a stable government job this month
to pursue my career in art. It's taken me a lot
of time to realize that this is what I want to do,
and I'm excited about it. But I'm feeling terrified
and overwhelmed and like I'm not fully ready
to quit this great job. And I also feel that it's
necessary—I know I need to take a risk and
jump in with both feet. I'm just having a hard
time trusting myself. What do I do?*

AMANDA: You're trying to decide whether to quit or not, but the truth is: You'll be quitting either way. If you pursue your art, you'll be quitting your job. But if you stay in your job, you'll be quitting your art. You said you've been excited and preparing and your heart wants to pursue art. You'll be quitting *that* if you stay at your job. So which one do you want to quit? It sounds like you're deciding that being free of the stable job allows you to not quit the risky dream, and that sounds amazing.

GLENNON: Yes! Let's frame every decision like that: It's quitting either way! So you quit your job or you quit your dream—which quit do you choose? It's like when people say, "I want to leave this toxic relationship, but it's too hard to leave." The follow-up question is: "Well, isn't it too hard to stay?" It's hard either way. Are you going to quit the relationship, or are you going to quit your idea that you deserve to be loved well? Leaving and rocking the boat is hard, but so is staying and slowly dying inside. Which hard are you going to choose?

Often, when making decisions, I try to put myself on my deathbed and consider whether I'll be happy I did it, sad I didn't do it, or whether it will even matter.

I say, "This thing that I'm doing, how important is it going to be to me on my deathbed?" I futurecast my way to the end. It helps for a lot of things—like a breakup, for example.

On my deathbed, will I be happy we broke up? Will I be sad I didn't do it? Or will it not even matter? If any of those are the case, go ahead and break up, girl.

ALUA ARTHUR

Seven

How do I do the hard thing?

Most of my suffering eras began because I was avoiding doing a single hard thing that I knew I had to do. We do that, right?

We suffer in a miserable marriage to avoid the painful breakup. We stay in an unfulfilling job because we're afraid of the uncertainty after quitting. We keep a toxic friendship to avoid the awkward goodbye.

We choose long-term suffering instead of short-term pain. It's a strange choice. I know this, and still, very often, the gap between what I know I must do and actually doing that thing feels uncrossable.

Why is it so hard to do what we must do?

GLENNON

I always talk about this Fannie Lou Hamer quote as the way that I orient around the right kind of hard. She says, "If I fall, I'll fall five feet four inches forward in the fight for freedom." That's how I know it's the right kind of hard. It doesn't mean my knees ain't scraped up; it doesn't mean I didn't lose some skin. I might be bleeding; I might have broke something. But am I closer toward my own revelation of my divinity than I was before I started? If so, then I'm doing the right kind of hard. I'm doing the work of reclaiming my liberation.

A lot of people don't do this work because they're like "It's so hard." Of course it's hard. It's tiring. Sometimes it's expensive. It's lonely. It can be frightening. It's all of those things. But it's like that anyway. You are lonely and frightened and fearful and exhausted right now, believing you're not enough. So if you're going to be that anyway, if you're going to do that anyway, fall forward toward your liberation.

SONYA RENEE TAYLOR

Almost all of us are steeped in communities and cultures and families that say telling the truth is dangerous, telling the truth will cause trouble, telling the truth will hurt other people, telling the truth will, in some way, cast you out of the circle of belonging. I actually think that the reverse is true. Truth always leads us in the direction of who we are meant to become.

My mind spins with so many examples of this. Think about every LGBTQ kid who was told growing up, "You're not allowed to be that. You're not allowed to want that," and how toxic it is to hold that lie, and how liberating, how beautiful, how powerful, how illuminating it is to say, "No, that's not true. I'm going to tell the truth about who I am." Or the lie of an addiction: "This is what I need to live. This is the thing that makes me feel okay." No, that's not true.

Lies never keep us safe. They only lead us to harm. I know all of us have lived in lies. But when you bring things into the light, when you speak your truth, when you live out what you know is the right way, that puts you in the safer zone, because then you're aligned.

The most painful thing is to be misaligned, to have your life out there be different from your life in here.

CHERYL STRAYED

To do the hard thing
I tell the truth.

I cannot imagine the suffering and sorrow that I could have avoided if I would've just told the truth about my marriage. In parenting, you get to reach sideways for help. We have each other in that. But in marriage, it is you and it's the other person. So when things are so, so broken, it's scary and it's isolating, and that's the easiest place, at least for me, to lie to myself about what's real. But saying the truth of how I felt out loud was the beginning of the end, in a good way. I can't believe I can say that, but I mean it now.

JEN HATMAKER

Rayya was the love of my life. But I came to accept, in some part of myself, that there was absolutely nothing that I was going to ever do about that because of my care and respect for her and for my husband. Then Rayya was diagnosed with terminal pancreatic and liver cancer and given six months to live and my world blew up. My heart blew up. My head blew up. The bottom fell out of my earth. I knew that I would be with her at the moment of her death. And the image I had in my head of holding her hand while she died without ever having told her what she was to me—what I felt for her—was so violently offensive to my soul that it felt like a crime against humanity. I simply could not allow that. Rayya was the person I needed the most in the entire world, and I was at a point where I didn't know how to do life without her. I couldn't imagine how I was possibly going to live, but I knew that if I let her go without telling her that and without telling my husband that, my marriage would be over anyway. Nothing was ever going to work again unless that truth was spoken.

ELIZABETH GILBERT

I define boundaries as "needs that need to be expressed verbally or through your behavior." We're *all* needy. We all need stuff. But sometimes we diminish that part of ourselves because we don't want to present as needy. Guess what? One hundred percent of humans are needy. We have all sorts of preferences in order to feel safe and supported. So how do we get better at expressing that?

NEDRA GLOVER TAWWAB

Sometimes we make the mistake of thinking it's our job to constantly convince everybody on our little island, in our little world, to love and respect and accept us and our family. No, thank you. I'm not spending another minute of my life hustling or convincing anybody of my or my kids' worthiness. If you don't respect and love us, you're not even invited on our island. We've got a pretty strong drawbridge these days.

GLENNON

To do the hard thing
I set and keep boundaries.

—

GLENNON: Let's practice how to set boundaries. Say I'm a person who is single and about to visit my family, and my mom is always bringing up marriage in ways that make me uncomfortable. How do I talk to my mom about it?

BRENÉ BROWN: You can say, "Hey, Mom, I'm super excited. I'm going to get in on Wednesday. I cannot wait to see y'all. One thing I want to let you know is, I know you love me, and I know you think a lot about me finding a partner, and I love that you think about me and you worry about me. It's okay to do that. What's not okay is to talk about it with me. You can worry about me, you can think about it all the time, you can have a ton of questions, that's okay. What's not okay is to bring the questions to me and to talk about it in front of or even with me. You can talk about it with Aunt Julie, you can talk about it with whomever. I don't want to be in that conversation."

GLENNON: In your research, what is the next thing that Mom says that is hurtful and not accepting of this boundary? Like "Well, you're so sensitive"?

BRENÉ: "Oh, come on. Come on. We love you and we're just having a good time and I just think you're such a catch." You can say, "I hear you and I love you, too, and I love that you think I'm a great catch. That means the world to me. I'm going to ask you again, I don't want to talk about that. It's hurtful to me. I'm going to say again, it's okay that you think about it and worry about it. It's not okay that we talk about it at dinner."

—

The hard part of setting boundaries is not the setting of the boundary; it's withstanding the discomfort of whatever happens next.

The outcome of setting a boundary is that people have feelings about it. People get upset. They go cold. They gossip. They disapprove. That can make us panic and want to take back the boundary or overexplain and justify the boundary to make sure everyone feels a certain way about us and our boundaries. None of that is part of healthy boundary setting.

Setting boundaries comes in two simple parts. The first part is saying the thing. The second part is being a strong little tree in a storm, staying rooted and grounded until everybody's feelings settle. We're responsible for telling our truth with love. We are not responsible for the way the world receives our truth.

GLENNON

If you haven't set boundaries before, I can't sugarcoat it: It's hard. But it's the type of hard that is worth doing. When you set boundaries, there are two processes going on. There's the very tactical, operational: communicating the boundary. But the other process that's going on is the feelings part: the feelings of guilt, of frustration, of anger.

The person you're setting the boundary with cannot take care of your feelings about setting the boundary.

You need to take those feelings somewhere else, whether it's a friend, a coach, or a therapist. I make little notes on my phone—a log of the boundaries I set and the feelings that come after. So you write down: *That time when I said no to making cupcakes for my kids' school, I felt like this. And then two days later, I felt like that.* That's a nice reminder for yourself for the next time you're wanting to push back against the social expectations. You can remember: *Hey, I've done this before, and it felt bad that last time. But then after a couple of days, it felt a little bit better.* And that's how you train yourself.

The guilt you feel after you set a boundary is not actually yours. It does not belong to you. So whenever you feel guilt after setting a boundary, imagine it as a faulty check engine light on your car dashboard. It's a flashing light. It doesn't really give you any meaningful information. It's just there. It's going off. So you can just let it be in the background. Guilt doesn't need to be your moral compass.

DR. POOJA LAKSHMIN

—

AMANDA: After we make a big decision in our lives, we often spend so much time imagining what life would look like on the road not taken. But we have to be careful about misconstruing that doubt and pain as regret. Just because we feel pain and loss on this path doesn't mean the other path would have been pain free. We have to be humble enough to admit that the imagined reality is not actually reliable, and we most likely would have a lot of the same pain and confusion and hurt on the path we didn't take.

GLENNON: There is an image of a woman who has just leaped off a cliff. Behind her is a big hand—the hand of the universe—which has pushed her off the cliff. There's a second big hand beneath her; it's about to catch her. That is the other hand of the universe. The universe pushes you off the cliff, and the universe will catch you before you hit the ground. But the fall is still so scary that it's tempting to panic, turn around, and try to claw your way back up the cliff. That climbing back is trying to unknow what became clear to you once. Your knowing has led you to do something so scary and hard that you wonder if it'd be easier to go back and pretend not to know. But the thing is, you *do* know. So you gotta let yourself keep falling.

AMANDA: If we view doubt and pain as inevitable consequences of making a tough decision, then we won't think that those feelings mean we made the wrong decision.

GLENNON: Yes. All pain is not regret. When it's time for my kids to go back to their dad's—when I see their little overnight bags all lined up in the foyer— I still have deep pain pangs. But it's not regret that I'm feeling. It's not that any of us made the wrong choice. It's just that things can be hard and painful and exactly right at the same time. We think that if we make the "right" decisions, everything will be easy and pain free. That's not my experience. Even the absolute best decisions come with some pain. It can hurt and still be right.

—

To do the hard thing

I accept that decisions can be painful and still be right.

Kelly Clarkson: I know we can do hard things— that's why we're here right now. But sometimes I just want to go straight to the happy ending.

Glennon: Yeah. We call that trying to skip the crucifixion and jump straight to the resurrection. I wish it worked that way but it never seems to. For me it's always: First the pain, then the waiting, then the rising.

—

We don't talk enough about grief as a part of change. And that does people a real disservice because then, when they hit grief, they think they've done something wrong.

I've done everything from completely losing relationships to reconfiguring and recalibrating relationships in a way where they exist but they don't look or feel like they used to. There's always been some grief in that, and I've questioned myself.

If we don't understand that grief is going to be a part of change and that loss is going to be a part of change, I don't think we can successfully evolve. We're not doing people a favor by pretending like there's going to be no loss in change. Change always includes a series of sometimes small, and sometimes large, deaths.

BRENÉ BROWN

GLENNON: I consider invitations into recovery to be some kind of cosmic honor. I feel honored when it happens because it's the universe looking at me and all my coping mechanisms and saying: She's ready now. She's ready to live without this blocker. She's ready to level up. She's ready to enter into this leap of faith.

AMANDA: Recovery is so courageous and nonsensically faithful and wild because it is deciding, with no evidence, to live without something that you cannot live without. The reason you're so worried about your drinking is because you know you can't stop drinking. The reason you need to live without it is because you can't live without it. And so you're just deciding: *Okay, I'm going to do that thing that I cannot do.* That's the miracle of it. It's the biggest act of faith.

ABBY: For those that are still struggling, that haven't made the choice, this is the hardest step to take.

GLENNON: When people say to me, "Well, I cannot stop this thing. I cannot stop drinking. I cannot quit this person," I'm like "Yes, you are correct. I get that. You are absolutely right. The person you are right now cannot live without this thing. But it seems that perhaps you are sensing a future self that can, though? And you're wondering if you're being called to become her?" Recovery is throwing yourself into the abyss, trusting that the person that comes out is going to be the one that *can* live without the booze. A new self will be born. There's a quote by Baal Shem Tov: "Let me fall if I must, the one I will become will catch me."

AMANDA: This applies not just to recovery things. When you think about needing to leave your spouse, but you absolutely cannot leave your spouse, that's the same thing. ⟶

To do the hard thing

I do the hard thing I cannot do.

GLENNON: That's recovery, too! Recovery is just recovering who you were meant to be. Those of us who have been through recovery know that first, you have to take this leap. Next, you get rewarded for that act of courage with withdrawal. Withdrawal is a dark night of the soul. It's a slice of hell on earth. When it's a drug, it's very obvious. It's very literal. When you're leaving a relationship or breaking habits, the withdrawal is much different. It's just as hellacious, but it's this long, drawn-out, terrible time when your coping mechanism is gone, so you cannot cope. It's a transition period where you've stopped doing the thing that you needed to live and you haven't replaced it with anything else yet and you haven't become the person you need to be in order to not need a replacement. It's very tempting to want to turn around and just sort of crawl your way back to where you were and decide to live there. You are just this sniffling, shaky, cranky, terrified, sweaty, newborn self.

ABBY: You're like a little baby deer.

GLENNON: Yes. And as you well know, I'm usually a nasty little baby deer. But then when I get out of the first parts of withdrawal, I can sort of feel my new self being born. There's this period when I can start to sense a new version of myself on the periphery of my consciousness. It's unclear, but it's there. The more work I do, the more I stay with myself and let myself fall without grabbing for old ways, the clearer the outline of that new self becomes, and then it starts to become colored in, and then I start to feel that it's real. I start to feel myself becoming. And at some point, that new self becomes more real to me than the old self behind me. Eventually, I am solidly her. The new me is the treasure. She is the prize. And she is always, always worth the hell I paid to become her.

I had a moment when I had to decide whether to return to my broken marriage or honor the self that rose up when I fell in love with Abby. The question wasn't: *Should I go back to my marriage, or should I love Abby?* That was not it. It was: *Should I go back to my broken life where I'm slowly dying so that I don't rock the boat, so I keep everyone else comfortable, so I continue to honor everyone's expectations of me, or do I break everybody's hearts, hurt my kids, blow up my little perfect-on-the-outside family so that I don't have to abandon myself again?*

Do I abandon everyone's expectations of me and honor myself, or do I continue to honor everyone's expectations of me and abandon myself?

It felt like a life-or-death situation. It was. It was about whether I was going to let myself—my real self—live. I almost decided to go back to my broken life so that I didn't have to hurt my children. Then I had this moment with my daughter when I looked at her and I thought: *Oh, my God, I'm staying in this marriage for her, but would I want this marriage for her? And if I would not want this marriage for my little girl, then why am I modeling that bad love is good enough and that abandoning yourself is good parenting?*

I decided to be a model instead of a martyr. I decided to live.
I hope she does, too.

GLENNON

To do the hard thing
I choose the right kind of hard.

I was in a big relationship a couple years ago. I thought I was going to get married. But there was a realization around what I needed. I was like: *I love this person. But it takes so much time and attention and there's a lot of instability inside of it, and I can't write. I'm spending all of my creative work trying to get this relationship to function.*

And I realized: *Oh, I have to let this go even though I'm breaking my own heart to do so. I actually have to trust that my calling is this writing thing and I'm not going to be satisfied if I'm not doing it or if I'm trying to just do it on the edges.*

ADRIENNE MAREE BROWN

I have a sister who I was so close with for forty-three years. But I chose to leave our family's religion when we found out that our daughter was gay and suicidal because of the teachings of that church. My sister decided that she cannot maintain a relationship with us. I am wondering if you have any advice on how to move past that. It's been five years. How do I heal? How do I manage losing her children, who felt like my babies, too, and recover from her rejecting my children? ⌇

To do the hard thing **I choose the right kind of hard.**

GLENNON: You are a hero. What you have sacrificed for your baby is heroic. There are these life moments when we have to choose what we will be: A mother or a daughter? A mother or a sister? To whom will we be loyal? When one is a parent, the right choice is to choose parent over anyone who is forcing that ridiculous choice.

Loyalty is important to people. I always hear folks saying, "I don't agree with them, but I have to make it work because I'm a loyal person." And I wonder: *Okay. But loyal to whom?* When we choose loyalty to people with old ideas that hurt us and our children, aren't we being disloyal to our kids? To ourselves? To truth and love? Sure, be loyal. But choose carefully to whom and what to be loyal. Sometimes "loyalty" can just be backward control. Loyalty can be the death grip of bad, old ideas. Instead of abandoning her in the name of old loyalty, you forged a new, better loyalty: Loyalty between you and your daughter. Loyalty to freedom, to love, to wholeness. With this decision, you became a cycle breaker for your entire lineage. I imagine your ancestors are singing.

Life doesn't give us easy choices: good or bad, right or wrong, hard or easy. We have to choose what is the right kind of hard. You could have chosen the hard in which you continued your relationship with your sister and your daughter paid the price. She would've had to hide herself or wonder why her mother allowed that pain into her life. But you chose a different kind of hard, one in which you are missing one of the most important relationships in your life but your daughter is free and has no confusion about what her mother believes about her. You taught her what she deserves from people. Now she knows.

I don't know what healing between you and your sister will look like. But I can imagine what healing from this trauma will look like for you and your daughter. I imagine you will heal by watching your daughter blossom into herself with freedom and confidence. I imagine you will both heal inside a lifelong relationship of trust—in which your girl knows she can always bring her full self to you—because her mama has her back. And when one of your sister's children needs a safe place to show their full self—they'll know where to turn. They'll turn to you.

I know this is hard. I also know you chose the right kind of hard.
Well done, Mama.

It takes so much energy to show up, to say the thing bravely, and to continue without lying down and taking a break. You got to do that day after day after day after day.

I had to give myself a pep talk the other day. I looked at myself in the mirror and was like "Girl, you are just a miracle. You are a miracle. The fact that you are where you are, from where you came from, having withstood what you've been through, it is a miracle that you're here smiling with that clear-ass melanin skin of yours, looking as good as you do, having a happy spirit, raising an incredible daughter, being an awesome friend. You are a miracle. Go on ahead, keep your head up."

BOZOMA SAINT JOHN

Eight

How do I let go?

I was listening to a relationship expert talk about the importance of letting go of what has happened to us. I thought: *You know what? I don't think I've ever truly let go of a single thing that has happened to me. Not a single thing. I have never gotten over anything, I am still under everything.*

Every time someone has hurt me and every time I've hurt someone else—and everything that could hurt me in the future—it's all right here inside of me right now. I hold on to it all, and I hold so tightly. It's all so heavy. I can't imagine how wonderful it would feel to somehow put it all down.

GLENNON

Melody Beattie: I have learned that surrender is one of the few things in life that hurts most before I do it. It's my resistance. When I'm in a state of resistance to a situation, to an emotion, to anything in life, when I'm resisting it, I'm putting myself through pain.

Glennon: It's not the surrender that hurts; it's the considering surrender that hurts.

Melody: Yes. Contemplating the fact that we're not really in control.

Amanda: That is the grief. Because if we get to a place of surrender—of accepting our reality, ourselves, and the people in our lives as they are in this moment—the grief we have to go through to get to that place is the grief that we can't make ourselves and our lives and other people any different than they are.

Glennon: The good news is we're not God. The bad news is we're not God.

We've got to put down what was never ours to carry so we can start living light and free. We deserve that.

GLENNON

I love this idea that the thing
that screws us up the most is the
picture in our head of how things
are supposed to be.

GLENNON

I try to script my life right
down to the final scene.
And then, my dear
beloved friend Life is like:
Oh, no, no, no.
Oh, it's not going to be like that.
It's going to be like this.
Now what's your move?

ELIZABETH GILBERT

To let go

I release what was *supposed* to be.

My therapist asked me why I feel so much overwhelm, stress, and anxiety during the holidays. I explained to her that I always feel like I have to make every moment and every gift perfect and beautiful and the best thing ever. Like it all has to be magic and since I'm the mom, I'm responsible for being the magic maker. Every year has to be the *best Christmas ever,* so I'm frantically creating this *big thing.*

And my therapist asked, "What if *you* are the thing? What if with your family, when you're on a stage speaking, when you're writing, when you're with your kids getting ready for Christmas, what if *you are the thing*? What if you don't have to constantly prepare perfection? And what if—in obsessing about saying the right thing, doing the right thing, presenting the right thing—all of your buzzy perfecting energy actually means that you're not there at all? And what if that means that it would be so much better for everyone if everything were *not* perfect—but you were actually *there*?"

GLENNON

Several months ago, we planned a lovely fiftieth anniversary surprise party for our parents. One of the ways my family expresses love is through large productions of things: a major toast, a perfect presentation, a big offering that has required a lot of preparation.

This interesting thing happened during the lead-up to the party: I found myself not preparing anything. I wasn't making a big gift or writing a fancy toast. I wasn't hounding my kids to prepare anything. I felt kind of scared, like: *Wait, what am I doing? I'm not prepared! This is crazy.* I decided: *It's okay. I'll prepare something on the plane.*

Then I'm sitting on the plane, and Abby pulls out her computer. She's going to watch a movie, and she looks so cozy, and I think: *I want to snuggle up and watch that movie with her.* So I did, and I felt so happy. And then the movie was over, and I thought: *I just really want to read my book now.* And the whole flight, I kept not writing anything and thinking: *What is going to happen? I am being so irresponsible. This is crazy.*

The party started, and it was so lovely. When toast time came, I just stood up and said something like "Hi, everybody. It's amazing that you're here. We love you so much." Then I said something kind about my mom and dad, and I sat down. My sister stood up and gave a beautiful prepared speech. I felt a little bit bad. I thought: *Oh, God, maybe what I did wasn't honoring enough, maybe it wasn't good enough.* But the evening went on, and the rest was beautiful—everyone had such a wonderful time. My cousin Beth, who has known me since birth, came up to me at the end of the party and said, "I have to tell you that I've never seen you so calm. So peaceful. It's incredible. You're like a different person." ⁓

⌒ Then my dad stood up to give his toast. As soon as he began speaking, something felt very different. His toasts are epically good. He's an incredible writer and performer. But there is always an edge there, a feeling of stress, of performance. But this toast, he was just present, not performing at all. And I thought: *Oh, my God, he's in the moment. He's very vulnerable. His words are less clever but more real. He's with us. He's a little bit emotional.*

Afterward, everybody else was emotional, too. He was so tender, and it touched us deeply. And I realized that it was because the party was a surprise. He couldn't prepare anything, so he couldn't perform anything. He had to just be there with us. And because he was there with us, he wasn't in his mind for the whole previous two hours focused on this thing that he was going to deliver to us. He was with us the whole time.

All I could think about on the plane home was: *I was not amazing. I did not nail anything. I did not perform anything. I did not deliver anything. And I was so happy and I was so* with *the people who were there. And they noticed, too. And they seemed to be happy with me, too.*

The shadow side of performing my love is that I am not *with*; I am not connecting with my people.

The idea that being in that space as I was—without performing or delivering anything at all—was not just *enough*, but perhaps the *best* thing: It felt almost too good to be true. But it *was* true.

GLENNON

GLENNON: As a mom and a controlling human being who truly believes I can make everything okay if I just worry enough, I resonate with the idea that "I am the center that must hold." Kate, you've said that you've felt that way in the past. Do you still feel that? How do we let go of that, of the illusion of control?

KATE BOWLER: I mean, who's going to make sure we all have towels? Who's going to remember the two million errands? It is so difficult to see all the weight that you carry and imagine that life would still go on if we were not doing that work or smiling that smile. It feels like I'm turning the big wheel so that everybody else's lives can function. But my cancer diagnosis forced me to let go of that. I had put myself in the center of the world, and then my world was ending.

Tragedy is the time when you're forced to rewrite all of the rules about how your ecosystem works because you don't get to have the pride of making sure everybody else's needs are met before your own. It has humbled me in my view of what I can even do in a day, but also how much I really do need other people and how much I was unwilling to let anyone else carry anything—mostly because of years of deeply ingrained patriarchy.

I've needed food, I've needed people to physically wash my hair, to carry me, to push my wheelchair, to pick up my kid—that was the worst, to ask someone to pick up my kid. All those things felt impossible. In there, though, was a challenge to the story that I was always going to be the only person who could love my people. Having a bigger picture of that has been an important truth—and a hard truth for me to hear.

—

To let go

I release the belief that it's all on me to make things okay.

I feel so much love and heartache toward anyone who asks me how I helped get Glennon sober. I want to make very, very clear what I did to get her into recovery: nothing. No one has ever loved, prayed, suffered, or strategized anyone into recovery. Not in the history of the world. What I did was I loved her and I lived my life with some healthy boundaries so that when she was ready for recovery, our relationship was not irretrievably scarred from the pain of the drinking days. And when she was ready, I answered the phone and supported her sobriety miracle.

That's how I see her sobriety—as a miracle. As far as I can see, there's no ascertainable reason why some recover and some don't—why I get to do life with my best friend and some of you lost yours. It's a miracle that I did nothing to earn or deserve more than any of you trying so hard right now. I couldn't do anything to lead her toward that miracle; I was just there when she became it. You don't earn a miracle, you just accept it with deep gratitude and you wish it for others. That is my wish for you, that you would get that miracle. But until you do, I wish you freedom—not to wear yourself down endlessly trying to earn it—so that there will be more left of you to celebrate when your miracle arrives.

AMANDA

I'm working on giving up on certainty. Certainty isn't real. It's okay that it's not real, and acknowledging that it's not real does not actually change anything about my reality. It doesn't make me less safe to acknowledge that the kind of safety I'm seeking doesn't exist. Because if it never existed, believing in it never made me safer. So I can just let it go. It's about un-Godding myself. It's okay to accept that I am not always the architect of this moment, but I can figure out what I can do, where I can move, and what I can change if I want to.

ASHLEY C. FORD

I did not know I was codependent. I thought I was just being helpful. I did not realize how much I'd stunted anyone's ability to grow. My personal work for the last year and a half is figuring out how to let other human people just be human people. All the way. Good, bad, hard, making good choices, making terrible choices. Because they're a person, and that's their life. It's not my life.

JEN HATMAKER

To let go

I accept that I can't fix someone and love them at the same time.

For years, I was so focused on *helping* my son that I almost missed *knowing* my son. I was so desperate to protect him that my energy went into managing him, not loving him. I was in a relationship with his behaviors, not with *him*. My eye was so trained to see what was missing that I almost missed seeing what was actually there: the hilarious, kind, handsome, fiercely loyal and loving human standing right in front of me— who, at his core, needs precisely zero fixing.

Instead of using my energy to worry about my boy, I started using my energy to get to know him. Instead of being in a relationship with his *behavior*, I started being in a relationship with *him*. Instead of using my love to help my boy, I started using my love to love my boy. Which is maybe the only help he's needed all along.

Now I can actually *see* him. And knowing him as the fascinating, miraculous puzzle he is is the delight of my life. It's so scary that I almost missed it.

It's scary to know that I could do the same thing with my own life—that I could become so focused on what needs to be fixed that I don't see the beauty of my life that needs no fixing. That I could be so busy managing my life that I miss it.

AMANDA

A while back, I was working on my spirituality and my meditation practice with a few people. The theme of my journey was surrender. It helped me identify what it was that I wanted the most, and then I had to let it go. While traveling with the national team, I would get on my hands and knees every morning and say, "I surrender the need for my mother's approval." Even as a full-grown adult, I was still feeling that I was playing for her. And I almost lost my love of the game because of it. One day I was on my hands and knees, and I got up and asked myself: *What if I'm wrong? What if my mother actually already loves and accepts me? What if it's me who's miscalibrating and projecting all my own fear on her?* I ended up sharing this experience with my mother, and we had an *Aha!* Moment together. It just hit me that my mom already accepted me. And it hit her that I didn't need some of the things she thought I needed. We were both able to move on.

CHRISTEN PRESS

When people don't accept you, it's an indication of where they're at, not where you're at. It has 100 percent to do with them and nothing to do with you. There's nothing wrong with you. Other people have been told that they can't be free or happy. When they see you being free and happy, they get really nervous because they have to hold a mirror to themselves. They wonder: *Maybe I'm not as free and happy as I thought.* What I always try to remind myself is: *This is not my fear.* I say that to myself, *This is not my fear,* and then I go find other people who are investing in love over fear.

ALOK

To let go

I stop taking on what is not mine.

I'm often in a situation where somebody is saying a cruel or dismissive thing and I'm taking on that hurt as if they've located some visible flaw in me and my character when, in fact, they're only speaking from their own hurt. That doesn't mean that I have to forgive them, be complicit in what they've said, or that I don't hold them accountable.

I just don't have to take on their pain.

My book begins with men in a bar telling me my life is not worth living. I took all that pain on and allowed it to isolate me from my life. So the ending of my book was very purposeful. It concludes in a bar with another man asking me, "How is it possible that your husband manages the burden of your body?"

Those two moments bookending my story show that the world is not magically better. The men in the bar are always going to exist. I'm always going to have to navigate that. But I did get a little bit better at not carrying that pain.

By the end, when the man said, "How do people deal with the burden of your body?," I could see that he was speaking from his own limitations, ignorance, pain, and intoxication. It really had nothing to do with me. I could say good night to him and then go on and enjoy the rest of my life.

CHLOÉ COOPER JONES

I built my life and career by refusing to quit. As a professional athlete, I was taught that quitters never win. But then nine years ago, I quit soccer. I quit my marriage. I quit drinking. I did all of that within a five-month period. Had I not done all those things, Glennon and I would have missed each other.

I owe so much of my happiness now to breaking points that made me quit, moments in my life that stopped working for me and I had to stop. To let go of something no longer meant for me meant that I had the ability to grab on to something new and beautiful. I'm so grateful that I learned how to quit.

ABBY

To let go

I walk away from what's not working for me.

Quitting, for me, is the ultimate version of living responsibly. Through almost dying from addiction—alcoholism, work addiction, social media addiction—I've learned that nobody's going to handle my shit for me. I almost died. Nobody is going to look at my life and say, "That's not working for you." Nobody is going to protect me but me. That's *my* job.

When something stops working for me, when something actually starts to affect my peace, it's my responsibility to stop and start something else. It's the definition of the word *responsible,* meaning "able to respond." My job as a sober person is to protect my peace so that when something—a relationship, a way of life, or an idea—threatens my stability, I can respond to that truth and get rid of it.

GLENNON

LUVVIE AJAYI JONES: I've had friendship losses over the years. Before letting go of a friend completely, I think it's important to let them know when they do something that hurts me. If they don't repair, that's a data point. If we get to a point where I'm like: *This person is not hearing me, they're not doing anything different, I really can't trust them,* then I decide to let them go. I become less available to them.

GLENNON: Yes. I think sometimes we don't end things, or we end things wrong, because we're trying to control the narrative. We're trying to fit into the narrative of "I'm the good guy and you're the bad guy," and I have to wait until I can prove that perfectly. But that's not real. Sometimes it's not you, it's not me, it's the energy between us. It's just not working.

LUVVIE: Yes. And you can release each other without even having hard feelings. You don't have to be like "Oh, I hate her." You can just be like "No, we drifted apart." And that's fine. Every friendship breakup doesn't have to be this dramatic bomb that just went off.

GLENNON: Yeah. I love your advice: You don't always have to decide whether or not you like the other person. You *do* have to decide if you like yourself around that person. And if you don't like or trust yourself or feel calm or safe, then that's enough information.

—

I love endings. We should celebrate them just as much as we celebrate beginnings. Because it's just as important, wise, and brave to know and accept when something beautiful should end as it is to know when something beautiful should begin. An ending shouldn't be thought of as failure. Endings are a necessary, beautiful stage of a creative life.

GLENNON

To let go I walk away from what's not working for me.

Sometimes you may decide that a relationship was a beautiful love story, but it may not be a life story. You don't have to squash the love in order to move on. You may just say, "This love is precious, I will hold it dearly, but it is not going to be my life."

There are beautiful rituals to honor the intimacy while also inviting the relationship to end or transition. You can start with "I'm here to say goodbye, and this is what I wish for you." And bring an object to represent what you want the other person to take with them. "When I think of us, these are some of the main images, memories, associations that I will have. All the things that we shared that I'll take with me, and that I hope you will take with you." Choose an object that you can hold, touch, smell, listen to so that you, too, can take away with you a visceral memory.

There may be grief or sadness at this closure. These are the feelings that often accompany endings. Let them be in you and then come through you. You may want to have an object that represents grief. A ritual I have often used is to throw something into the water. Often it is bread, so that other creatures can feed themselves on what you let go of. Relationships are filled with rituals from the beginning, but the way you end will do everything for what will follow.

ESTHER PEREL

I was madly in love with my first husband, and our marriage ended via an email message and two five-minute conversations—and I've never seen him or talked to him since. There was no shared grieving. No processing. No answers. No closure. The center of my world vanished in an instant.

That's called ambiguous loss: loss that can't be defined or processed, where there's no closure or clear understanding of what happened. It leaves you in a constant search for answers. You can't resolve your grief because you don't have the answers to begin to even understand your own situation.

My ambiguous loss resulted in massive self-blame and self-doubt, crushing confusion, and an excruciating whiplash of grief. Then, while I was still clearing out the home my husband and I had shared, a package was delivered. It was a note congratulating him, and a "Baby's First Christmas" ornament. That evening, I found the online baby registry. And that's how I learned that I would *never* actually know the story of my marriage, nor the story of the end of my marriage. Having to accept that I would never have the answers I needed—that I would never actually know my own story—was the hardest part.

I had to choose whether to continue to rail against that impossible unfairness or choose to release it into mystery. I worked really hard to release it. Because even if I learned every fact, date, time, event, and answer I craved, it wouldn't be *The Truth*. It wouldn't be my ex-husband's truth or his new wife's truth or their new child's truth. It would just be a version of the truth I used to survive sorrow.

I found a little peace by releasing it into mystery. And as hard as that is, I think it's actually more aligned with the reality of life. The truth is that most of life is a mystery, and acceptance of that mystery might be as close as we get to peace. And, in celebration of my hard-won miraculous peace, every single Christmas I hang that ornament on my tree.

AMANDA

To let go

I stop seeking closure from others and I give it to myself.

Sometimes the goodbye is done with
the person present, and sometimes the
goodbye is done with the person that
you carry inside of you.

ESTHER PEREL

In general, I have difficulty not wanting to know absolutely everything. Some of it is curiosity, some of it is pathological. But, I have this desire for information in my everyday relationships, so it makes sense that I had it in grief. What I've come to realize is you just have to accept what you don't know, what you cannot know and will never know. You have to let those questions go after a while. I spent so much time after my friend's death focused on the "why" and "what I missed" that eventually I realized it was cannibalizing his life instead of honoring it. Those questions are not the entirety of his life and your relationship and memory. I eventually let the questions go, and that was a more fitting tribute to him.

SLOANE CROSLEY

True belonging has forever felt inaccessible to me. As far back as I can remember, I have felt like a little bit of an alien, like an outsider looking in. My inner voice is always saying: *I don't belong here I don't belong here why can't I belong here?* The only real belongingness I've ever felt in my entire life is in my home with these four particular people. So as my kids grow up, it's not just a loss of identity that I'm struggling with but a loss of the only belongingness I've ever felt. It's really hard.

As they move on and out and away, my energy is suddenly desperate. I am chasing everybody. I'm just reaching out and grabbing at them over and over again. Too many calls too many texts too many hugs too many bids for attention. That is not how I want to be. I don't want to spend the rest of my life chasing my butterflies, I want to create a butterfly garden that's so beautiful they can't help but come back.

To do that, I need to find a way to embody the centeredness and peace of a person who has done her job well—and now gets to rest and live and know her babies will return when they want to, not because they sense that I need them to. I need to embody the knowing that at every moment of this life with them, I have loved them, sometimes poorly, sometimes amazingly, but always with my entire heart and mind and body and soul. I need to get busy building my next era with Abby so they can see my juicy, beautiful life and trust it and want it enough to ask for my help and my thoughts. I want them to see me as a steady resource to return to and refuel with, so they can go back out into their lives and become what they dream of becoming. In order for them to go be okay, they need to see me okay. I need to see me okay, too.

GLENNON

To let go

I set my kids free.

Abby: For me, the hardest part about these children growing up is that they now start to have private lives, not only interior lives but private lives with their friendships and their new partners and their new communities that they're forging for themselves. That feels hard because it leaves us out and that's uncomfortable. We have to trust and believe that we did the very best that we could and let them go. I feel confident that they'll come back eventually—if only to file their grievances.

Amanda: It truly is the most heartbreaking paradox of life that, if you are lucky, your children will not need you—but what you want most in the world is for them to need you. And tragically, it seems as if the sure-fire way to ensure your kids won't want you is for you to need them.

BRENÉ BROWN: If my kid comes home and says, "Hey, I got in trouble today because I was talking while the teacher was talking. They said I was being disrespectful," I could respond with control: "You need to go upstairs. And you need to send an email to this teacher. Apologize for being disrespectful." But that is control as opposed to connection, which is "God, that must have been really hard." Then you hear "Yeah, I was just asking if they had an extra pencil. I'm really sorry."

You have to ask: What does support look like? What can I do? I can listen. I can help. I can say, "I know you're not inherently disrespectful, and I know it means a lot to you, so that had to have been really tough and maybe embarrassing."

AMANDA: And what are you controlling in that situation, Brené? Because what I would be controlling in that situation is my *own* embarrassment.

BRENÉ: That's it. It's how you're perceived as a parent. I want to be the parent who has the kid that's not disrespectful, that apologizes via email. Everything around control really comes back to some level of fragility around our own worth.

—

To let go

I stay focused on my own work and let others do theirs.

There is a time that comes later in life when loss after loss arrives and it feels like an unraveling of everything you've built and everyone who built you. For me it began when we lost Abby's beloved brother Peter, then discovered Amanda's cancer, then lost my beloved Aunt Peggy, the matriarch of our extended family. My parents started visibly getting older. The kids started living bigger lives, and coparenting entered a different, difficult phase. Everyone was making decisions that scared me, and I had no concept of how involved I was supposed to be in others' lives anymore. I realized: I don't know how to live among people who are going to do whatever the hell they're going to do without losing my mind. I don't know how to love people without trying to control them. I don't know how to lose people without losing myself.

That's how I ended up at my first online Al-Anon meeting. Somebody had a little thing on their screen that said, "Don't fight it, don't fix it, don't figure it out." I took a picture of that and sent it to my friend Alex with a text that said, "Excuse me? Is this for real? What the hell am I supposed to do all day?" Slowly, I am learning that it's my job to make myself okay. It is not my job to control other people's decisions and lives so that I can feel okay. The question is: How do I be okay without using people to get me there? How do I make *myself* okay?

Each morning I wake up with all my million worries and I sit down and make two to-do lists. The first is God's to-do list. The second is mine. One at a time I write down every single worry that I have absolutely no control over under God's name. God's list is usually like: My kids' safety! Chase's future! Tish's career! Amma's friendships! My parents' health! War, famine! ARE MY DOGS GONNA DIE? There are usually about three worries left for my list, and they're always simple things like: Call your mom. Take a walk. Write that article. It's always such a relief, looking at those lists. Every morning I think: *God, I'm so glad I'm not God.*

GLENNON

We try to control everything so nothing changes. We're terrified of change. We waste so much of our time on these profoundly absurd fictions when the only true thing we absolutely know is that we're going to die. We try to hold everything still, because to embrace the fundamental currency of change would instigate us to have to speak frankly about death. That's what I've come to: The fear of losing control is actually the fear of death, and the fear that what we have right now is impermanent. All of this control is actually about our fear of death. That fear causes us to control each other in ways that look like safety, but are not. So how do we let go of that fear? People I love died and it undid me. It forced me to confront that every single time I make connection, it's going to end. And then I had to make the choice to make connection again and again and again anyway. Navigating the concept of death is actually about surrender—fully showing up and having faith that it's going to be okay in the end.

ALOK

Our mortality is what makes this life rich. I remember being really young in church and hearing that hell was burning for eternity. All the kids in my Sunday school class were terrified of the burning, but I was freaking out about the word eternity. I knew at a young age that anything happening forever would be hell, but what I didn't know at that time, which I've learned this year, is that that applies to living too—if we were to live forever, that would be hell. There is something that makes this life beautiful, and that is the brevity of it.

ANDREA GIBSON

It's funny to me when people are like: *It's unrealistic to believe there's an afterlife, another world, another existence.* Okay, but aren't we in an existence, a world, right now? If this one exists, isn't it perfectly logical to consider that another one might? It would be weird for somebody at a party to roll their eyes and say: *It's insane to believe an after-party might happen. There is absolutely no way other parties exist!*

GLENNON

To let go

I allow life's brevity to be its magic.

We imagine death with so much fear and the worst-case scenario—fire and brimstone and hell. But none of us knows what it is. Nobody who has lived has gone all the way there and come all the way back.

So what if death was the best thing you could ever experience? What if it's actually really joyful to watch your kids grow up from the other side? What if you get to be more intimately connected with the people you love when you're dead? We can fill that concept with anything we want, yet we choose pain, we choose the horror of it all.

When people come up with an idea of the other side that feels good for them and can rest in it, they feel comforted; these people are the most at peace. The people that are still unsure suffer the most.

I have a belief I'm playing with about what happens after death, just because it's kind of fun: At the moment of my death, I can feel every feeling I've ever felt in my life. All of it. The grief and the sorrow and the pain, but also the joy and an orange I ate and the sun on my skin when I was in Venezuela and that one really incredible orgasm—all the things at the same time. And then I explode into glitter everywhere. The glitter goes up—this is biodegradable, good-for-the-earth glitter—and then it falls down like a soft snow shower.

And then the *me* that observes, the *me* that is not tied to my experiences in my human body, is watching it all come down and feeling really joyful that every little bit of human expression, every little bit of humanity I let myself lean in to during my life, is now settled onto this big, huge glitter wave that just coasts for all of eternity. Could that not be pretty rad?

ALUA ARTHUR

I think control and love are opposites. Because love requires trust. We only control things or people we don't trust fully. We can love people or control them, but we cannot do both.

So I am practicing loving Abby instead of controlling her, loving my children instead of controlling them, loving my body instead of controlling it, loving my life instead of controlling my life, loving myself instead of controlling myself.

It's still hard. It's scary for me to trust. But it's also the biggest relief of my life. I've been holding my breath to hold it all together for so long. Trusting feels like breathing again.

GLENNON

Nine

How do I go on?

After my brother died, Glennon left a note on our bed with a Samuel Beckett quote: "You must go on. I can't go on. I'll go on."

That makes sense to me in my bones. I know I'll find a way to go on, but right now I just don't know how. I'm scared I'll never feel real joy again, like unburdened happiness is just over for me.

I miss my brother, and that missing takes up all of me. I hate it. I just hate it.

ABBY

Glennon: You've said, "Part of being able to bear the things we can't bear is not about tossing them off. Not about making the weight lighter, but simply learning that we have the capacity to carry it."

Cheryl Strayed: What I learned through writing *Wild*—what it's about at its core—is that we can bear the unbearable. Of course that was true when it came to lifting a backpack that I literally couldn't lift and carrying it through the wilderness. But it was also true in a more emotional and metaphorical sense. When my mother died, I thought I couldn't live without her. And everyone out there who's lost anyone who was essential to them thinks: *I can't live without that person.* And then what's true is that we can, and we will, and we do.

Amanda: What's cool about that is you don't have to believe you'll be okay to make it true that you will be okay—in fact, part of grief is that you *can't* believe it. You can't believe that you can live without your mother. It's just one step at a time, one day at a time. And then you realize that even though you can't go on, you are, and therefore you can.

Cheryl: It's also about rejecting the dichotomy of those who can and can't. It's not like there's one category of people who are the strong ones who can endure tremendous loss or face very difficult physical circumstances or whatever the hard thing is and then another category who can't face it. We can embrace that both things can be true at once: This is a hard thing that I don't want to do, but I'm doing it—I will, and I can.

AMANDA: After your mom died, you wrote an email to all the people who were reaching out to try to support you. You said, "Listen, I'm not writing any of you back. But I still want you to write to me. I still want you to reach out and invite me to things. But I need you to expect that I'm not going to write you back right now. I'm not going to be able to reciprocate, but I feel you."

MARISA RENEE LEE: Yes. It's permission to let go of the expectations that you have for yourself. For me, it was about friendship. But it can also be about work. It can be about how you show up as a parent. Because when grief arrives, it takes over. You are not in charge. Permission to just let grief lead is a big, big, big part of the healing process.

GLENNON: You have permission to let your personality and your expectations and your standards disappear and to let grief guide you.

—

Throughout my grieving, I wasn't feeling or crying as much as I thought I would. I was questioning whether I had lost a part of my sensitivity. It hit me two months later. It was snowing. I was taking my dog for a walk, and it was one of those beautiful nights where the snowflakes are huge and they're falling at a very slow, cinematic pace. The visual, the beauty of the earth continuing despite my struggle, despite anything else—I realized that life moves on. You can spend your time worrying about whether you're doing it right or wrong, or you can just let yourself feel. That cracked me open.

DAN LEVY

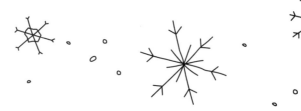

To go on

I let my grief lead.

There's a lot of instruction on grieving, and there's a lot of shaming around people grieving wrong.

The way I did it was the way I needed to do it. And the way I did it was that I threw myself back into life full on, because that felt right to me at the time. To this day, I say it was the right thing to do.

I thought that it would feel like depression, but it was a very vibrant time for me. I was keenly alive and I was also in a lot of emotion, but the emotion was very hot and fiery. It wasn't like a dampness, like the way that I've experienced depression. So when I wept, I wept hard and big and ugly and riotous tears.

When I was angry at people and at Rayya and at me and at God, that anger was hot and fiery. It was very vivid. And there were also lots of feelings of rejoicing and celebration. I've heard it said that all true grief has a weird element of rejoicing underneath it, because you're rejoicing at how much you loved that person and how impactful they were. There's something huge about it.

I really thought that it was going to be a much quieter thing. And of course it was grief for Rayya. Nothing about Rayya was small or quiet or damp, so it made sense that the scale felt like that.

I had a big year. But grief is a bill that has to be paid eventually. And I was a little bit putting that bill off. I also don't want to judge myself for that because that's what I needed to do. I couldn't pay that bill right away. It was too big.

ELIZABETH GILBERT

As far as I can tell, grief is forever. Grief is the repeated experience of learning to live in the midst of a significant loss.

The love that we share with people is something that leaves a permanent imprint on our brains. And the best way for us to live with loss is to find a way to continue our relationship with the deceased. I definitely talk to my mom sometimes. I make an intentional effort to include her in our family and to share her with my husband and my son. The week I published my book, we celebrated by giving our son his first pancakes. Pancakes were my mom's thing. Sunday mornings, before church, she would make us pancakes pretty religiously, even when she was sick. We wanted to find our own way to include her in this special week. There was a lot of joy there.

That's the thing about grief. It doesn't always show up as sadness and wailing and depression. Sometimes it's just love and peace and inclusion. I want my husband and my son to know my mother. My husband and my son *will* know my mother.

MARISA RENEE LEE

To go on

I don't try to get over it.

When my mom passed, I got really good advice from a family friend. Reflecting on his own experience of losing his mother, he shared with me that the moment she died, she was with him forever. When people are alive, you have to physically go to see them in order to spend time with them. But when someone's no longer alive, you never have to travel to see them. They're always there. That articulation is exactly what my experience has been. My mom is always with me.

Sometimes when things are hard and I feel like I've failed or let people down, I can look up to the sky and think: *My mom is here, and she doesn't care about this.* I have this relationship with my mom that's growing. I can still revert to those old pathways where I'm like: *I missed the goal. My mom must be disappointed.* But now I'm trying to cultivate this new pathway that is: When you're omnipresent and when you're transcendental, which I think is what happens when someone passes, there is no longer a limited human nature.

Now I get to experience this relationship with my mom where I know 100 percent that she's proud of me, she accepts me. I get to live my life with that freedom, and I get to talk to her in a way that I often couldn't when she was alive, because I had fear of my flaws, fear of her flaws. And now the fear is gone, because she sees me at my worst. There's no hiding from her. There's no hiding anymore.

CHRISTEN PRESS

We do not have enough words for sadness. When I taught third grade, one of my students lost her mother. It was just a year of sadness with this little one. I remember sitting and talking about her feelings during art. We were using blue paint and talking about sadness as blue.

She put a bunch of blue on the paper, and I said, "Your sadness is blue?" She said, "Yes, but it's not all blue." She added some yellow because sad can have hope in it, right?

She added some red because her sadness was sometimes so angry. She once looked at the rest of the class and said to me, "Why do all these other kids get to keep their moms?"

There was blue but with orange for her, too, because she said, "I'm so scared. Who's going to take care of me now?"

Sadness is so many things. Some of us are blue with sadness, but there's gold leaf inside the blue. We're so sad because we lost something that we love so much, but that means we had that golden kind of love.

GLENNON

To go on
I let myself feel it all.

When we do actually surrender to our feelings, when we name them, write them out, share them with a friend, that is actually when they become easier to deal with.

MARISA RENEE LEE

My brother's funeral was a traditional ceremony in the church. I felt nervous because the church has been a painful place for me. My family had actually discussed skipping the funeral altogether and moving right to a celebration of life. But I remember sitting in that church at Peter's funeral, surrounded by the masses of grieving people who loved him, the serious music, the crucifixes on the stained-glass windows, the incense, the ritual of it all, and thinking: *This is so painful—and it's exactly right.* It was a container for all of our energy and all of our sadness to be in the same place and to let it be on the outside as dramatic and sacred as it felt on the inside. Everyone was allowed to be sad. Everyone was allowed to be angry, even. Everyone was allowed to stop and honor and mourn the loss first. We needed that step to be able to truly move on to celebrating his life. As Glennon says: First the pain, then the rising.

ABBY

Mourning is about feeling all of our feelings. When I am in grief, I think: *I'm feeling all these feelings; therefore I need to mourn so I can stop feeling all these feelings.* But mourning isn't about banishing the messy feelings and getting to the other side as quickly as humanly possible. The messy feelings, the conflict, the grossness—that *is* the mourning.

AMANDA

—

GLENNON: I have often felt that grief is less like something that comes and haunts me like a visitor and more like I'm the visitor and the sadness is a room inside of me. It's like my body is a house and there is one big room inside of me where the knowing lives; the sad, wild remembering of how beautiful and terrible and temporary and fleeting everything is. I spent decades of my life keeping that room locked: Do not enter. Caution tape. My job was just to walk by it lightly on tiptoes. Then I started letting myself visit the room. I was like: *Oh, maybe this is a good place to visit. Maybe it is in my house for a reason.* I would go there—only when I made art—and then leave quickly. After I was done writing, I'd tidy up and leave, because I'd have to go back to the regular world where people don't want to talk about this shit all the time.

But now it feels like I have emptied this room and put stuff from it into every room in my inner home. I have decorated every room with the wild ruinous knowing, and I live among the knowing every day, and it's beautiful and difficult, and I wouldn't have it any other way.

AMANDA: So you're no longer compartmentalizing the sadness and the knowing. The deepest existential woe is now in the joy room and also in the peace-and-comfort room. It's everywhere.

ABBY: Open floor plan.

—

Sadness is the distance between our inner vision of how beautiful things could be and what is visible to us on the outside—in our families, in our communities, in our world, in our lives. If we did not have a beautiful vision, we would not feel so sad that the beauty is not yet manifest in reality. Sadness is the gap between the seen and unseen—between what we know could be, what should be, and what actually is. This is why so many visionaries have such big sadness: They ache at the way things are because they have such a strong, haunting vision of the way it *could* be.

People who have the sadness can become warriors for truth and beauty and peace and love. Because what the sadness is making inside of us soon steps out of us. That's how it works for me. When I am very sad on the inside, I know I'm about to forge big change on the outside. And if I've honored that inner aching sadness, stayed with her, paid attention to what that sadness has done inside of me, when that future self steps out and does something brave and amazing to help close the gap, I can look at her and say: *There she is. I recognize her. She was rising up inside of me before she was outside of me.*

GLENNON

There she is.

It makes sense that the antidote to the absurdity of life is the absurdity of life.

AMANDA

—

SAMANTHA IRBY: My philosophy to this day is that even in the most bleak of circumstances, I have to find the joke in order to keep going. I am not a traditionally hopeful person. The laughter keeps me going.

GLENNON: Your theory is: I can't make life bearable, but I can make the next five minutes more bearable.

SAMANTHA: Yes. Both my parents died when I was eighteen. My sisters and I were at my mom's funeral, and it was really sad. We were sitting in the front row. And the minister who was performing the service didn't know my mom very well, but he knew my sister. And my sister's name is Carmen. But the minister kept referring to my dead mom as Carmen. And when I tell you I was screaming laughing, by the fourth time I was falling over in the pew, laughing. And my sisters were laughing, and I was just like: *Okay, this is how we get through this.* It's terrible, and we're going to have to sort through her stuff and figure out how much debt she was in and all that stuff. But to get through that moment, we just were crying laughing at this dude. And Carmen, I felt bad for her. I kept asking her, pointing to the casket, "Shouldn't you climb in there?" It was hilarious. You have to find the one absurd thing and just cling to that until you get through to a good place.

—

To go on

I stop trying to make everything make sense.

Being immunocompromised due to the cancer and chemo, I couldn't be around a lot of people. So I just started driving around visiting the world's largest statues of things. Like the world's largest northern lake trout. Recently, I saw the world's largest replica of the world's largest lighthouse. And the replica was really small. It was not big. But I was just doing stupid things that made me feel like I was soaking up life again. I think that's one of the only things that helped me cut through the noise of being scared about finitude. You just kind of get off the math paradigm altogether.

KATE BOWLER

One of my favorite words in the English language is *alchemy*. For me, it's about taking the thing that you're most afraid of and transforming it into something meaningful and useful, maybe even beautiful. During the moments in my life when I've felt most powerless, that process of alchemy has given me a sense of agency. When I came out of the hospital after my second bone marrow transplant, I needed to use a walker—which was not something I ever thought that I would have to do at the age of thirty-four—and I was embarrassed by it. It reminded me of how weak I'd become. So I ordered a giant bag of colorful rhinestones and a hot glue gun, and I bedazzled it. Then, instead of people looking at me with pity, they would laugh or comment on how beautiful the rhinestones were. Alchemizing pain into something creative has become a guiding principle in my life.

SULEIKA JAOUAD

I was on my book tour, and I was in the hotel room. I was supposed to go out and speak to a bunch of people about my book, but I was feeling really anxious.

I was looking out the window, and I could see Times Square. I kept going back and forth from my window to my door, and every time I would get stuck and I would be like: *I cannot do it. I cannot leave this hotel room. I cannot make myself leave here. My anxiety is too strong.* I just felt like such a failure. I sat down next to the window and opened it up and was like: *At least I can feel like I'm kind of in New York. I can hear the noise.*

I look down, and there's this big fountain. It's fountains on fountains and it's so pretty and I notice that there is this rainbow fire coming up off of this fountain and I am trying to figure out what it is and I realize that it's a prism effect.

I've never seen anything so beautiful. ⁓

And everybody is walking past it as if they couldn't care at all. And I just thought: *Maybe they're just so used to it that they don't even see it anymore.* Then I realized that that wasn't what was happening at all. Since I was so high up in my building, I was the only one that could see the light hit it in that certain way. No one else could see this amazing, fantastic thing that was greater than anything I would have seen out there. I was so grateful that I was there in that moment.

Sometimes life creates a path for you and it ends up being the right path.

JENNY LAWSON

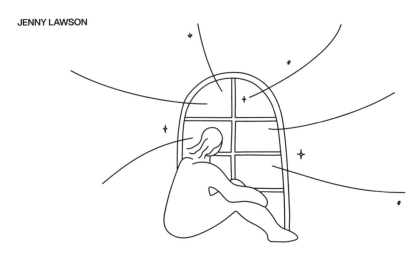

LAURA MCKOWEN: I couldn't get sober alone. I tried very hard. I did not want anyone to see what was happening to me inside of me. I always wanted to keep an extra 10 percent for myself. Until one of my best friends, Jim, said, "There's sanity in community." And that changed things for me. Because my mind does not always tell me the best things to do. I had to learn how to date and be in a healthy relationship by listening to other people. Because what my mind would tell me was so colored by trauma that it was skewed. And so if I didn't have the sanity that came from community, I would just keep repeating the same pattern over and over and over again.

ABBY: Community is so important. When I first got sober, I did not know where to turn. I didn't know a single sober person. I had gotten a DUI, and the world found out about my problem before I could even say, "I need help." I decided I was just going to open up and tell my story to people. That was hard because as a famous athlete, I was supposed to be a shiny superhero. Being admired is really lonely because it's never real. Admiration is like this fake pedestal that separates. But after I started telling my truth and admitting I was fully human, I got to be human with other people. I found out that I wasn't alone at all. I realized: *Oh, life isn't just something I have to suffer through silently.* Sometimes you don't know which communities to go to so you can ask for help. You just have to say the thing out loud and let the right people find you.

LAURA: It only ever starts with telling the truth to one person. If you can just start to tell the truth a little bit, you will start to have community, because we all want it desperately. We all want it, but we don't know how to do it or we're too afraid to do it. But man, the people that are ready for you and the people that want to be in your community, when they hear you speak the truth, they're going to find you.

—

To go on

I reach out to others.

We tell kids, "If you do the right things, get good grades, you're a good person, you're helpful, you're compassionate, good things are going to happen." When you take that mentality into fertility, you eat the weeds and take your supplements to prepare your body for the life and assume it'll just happen. But what if you do all of those things and it doesn't happen? What are you left with but the feeling of failure?

Fertility is a journey. Every month my period came, it felt like a little death and it felt like my body failed me, like the world failed me. Like every system I bought into was all BS. And when all this happens in the public eye, it feels like a flogging, it just feels so big. You're so covered in shame like syrup that you can't get out from. It feels like everyone can see everything: They can see you're a failure, a loser; they can see inside of your womb and inside of your heart to know you don't deserve it and that you must be doing something that is affecting your ability to conceive.

But as I was circling the drain of shame, I did a lot of therapy, listened to a lot of podcasts, and read a lot of books. This vulnerability and inner work made me want to seek community and talk to other people who are in this same space, like "Tell me how you got out. How did you see the light? Even if there wasn't a baby at the end of it, how did you get there?" And what I realized is that when you embrace radical transparency it breeds community, but when you embrace the lie and you embrace caginess and silence, it breeds isolation.

So I realized: *Yeah, it sucks. But what if I was honest about it? What if I just told the truth about what I feel to everybody and release the shame and humiliation?* I thought those things were protecting me from reality, but they weren't. They were delaying my reality—everything looks a thousand times worse when it's framed through the prism of shame. When I finally embraced the truth with radical transparency, holy shit, I freed myself. I freed myself to exist as I actually was.

GABRIELLE UNION

In the aftermath of my brother's death, one of my friends wrote me a text with a story about my brother. It was this tender lovely story, and I read it and smiled and cried because it reminded me of the uniqueness of my brother's beautiful life rather than being so focused on his death. The gift of that little story was so important to me. The friend who wrote it to me had lost her mother a couple of years prior, and she remembered what had helped her the most in her grief: the specifics; the memories; the stories. Now that's what I try to offer folks. A friend of mine lost her dad recently, and I wrote to her with a story about him. People always say, "There are no words." That's not true. There *are* words. You just have to sit and think about what they are.

ABBY

When we lost our pregnancy, one of my really good friends sent a box of gourmet cheese and stuff to go with it from our favorite cheese shop. She and I love cheese; cheese has been a big part of our relationship. When I got that package, I felt so seen because it wasn't about this horrible loss that I still hadn't even processed; it was about *me*. Show up in a way that reminds people who they are at their core.

MARISA RENEE LEE

To go on

I show up and allow others to show up for me.

The best kind of showing up is when you make an offer of specific help. You don't text someone and say, "Let me know if you need anything." Because if they're like me, they will never ask for help. And I think the best specific offer is the thing that you already love to do, maybe that only you can do. If you love dogs, you offer to walk someone's dogs. If you love mowing the lawn, you go and mow someone's lawn. I've been the recipient of so many beautiful acts of showing up. When I was undergoing my second transplant, I spent about six weeks in the hospital. I was limited to two visitors during very constrained visiting hours, so I was really isolated.

Then one day, my friend Behida called me and said, "Look outside your window." I looked down onto bustling York Avenue in Manhattan, and there she was, dancing like a maniac. She's not a professional dancer, but she loves to dance, and for about five minutes straight, she did little kicks and hops and turns as if nobody was looking—though of course, everyone who passed by was staring at her. I laughed and knocked on the window, and she waved up at me. It was a tiny, amazing moment of connection that filled my whole day with joy. Another was when our mutual friend Liz on Valentine's Day— quietly, without telling me anything—made a heart out of little LED lights out on the sidewalk. That was it. So simple but beautiful.

There's no right or wrong way to show up, but ultimately, I think the most powerful acts of showing up amount to this: *i'm here. i love you.* I'm going to keep being here.

SULEIKA JAOUAD

The one thing that I feel is most universal is the pain of losing your mother, watching your mother take her last breath. I think every son will go through that or experience the loss of someone who has mothered them. It changed my life, watching my mother die.

Because now I realize that everyone I see is going to watch someone who has mothered them die. And I suddenly feel so much closer to everyone because of that. There are strangers whose mothers have already passed. And all of a sudden I feel closer to them as well.

OCEAN VUONG

To go on
I remember that we all grieve and I am not alone.

After my brother passed, I was so terrified to go to my mom and dad's house. I walked in, and it was just lots of tears. Everybody was telling the story of how they found out that he'd died. It was so interesting how badly I wanted to know everybody's stories. When things like this happen, it's really important to mark it, to put a flag in the ground and say: *Okay, this happened, things will be different now.* Even though it's really sad, it's also really beautiful. We will all go on, but this moment is a touch tree that we will always go back to. It was ours. We will never forget it.

ABBY

My life was blown up when my son, Shane, went skiing on his twelfth birthday and never came home. My soul fell out of my heart. And I spent the next twenty years trying to find more light and get through it and understand it. One of the first lessons I learned after moving to California with my daughter was that I wasn't able to run into anyone on this planet who hadn't encountered some form of loss, some form of anguish. We're not alone in it. We're not singled out.

MELODY BEATTIE

Oftentimes grief can feel like this incredibly isolated experience. It's hitting you, and you leave your house, and you look around, and people are in the grocery store, and kids are laughing, and people are carrying on, and you are in grief. You're in pain. It's inescapable, insufferable, all-consuming pain. And when people around you are not experiencing that, it can send you into an even greater state of isolation because you think no one understands. But everybody is grieving something. Everybody in the room that you're in is grieving something. Everybody in the grocery store you're shopping at is grieving something, if you were to scratch the surface of their lives. And there's community in that if we can just be more open about it.

DAN LEVY

When a big event happens in your life, like losing someone you love, or receiving a diagnosis, or going through recovery, there's a portal that opens. It cracks you open to the truth of your own mortality—and that gives you access to remembering the kind of life you want to live. It's like a light that's shining above your head, and suddenly you have a bit more connection to the universe. Many of us don't want to be conscious, but there is a true gift in that consciousness.

Watching Glennon work through the grief that came up in her recovery and rebirth was miraculous. Some days it came in blips; for a moment I could actually see her embodiment happening. I'd look at her and think: *Oh, my gosh. She's landed. She's here. She feels safe, and she's taking a breath.* And then it went away; she'd get lost again in her head and her fear. Now her embodied moments are more frequent than her fear moments. It somehow feels like I can sense the little girl version of Glennon finally feeling safe on this earth to stay, to really be here with us, with me. Adult Glennon has worked so hard to create a life in which little girl Glennon feels safe enough to come out and exist. It's amazing to see adult Glennon become the person that little Glennon always needed to show up and fight for her. It's just a really hard-won magic.

ABBY

To go on
I find the beginnings in endings.

—

GLENNON: For a long time, you referred to the day you were paralyzed as your "death day." Then your sister said something to you that changed everything. What did she say?

CARSON TUELLER: We went on a little brother-sister date to get pretzel bites at the strip mall. At the time she was thirteen. We were talking, and I referred to the day of my accident as the day of my death. And she said, "What if we called that the day of your rebirth?" I thought it was cute but said, "No, we can't call it that." But as I drove home, it stuck with me. I thought: *Well, who's to say? Am I right? Is she right?* Over the course of three hours, I had a powerful paradigm shift. I had a profound experience, realizing that the only thing that happened to me was that the bones in my neck moved. They hit my spinal cord, and my body now works the way it does and doesn't. No drama, no brokenness there; that's simply all that happened. And I have added all the rest of the meaning. That left me with the realization that I can create the meaning around every event that I previously thought had fixed meaning. I left the gym that day saying, "That's the day of my rebirth. That's the day of my rebirth. That's the day that the stars aligned and I became exactly who I was supposed to be." This is Plan A. Is it true? No. Is it false? No. Calling it the day of my death, the day I was devastated, the day that I lost everything and veered from the path I was destined to be on is as true as: *This is exactly where I'm supposed to be.* But living inside of one of those paradigms produces a very different result and a very different way of being from the other.

Suddenly, when I claimed this as Plan A, I had access to whole new ways of being and acting that were unprecedented. I started going on dates, I started taking risks. I started telling people to carry me up the stairs. I started doing all the things that I wasn't doing before because I was broken. I was this tragic hero. And it all changed just by changing this story or interpretation about the actual event.

—

Grief is its own deal, and it will do what it wants in our bodies; it affects us all differently. In my experience, it came in waves. At the beginning it was just a tsunami, an endless, relentless wave, pressing me up against the wall, drowning me in debris. It felt like there was no escape, like I was going to die. And then it began to ebb and flow a little bit. I would notice that all of a sudden I would have an afternoon where I felt genuine joy and I laughed and I didn't have a single bad thought for forty-nine minutes. And I was like: *I just did forty-nine minutes. That's my longest stretch. Let's write it down.* A sense of stability was growing in me, and I was pulling my way on a rope bit by bit. I don't think there's any one path through recovery, but right around the one-year mark is when I thought: *I'm going to live.* That's when I knew that I was past survival and that I was going to thrive.

JEN HATMAKER

—

GLENNON: It was so beautiful when you said, "When I find myself longing for my mother, when all I want is to put my head in her lap and have her rub my back and tell me everything will be okay, I ask myself: *What is it that I'm truly longing for? Is it comfort, consolation, a loving touch?* I let the answer guide me toward what I can provide for myself, and I give myself permission to access it."

MARISA RENEE LEE: When I feel that way, I close my eyes. I take a deep breath. I think: *Okay, what do you really need?* I would love to be able to pick up the phone and call my mom, and I can't do that. But I know what she would tell me to do: "Take care of yourself. Slow down."

—

To go on

I move forward one step at a time.

I had a conversation with a professor named Jerry Sittser. Twenty-some years ago, he lost his mom and his wife and his daughter in the same car accident. There's no math on a loss that devastating. But he said with such strength and dignity: "I have really learned how to carry it." And I think that the big hope we can have for ourselves is having lives that are beautiful and meaningful and true. That we can suffer devastating loss and still carry it.

KATE BOWLER

Maybe we don't ever get over it. Maybe we just go on and take it all with us.

AMANDA

I refuse to spend the end of my life—no matter how much time it is, whether it's two months or twenty years—not loving my life, and that doesn't mean not feeling. My therapist taught me years ago that you can't shut yourself off to grief without also shutting yourself off to joy.

You have to think of it like a kink in the hose: If you stop the flow of sadness, you stop the flow of happiness at the same time.

So I'm crying about twice an hour. Then I'm bursting into laughter.

ANDREA GIBSON

Ten

How do I make peace with my body?

My entire adult life, I have moved every two or three years, trying to find the perfect home and city where I'll finally feel comfortable. It just hit me last year, at forty-eight years old, that the reason I can't find comfort anywhere is that I'm not comfortable in my real home: my body. Moving is never going to help me because wherever I go, there I am, in my body. My body has been my only home since the day I was born and will be my only home until the day I die. The work of my life is finding peace and comfort here, now, in my own skin. I want to learn how to feel cozy and safe in here.

GLENNON

The importance of beauty is planted in us young, and some of us spend our lives chasing it to earn worthiness and power. When you're a kid, you start to learn how to make your way in the world by making people happy, by being pleasing. One thing I learned early about myself was that I was cute and that my cuteness was currency. My cuteness earned praise and approval from grown-ups. I could see it in their faces. I could see them open up to me. It was so painful to turn ten and start slowly losing all my adorableness and power.

I became greasy, oily, chunky, frizzy, zitty, and I can still feel that shift viscerally—watching adults pull back from me instead of lean in. A little girl inevitably becomes fully human instead of a doll. For me that felt like a devastating fall from grace. I went from the world adoring me to the world looking away from me. I had lost all of that love, all of that power—and I had no idea how to get it back.

GLENNON

When my grandma was in elementary school, her teacher sent a note home that said, "Phyllis can't run in the playground. Needs bra." My grandma had to look at her teacher, knowing that she was hated because of her body. At home, my grandma was also surrounded by all sorts of abuse. She became so disconnected from her body. She stopped eating at mealtimes. She stopped running on the playground. She said she would sometimes look down and think: *Is that my hand? Is that hand mine?* Or she would pass herself in a window and do a double take because she was so disconnected from the sight of her own face and the sight of her own flesh.

COLE ARTHUR RILEY

The first time I became aware of my body as different in any way, I was nine years old. I can remember exactly what I was wearing, exactly where I was standing. My uncle said, "You've got a real potbelly over there, don't you?" I looked to my mom, who rushed me upstairs to safety away from that comment. Sometimes I wonder what it might've been like if she had said, "Oh, whatever." It was almost like when a child falls and they look to their parent to confirm the damage. I think my mom's reaction amplified it in my mind.

MEGAN FALLEY

I was told at a very formative moment, "No one wants to marry a fat girl." It was right as I had started to put on a couple of pounds. So it was very tied to my sense of what was going to give my life value. For me, there was a rebelliousness in saying, "Oh, no one wants to marry a fat girl? I don't care. I'm going to eat everything." Since I was raised in diet culture, I'm going to try to diet, but then I'm also going to rebel against that and eat everything.

ADRIENNE MAREE BROWN

To make peace with my body

I realize I wasn't born ashamed of my body, I was *taught* to be.

My first year of college, I gained probably twenty pounds. When I came home that summer, I remember looks of pity. At the mall, I ran into some guy I vaguely knew from high school who looked horrified as he said, "You used to be so pretty." My good friend sat me down to explain to me why I shouldn't *let myself go.*

That was the moment I understood that *myself* was the way that I appeared. And *letting myself go* was letting my body be what people didn't want it to be. Never mind that I had gone to college, adjusted to a brand-new world, made new friends, and earned straight A's. That was not relevant if I didn't also look the way I was supposed to look.

AMANDA

When my daughter was thirteen, she showed me a meme on Instagram that said, "Love your cellulite, ladies!" She said to me, "Wait, what? I didn't even know I *wasn't* supposed to love my cellulite until I saw this."

GLENNON

The thing that's been reinforced over and over again is: There's no space for you. We don't make space for disabled bodies. We don't put bodies like yours on the cover of magazines. You are not ever going to be a romantic lead, and you're not going to see a body like yours in a romantic comedy. You're excluded even from conceptions of what diversity even is. So I thought: *Okay, well, I'm not a body. Nobody values my body. I won't be a body, I'll only be a mind, but let me tell you, I'm going to be the best possible mind in the world.* It was this plea: If I just get enough degrees, if I just get enough awards, if I just write a good enough essay, won't that be enough to see me as real and valuable?

CHLOÉ COOPER JONES

AUBREY GORDON: 97.9 percent of fat people say that they experience anti-fatness and that it comes from their families and their friends and the people that say they love them the most. People who are not fat say things they think are encouraging to fat people; in reality, they're all just different ways of calling us fat. Like "Hey, do you want a gym buddy?" That's not a thing you're generally offering to your thinner pals. Or "Oh, have you thought about wearing this? It's a little more slimming on you." All of this "I'm helping" is designed to make fat people look thinner and appear thinner, as if that's our pathway to success. And it's also designed to make thin people feel like they have done good things to earn the bodies that they have.

GLENNON: Once you were in a soccer stadium buying jerseys and you said, "There's no jerseys for fat people here," and the woman behind you in line tapped you on the shoulder and said, "Oh, you're not fat. Don't say that about yourself."

AUBREY: If I had said, "I'm Canadian," and someone went "You're not Canadian; you're smart and you're beautiful," you'd be like "What do you think about Canadians? What is your deal?" We're sort of all telling on ourselves about our attitudes toward fat people all the time without reckoning with how that lands for fat people. It really is a hierarchy that hurts us all; it pulls thinner people away from their relationships to fat people in a really meaningful, intense way that I think many folks don't even really clock is happening.

To make peace with my body I realize I wasn't born ashamed of my body, I was taught to be.

Growing up, I was at a distance from my body. That was my strength: to leave; to escape. Then, as I go into adolescence and I'm dancing, I'm in front of a mirror pretty much every day of the week. I can't escape the sight of my own face. So what do I do? I turn against it. And that distance from my own body eventually becomes disdain. It becomes self-hatred. That was the story of my bulimia—a hatred of my body. But more than that, a hatred of me, a hatred of myself. Destroying the body felt so necessary to my survival in the same way that leaving the body felt necessary to my survival.

COLE ARTHUR RILEY

When I was a kid, I didn't think that I could be both queer and Indian. I had to be cis, I had to be married. When I pierced my nose, my grandmother said, "How could you do this to me?" But when she said, "How could you do this to me?," what she was also saying was "How could you show me that freedom is possible?" Because it's easier to believe that this prison is a home. It's easier to believe that this misery is the only way to live. And in witnessing me own my own body, she had to confront the ways she's outsourced that ownership to other people, to culture, to identity. And so, so much of the trauma I experienced from my own people, I know at the root comes from these histories of unprocessed trauma from colonialism, from so many of the violences wrought on them that made them feel like they were never enough.

ALOK

I was sexually abused as a seven-year-old. I blocked it for a long, long time—I had to go through a lot to get back there. Abuse and sexual trauma, along with the pressure on women to be thin and perfect, can cause us to dissociate from our bodies. We block out the abuse and become self-hating. I felt judged by how I looked, even by my father, so I went through a lot of life wanting to be perfect. I developed eating disorders. I thought nobody would ever love me unless I was perfect. All the interesting, complicated, angry parts of myself moved out and took up residence outside of me somewhere. I had to work really, really, really hard to bring myself back into myself. Like a double image that's finally coming together. But in the end, I succeeded.

JANE FONDA

*To make peace with my body **I realize I wasn't born** ashamed of my body, I was taught to be.*

Many of us have these really early experiences of our bodily knowings being denied. As kids, we're told, "No, you're not feeling that." Or "You're not hungry." We see our parent upset, and they say, "Oh, I'm fine, I'm fine." The adults in our life—who we depend on for our survival—really start to make us doubt the things that we know intuitively. So we face a conflict: Do I stay connected to my body, or do I preserve the relationship that I'm in? The ability to be in relationship with people who approve of us and love us is so essential to our survival that we will sacrifice what's happening inside of us to make sure that we are safe relationally. But God bless our dissociation. I am so grateful for every single moment that I shut sensation out of my body, because I needed that to survive. It was the most important thing I could have done at that time. It was what kept me alive. But at some point, we get to update our systems and say: *I'm not in the moment that needs to be white knuckled and survived in the same way. I am with people who love me, who want to help me meet my needs. And it is okay for me to be seen in the fullness of who I am now.*

DR. HILLARY MCBRIDE

GLENNON: In the religion I grew up in, we were trained to believe that our bodies were not us. It was "You can't trust your body. Your body has evil tendencies, and it will lead you astray." It was just a relentless effort to separate us from our bodies.

SONYA RENEE TAYLOR: That's a great message if you desire to control a large number of bodies. What an amazing thing to be able to tell enslaved Africans, "Your body doesn't matter. You'll get your reward in Heaven." It's a wonderful way for me to continue to utilize your body for my profit and not have you be embodied enough to decide in a collective mass scale to uprise. The intention of that message is disconnection.

—

The BMI was designed by a statistician, sociologist, and astronomer looking to construct the "ideal man." He gathered data on the height and weight of white men in the French and Scottish militaries in the 1800s. Around the turn of the twentieth century, American insurance companies were looking for ways to charge some policyholders more, and the BMI offered a way to say, "This is the level of fat where we will charge you more." The BMI has nothing to do with your health. It's never been meaningfully tested or adjusted in any real way. It categorically does not work for Black and brown people. It incorrectly predicts health risks. And even among white people—the people that it was "designed for"—its high-water mark of being able to "detect obesity" is only 50 percent.

AUBREY GORDON

Skin bleaching, a way of life for so many women of color all over the world, is causing all kinds of cancers and illnesses. That's why skin-bleaching products are banned from use in Europe. Yet the large majority of these products are manufactured in Europe *specifically to be dumped in the so-called Third World.* We spend so much time focused on shaming the "choices" women make in the name of beauty without looking at the institutions that make and profit off these options for women in the first place.

DR. YABA BLAY

*To make peace with my body **I realize I wasn't born** ashamed of my body, I was **taught to be.***

As we obsessively try to control our own bodies—to make ourselves thin, keep our wrinkles at bay, hide our gray—extremist activist groups have obsessively stripped away our right to *actually* control our own bodies.

Our culture is obsessed with breasts—we're told a hundred different ways to lift, enlarge, or enhance them by the time we're sixteen—yet most of us have never been told our breast density, which determines our risk of cancer and whether or not a mammogram can even detect cancer in us.

We learn with great precision how to make our bodies more desirable, palatable, and valuable to others. But we don't learn what we need to know about our bodies in order to live our lives with vitality and peace and pleasure—like how we can best cope with the dramatic decades-long process of perimenopause and menopause or how we can consistently and effectively orgasm.

None of this is our fault, but it's all our responsibility. Because when we control ourselves, we lose ourselves; and when we lose ourselves, they control us.

AMANDA

It's real hard to think of a law that limits a man's control over any part of his body.

FORMER VICE PRESIDENT KAMALA HARRIS

As Dr. Amos Wilson says, "If you want to understand any problem in America, you need to focus on who profits from the problem, not who suffers from that problem."

ASHTON APPLEWHITE

It is expected that you pass on the system of body shame and body terrorism. It's no failure of ours that we've been indoctrinated into this system. It is by design. The gift of this moment now is that we have been born into a time unlike any other time before; we now have the tools and mechanisms to, on a massive scale, dispel the lie.

SONYA RENEE TAYLOR

It is a real challenge to push back on the classist and racist beauty standards of whiteness/thinness/blondness. It's a real challenge to push back on wellness culture, too. But when you start to track those ideas back to their sources, you begin to understand why they exist. They exist to keep us wasting all our resources—our money, our attention, our time—on the tiny myopic individualistic optimizing purifying project of self-perfection. When you figure that out, you begin to ask what other kinds of projects you might spend yourself on if you weren't so self-obsessed. You consider that some of your resources might be spent on individual and collective liberation. Then you realize the stakes. It dawns on you that breaking free from beauty standards and wellness obsession is a matter of life and death.

GLENNON

To make peace with my body

I reject anything that tells me to fear myself or that I'm broken.

Beauty is a made-up thing. It is not fixed. It is not universal. It is based on a culture's particular political and economic structure. It's like we're in Oz, and I want to scream, "There is no wizard! It's just a powerless man pulling knobs!" If we all decided not to participate in the beauty standard, it would go away—because all of our striving to achieve it is exactly what is maintaining it as the standard. If each of us just decided: *Nothing about me is broken, so I'm going to stop trying to fix what isn't broken,* there would actually not be a beauty standard. It only exists because we're all striving to achieve it.

AMANDA

It is super important to recognize that the thinking we have about our bodies and other bodies shapes our experience of being a body. Are we perpetuating these kinds of constricting narratives, or are we able to say: *Whoa, that's not an okay narrative to pass on about a body.* It can be as simple as: *I'm supposed to be sitting in a meeting all day. Maybe I'm going to stand.* It's about disobeying.

DR. HILLARY MCBRIDE

The hardest part of healing is looking at your own attitudes about beauty, age, and aging. No one wants to acknowledge that they're biased. It's uncomfortable. But the cool thing is, once you come together and share your experiences, you realize: *Oh, it's not me. It's not that my tits are too small or my forehead is too wrinkly.* These are widely shared social and political experiences that we can come together and do something about. And that is really liberating. Once you're able to look at your own brainwashing and collusion, you're off and running.

ASHTON APPLEWHITE

*To make peace with my body **I reject anything that tells me to fear myself or that I'm broken.***

Fear of self or fear of the other never comes from our truest self. That kind of fear comes from our conditioning. So instead of being carried away by false fear, we can pause and interrogate it. That pause always helps me get freer. I was looking in a mirror the other day and noticed that my neck looked a little bit different—kind of wrinkly and saggy. It made me feel panicky for a moment. Then it made me think about the book *I Feel Bad About My Neck*, which made me remember Nora Ephron and made me very happy. Then I had a moment of: *Oh, wait. Who taught me that my neck's not supposed to look like this?* And then: *Who benefits from my believing that?* Certainly not me. Just some guy somewhere running a lotion business. No, thanks. I love my neck. It's done such a good job for so long of holding up my head. I love you, sweet wrinkly neck. You're perfect to me.

GLENNON

Your capital-S Self will never tell you that you're broken, it will never tell you something is wrong with your body, whether that's its shape or size or color or anything about its function. That is never coming from the Self. There is a you that is present and always speaking. And there's no greater or more important task in this life than to know how to find that voice, hear it, and then live consistently with it. That has proven to be the most important thing I've ever done with my life.

CARSON TUELLER

In a world that wants us to be machines, it is easy to think of ourselves as machines. Kaitlin Curtice writes about talking to her begonias as she gives them water and they soak it up: "Oh, you were so thirsty."

She says, "I wonder if we let others know when we need a drink or a break from the heat." I don't think we do. I don't think we even know how thirsty we are. It made me cry to imagine myself soaking up water while someone says tenderly, "Oh, love, you were so thirsty."

AMANDA

To make peace with my body

I listen closely to my body's needs and I honor them.

Listen to yourself when you are tired, when you are thirsty. I've just started keeping a glass of water on my desk. When I notice I'm thirsty, that is me being embodied in a positive way. That's an attuned connection to myself. Am I pausing to notice that it's good for me to stretch and move? What are the places where I feel mastery in my body, and where I can experience myself as powerful? Can I do those more? Is there an activity that I do that I notice I feel better after doing?

When we start slowing down, we disrupt capitalism, we disrupt hustle culture. We start to go "Oh, that's not sustainable for me anymore." When I slow down, I'm noticing that the seasons are changing. I feel like I'm actually seeing daffodils come up in my garden. What it's doing is making me feel connected to the earth. And the more I'm connected to the earth, the more I want to be in relationship with the earth. It takes us into a kind of mystical oneness if we take it to its full extent.

Embodiment actually brings us into relationship with all life, because it's life that is in our bodies. And when we start to encounter that, we start to see it everywhere.

DR. HILLARY MCBRIDE

What
if every
single thing
that I have learned
about who I am is wrong?
What if it's not: I think,
therefore I am.

What if it's:
I feel, I see, I vibrate,
I hug, I eat, I rest, I orgasm,
I smell, I touch, therefore I am.

What if I do not have to learn to love
my body because my body is not separate
from me? It *is* me. What if the only thing
I have to learn how to love is having the
experience of living through this body?

I don't want to perfect my body.

I want to look out from in here
and experience it all.

I want to be in here and have
the full experience of being a body.

I don't want to love my body.

I just want to body.

I want to be.

GLENNON

In embodiment work, we practice centering. You practice getting into that state where your body is somewhat relaxed. It doesn't mean that you're happy or calm, but your body's just there.

And you can start to see when things activate you. *Oh, that took me a little bit out of myself. How did I do that? What did I do?* And a lot of times, we tend to do similar things over and over again because we practice them. So someone might come toward you and you're like: *Oh, I just went way in the back. How did I do that? I tightened around my eyes, I closed off my chest.* There are all these subtle, subtle ways.

Making time to practice listening to and being attentive to ourselves and what we're doing—that is embodiment. There are always sensations, there are always responses, there's always information about who you are right now. But we are often trained to be so externally focused that we're not very good at listening to the signals that our body is sending out. So practice. Practice.

PRENTIS HEMPHILL

I always thought that my body was just an unfortunate container carrying around my brain. Embodiment is new to me. Hillary McBride said, "Why don't you stop calling your body 'it' and start calling your body 'she' and 'her'? Because she *is* you. She isn't separate from your brain and from your heart and soul, she is you. And she is Team You and only Team You, and her only agenda in this entire world is to keep you safe and flourishing. She won't tell you a lie." So I started referring to my body as "her," and I talk to her in the most loving of ways. And when she tells me something, I'm going to listen. I'm going to pay attention to her wisdom, knowing that that is the highest good for my life.

JEN HATMAKER

I'm practicing listening to the feelings and sensations inside my body. I get a signal inside of my body when I'm full. I also get a signal when I eat something that my body is like: *That's not good for me.* The same thing happens in my life when I'm sitting down with someone. If I feel: *This person is not authentic*, it's not going to work for me. It literally shows up as a sensation in my system, and now I'm learning to feel it. I've spent ten years learning to feel again, and now I'm like: *Oh, I can feel that.* God, I wish someone had showed me that when I was five.

ADRIENNE MAREE BROWN

To make peace with my body **I listen closely to my** *body's needs and I honor them.*

In young adulthood I was so disembodied. I was so lacking in how to communicate well and how to love others and myself. Then I started therapy, and I started noticing the pain in my body. My lower stomach hurt, my lower back hurt, I would get headaches. I went to the worst extremes looking everything up. And then I had to stop and realize, maybe my body's just saying: *Oh, this thing is really painful and you've been thinking about it a lot. This is a trauma response, a stress response.* It took me so long to realize that the trauma I've carried in my body since I was little still manifests in my adult body. My adult body is still trying to tell me things just like my child body was trying to tell me things. What if I go slower, stop, learn to breathe, and listen to what she is telling me?

KAITLIN CURTICE

I had to meditate for a year before I really started to feel like the messages my body was sending me were a lot clearer. I went through a whole process of really listening. At first I couldn't hear anything. All I could hear was: *I don't feel good.* But slowly, over time, it became so much more clear. *Oh, I'm thirsty. I need water. I need to stretch. I need to go on a hike. I need to move my body. I need to dance. I need to sing. I need to make love. I need to have a deep conversation with somebody I care about.* I am so much healthier and so much happier after learning to listen to my body.

JUSTINA BLAKENEY

Kids are natural, intuitive eaters. But, as adults, so many people outsource their eating decisions to some expert or some meal plan at the expense of losing trust in themselves. But we can actually eat by listening to the messages of our bodies. Our bodies give us these amazing messages, letting us know how we're feeling, whether we have to go to the bathroom, whether we're hungry or full. And when we're in touch with that, it's powerful, powerful information.

EVELYN TRIBOLE

GLENNON: At first I thought my anorexia was just extreme vanity—an obsession with appearance. I decided to undo that through renunciation, by becoming an appearance monk. No more Botox. No more dyeing my roots. No more makeup. One day my daughter looked at me and said, "Do you think it's wise for you to keep all these hard rules for yourself while you're already trying to beat such a hard disease?" I looked at her and then called my hairdresser to touch up my roots. People without a strong inner locus of self-trust tend to look for outer loci of control. That's what I was doing: replacing one set of rigid rules for another set instead of replacing rigid outer rules with inner self-trust—with embodiment. Because even though I really *want* to be a woman who doesn't want to get Botox, I actually *do* want to get Botox. Even though I *want* to not want to dye my hair, I actually *do* want to. By banning these things, I wasn't following my true desire, I was disciplining myself. That's not how I want to live. I don't want to be so afraid of what I want that I make a million cages for myself. I want to stop being afraid of myself. So I decided I wasn't going to stop getting Botox until I *actually didn't want to.* I was just going to be gentle and kind to myself and do what I wanted to do, one thing at a time. I decided to try accepting who I *actually* am and what I *actually* want. When I decided that, I instantly felt calmer.

AMANDA: It's denial of yourself—denying what you want, denying what you need—which is the same thing as anorexia, right? As opposed to thinking: *How can I get to the place where I don't even want or need that thing?* Then, if you do arrive to that place, it's not a denial; it's actually an honoring of yourself to *not* do it.

GLENNON: Yes. And the amazing thing is that it took a year, but one day I looked at my Botox appointment coming up the following day and I thought: *I don't want to go. I don't want to leave my cozy home and wife and dogs and pay somebody to stick a needle in my face.* So I canceled, because it suddenly felt so silly. We grow and we learn, and slowly and suddenly, things we've done forever feel silly. So I guess I'd just say to women, "Do exactly what you want and keep becoming, and then when you want something different, do that. But you don't have to discipline yourself. You can wait for your wanting to change."

To make peace with my body

I trust my body,
I don't control it.

This is spiritual work. This is healing work. Do I trust this vessel that has brought me here? We can't get to trust until we realize our bodies are not our enemies. What does it mean to decide that my body and I are on the same team? Have I eliminated dominance, control, coercion, force from my relationship with my body? If I'm saying I want to practice justice, am I in a just relationship with my body? And when I'm in a relationship of trust, what do we do? How do we move?

SONYA RENEE TAYLOR

We fiercely control our bodies. We only control what we don't trust.
GLENNON

If we don't trust our bodies, we will never know their power.
AMANDA

Joy is loving what is true about your body—loving everything about the size and shape and beauty and gloriousness of your body; loving what's true, even when it's not what you were taught should be true or what you wish were true. The hard part is getting to a place of loving all the things you've been taught to hate because it means abandoning hope that you will ever be those things. You have to let go. You have to grieve. You have to have some rage about the fact that you were lied to for decades—and then you clear open the space to really explore the body that you actually have instead of the one you wish you had.

EMILY NAGOSKI

Anorexia is a commitment to being steel, to being unhuman, to being unmoving, to being a compliant robot. Anorexia is the opposite of *wabi-sabi*. *Wabi-sabi* is the Japanese concept that everything is always decaying, that everything's out of control, unfinished, and that's the most beautiful aesthetic in the world. Our culture is like "Freeze it. Perfect it. Filter it. Don't show time passing. Don't show mess. Don't show flaws." I want *wabi-sabi*. I want to show proof of life in my life.

GLENNON

To make peace with my body

I focus on what I like instead of what I look like.

Glennon: I had this weird moment recently when I thought: *Oh, my God, this is recovery.* I was at a store looking at these bracelets. I really like sparkly things, not because of the way they look to other people but because I like to look at sparkly things. So I was at a store, and I saw this silly beaded bracelet, and it was just sparkly, sparkly, sparkly. It was kind of silly, honestly. A bit cheesy. But I was like: *I want this, because I want to look at this.*

Amanda: You thought: *I don't think this will look good* on me. *I think this will look good* to me.

Glennon: Yes! That's it! I was in the store going: *Oh, my God. Is that what things are for? Am I supposed to have things that I love to look at on my body, in my life, in my house—not because someone else is going to think this thing is cool but because I like to look at this thing?* Now I just want things on me and around me that I like and that I like to look at. I don't care how they look to anyone else.

The vibe now isn't: What do I look like?

It's: what do I like?

Your body is not your masterpiece. Your life is.

It is suggested to us a million times a day that our bodies are projects. They aren't. Our lives are, our spirituality is, our love is, our relationships are, our work is. Stop spending all day obsessing, cursing, perfecting your body like it's all you've got to offer the world. Your body is not your art; it's your paintbrush. Whether your paintbrush is a tall paintbrush or a thin paintbrush or a stocky paintbrush or a scratched-up paintbrush is completely irrelevant.

What is relevant is that you have a paintbrush that can be used to transfer your insides onto the canvas of your life where others can see it and be inspired and comforted by it. Your body is an amazing instrument that you can use to create your offering each day. Don't curse your paintbrush. Don't sit in a corner wishing you had a different paintbrush. You're wasting time. You've got the one you've got. I don't want to go to any more classes where everybody is learning to love their paintbrushes.

I just want to paint.

GLENNON

Eleven

How do I make and keep real friends?

When the kids were really little, I remember seeing some women at daycare pickup. I liked their energy. So I emailed them and said, "Would you all like to come to my house? I'll have bagels and coffee." It was really kind of scary because they could have said no. But they didn't. More than a decade later, we're all still friends. I sometimes think: *What if I hadn't sent that email?* I would probably still be at school pickup, thinking: *Hey, y'all, I still like your energy. I still don't know you.*

AMANDA

I have this theory that souls are made in bunches. And someone, somewhere, in some beautiful gathering has these big cauldrons that they make souls in. And they're like "Okay, this one's going to have a little bit of heartbreak but a lot of joy. And these are going to be people who have really open hearts." And then when the little veggies arc cooked and they're souls, they sprinkle them out through time. Some of them are back in 1816, and one goes in a dog and one goes in a lizard and one goes in an Abby and one goes in a Glennon and one goes in an Amanda and they're all over the place.

And you don't know what's going to bring
you to a fellow sister from the cauldron.
But you meet someone, and you're like:
*I don't know what it is, but I feel like I've
known you forever. Oh, we're from the same
soup!* And although the time period we're
from or the town we're from doesn't match,
somehow we're still from the same
ingredients, the same soup.

TRACEE ELLIS ROSS

During my first therapy meeting, the therapist looked at me and asked, "How is the way you deal with food the same as the way you deal with people?" I rolled my eyes and thought: *Oh, come on.* But what I started to understand is that I avoided food and I avoided people. I was scared of both. Just like I had decided that there were only a few safe foods, I'd also decided that there were only a few safe people—everyone else needed to be kept at a distance. I was a person who didn't need food and didn't need friends. I really believed that. I have come to understand that I am, in fact, not some kind of sub/superhuman who is not hungry for food or friendship; it's just that I wasn't doing friendship in a way that allowed me to enjoy the real benefits of friendship. I wasn't making myself open, I wasn't letting anyone in. I'd always told myself: *I don't have enough time for friendship. I'm barely making it through the day as it is.* I learned that I need friendship *because* I can barely make it through the day as it is. Friendship, it turns out, is not something to do if I have extra energy; it's the thing that gives me the energy, creativity, happiness to actually enjoy life.

GLENNON

—

ESTHER PEREL: Trauma represents the tearing of the emotional and social fabric, a rupture of the connective tissue that isolates and silences us. Meaningful connections often offer a reparative experience that can offset the consequences of such fracturing experiences. People come together in many forms: They sing, wail, read, pray, light candles, hold vigils, tell stories, listen to each other, laugh, and relate. Fundamentally, what brings us back from trauma is that reconnection, a sense of aliveness and hopefulness that comes with it.

GLENNON: That is so beautiful because we tend to think that the way to get through trauma is to continuously go backward to it and keep mining it. But you're saying that moving toward what is warm and joyful and moving forward—toward other people—is also a way of healing.

—

To make and keep real friends

I prioritize connection.

Here's the thing about Black women's sisterhood that's really specific and important: Our sisterhoods are our lifelines. From the time we are born, Black women cleave onto each other. There's this connection that's kind of unspeakable. These friendships are a survival tool. Because if we didn't lean on each other, the world would've destroyed us by now. Black women have saved each other over and over again, and we are each other's breath. Our friendships mean something different.

LUVVIE AJAYI JONES

When I speak to the sisterhood of Black women, it's because we are called by our foremothers into a divine place that we should be so clear and forceful not to allow to be interrupted, because these are the things that have kept us alive. These are the things that have given us joy where there shouldn't have been any, creativity where it wasn't allowed, family where it was literally forbidden by law. It was through this sisterhood that we were able to create the spaces that saved us and that hold us and that heal us. And so we owe it to our ancestors to make them proud and to be as good of a descendant as the ancestors were becoming, right? I have a responsibility to those who built the space for me to exist in, and I have a responsibility to make sure that space is ever more safe, ever more beautiful, ever more powerful for anybody coming up after me, and I want people to rue the day that they ever thought they were going to come break us apart. Try it if you want to.

BRITTANY PACKNETT CUNNINGHAM

—

EMILY SALIERS: The more you have a community out there, like queer alliances, there's more of a sense of *I have a place where I can be.* When I was coming up, all I heard was: *You're different. You'll never be validated.* But some of the young people I know who come out are overjoyed and happy; they didn't have to fight this dark internal battle because they have community.

AMY RAY: Together, we can affirm our validity as human beings, our dignity. That's why we need community.

—

I used to take my kids to a cat shelter, and we'd go sit in the little room with all the kittens crawling everywhere. One day, a little orange kitten came up to Amma, a gray cat approached Tish, and a calico snuggled up to me. We all played with our cat and the other cats for hours. When we got back to the car, I asked, "Which cat did you all like the best? Which one was your favorite?" Each of us immediately identified our favorite cat as the one that had approached us first. I realized: *Oh, we each liked the one best who first liked us best.*

If we want to be liked, we have to *like*. That's it. Nobody leaves a party saying "My favorite person was that cool, aloof one." It's the person who approaches and shows interest in us.

I really, really think the secret to being loved is to love. And the secret to being interesting is to be interested. And the secret to having a friend is being a friend.

Why don't we want to believe that? We insist that we need to be the smartest or the most interesting or the most successful or the most beautiful to get people's attention. But maybe we don't. Maybe we just have to show a little interest. Maybe the surest way to be liked by people is simply to like people.

But that's a risk, right? To openly like someone? To admit to someone "I like you. I'd like to spend time with you" is to risk rejection. It's vulnerable. It's brave.

Be brave. Like somebody.

GLENNON

To make and keep real friends
I take risks.

When I'm making friends, I have to be brave, and being brave is just jumping. I imagine myself as a little kid jumping two feet into a cold pool. Once you get in there, it's not as cold as you thought it would be.

REESE WITHERSPOON

There was a study showing that people who think that friendship just "happens" are lonelier than people who think that friendship is something that takes effort. The people who know that friendship takes effort actually show up, make the effort, go out of their way to try to meet and connect with people.

DR. MARISA FRANCO

If you're standing in a circle of people and there is someone standing alone outside your circle, the thing to do is notice them, smile, move over a bit, and say, "Hi, come join us!" Better yet, let's stand in horseshoes instead of circles. Let's always leave space.

GLENNON

We need capital-F Friends and lowercase-f friends. My capital-F Friends are people I know inside out, who know me inside and out. My lowercase-f friends are people who I'm just like "Oh, Bob? Yeah, he's a good time." But I don't need to know Bob's soul.

People divide themselves into those categories for you. Around ten years ago, I posted that I was in the hospital. I had a friend, John, who I'd met through the internet. We were just internet friends. And he came to the hospital and visited me; he was the only person who visited. And I was like: *Oh, you want to be here during this stuff? Okay, we're real friends.*

SAMANTHA IRBY

To make and keep real friends

I make room for all different types of connection.

I have plenty of front yard friends, people I enjoy but don't know deeply. I can banter and laugh with these people but don't feel any sense of responsibility for them. Sometimes a front yard friend sparks a curiosity in me, so I invite her inside my home, maybe into the foyer first. Then, after plenty of foyer time, if I feel not only sustained interest but also sustained safety with her—if I feel warm and cared for and I sense my nervous system calming around her—I invite her to my couch. Couch friends are my true friends, the friends who've earned my trust, who share most of my values, who I feel safe with.

You get to decide as you invite people farther into your home and your life. Who makes you feel that you can exist the most?

GLENNON

The way I was doing friendship before is like this: I would get together with someone, and they would share something about themselves. Then they'd ask me how I was and I would tell a story about something that I had already solved, like "I was bulimic since I was ten and I was an alcoholic. Here's my vulnerable story . . ." I figured out how to take my trauma and pain and serve it up with a nice red bow. I thought that was connection. The problem was, I never shared what I was in the middle of; I never shared my uncertainty, my messy middle—just my before and after. That's not actual vulnerability, it's packaged vulnerability. That's not how to get help or guidance or wisdom or support. People can't help you with your stuff if you only share what you've already solved. Offering packaged vulnerability is like planning a road trip with a friend with the goal of spending time together. Then, instead of jumping into a car together, you book a flight and tell your friend you'll meet her there. Okay, but you missed the togetherness, the bonding, the connection, the working it all out together. You missed the whole point.

GLENNON

If we're never vulnerable, if we're never sharing the parts of ourselves that feel shame, then we will never trust love. If you don't know me, how can I trust that you love me? You don't know the value friends will bring to your life if you never allow yourself to experience it.

DR. MARISA FRANCO

To make and keep real friends

I stop hiding my mess.

There is something so incredibly honest and healing about sharing the most mortifying thing that has ever happened to you. When people laugh and say, "Oh, my God. You thought that was bad? Let me tell you what happened to me," all of a sudden you're making friends. Nobody's like "This person has really great hair, and so I want to be best friends with them." You want to be friends with the people who make you laugh, who make you feel safe, who make you feel comfortable. It's the authenticity of, "Hi, I'm screwed up. Can we be screwed up together?"

JENNY LAWSON

Abby and I went on a trip with Alex, who was a new friend at the time. At the end of the trip, Alex said, "Okay, so here's what I usually do after a social thing like this: I lie in bed and obsess over every single thing I said or did that I wish I didn't say or do and then I think: *Do they think I'm ridiculous for saying that?* I call that my postmortem. I just kinda die for a day. So what if we did it differently? What if we just did our postmortem now, together?" So we all sat at breakfast and talked about every single thing each of us had said and done over the three days that made us cringe in retrospect. That conversation was the one that made us closest. It cracked it all open.

GLENNON

I have a friend named Christine. I was in the delivery room when she had her baby; she helped me through my divorce. But we fell out of touch. A couple of years ago, her husband, Chris, learned that he had an aneurysm and a heart valve that needed to be replaced, which required this very complex, massive open-heart surgery. Christine would be in another state with him during the surgery, and they have two kids at home. She wrote to me saying, "This is what's happening. Would you be willing to help?" She gave me concrete things I could do.

A year after the surgery, Christine and Chris hosted a dinner. At the start of the evening, they both stood and said that the purpose of the night was not to celebrate Chris's recovery but to celebrate the people who had gotten them through that scariest time of their lives.

Christine said, "We just want everyone in this room to know what we learned from this experience: If you open yourself up to receiving help, your people will show up and make things okay. And if you are ever in a position where you need help, we will be among your people." It was beautiful; I was so thankful to be there. And I realized that if she had not taken the time to invite me to help, I never would have been there and been part of that magic, and I would have completely missed out on reconnecting with her.

Asking for help, and being open to help, is one of the most generous things you can do, because it brings a gift of connection. It made me wonder: *How many tables am I missing out on hosting, or showing up to, because I am caught in the lie that I can—or should—do it all myself?*

Maybe you need to let yourself fall apart to connect with people. I think my life has been smaller because I haven't been comfortable being seen when I don't have it all figured out.

AMANDA

To make and keep real friends

I am brave enough to ask for help.

A couple of years ago, I had a conversation with a woman who had a couple of kids, a very busy life. One day, her neighbor, who was a chef, offered to drop off a steak dinner for the whole family. He said, "I have this new recipe. I really want to try it out. I would love to bring it over for you guys." And her mouth was literally watering as she said no. "No, we couldn't. No, no, no." To me, that was such a powerful example of how, because we are so conditioned to view asking for help as a weakness, we actually turn away bids for connection. That was a bid from her neighbor to create community. In turning that away, she was rejecting that community.

DR. POOJA LAKSHMIN

When I call my friends and tell them I have a problem, I see it as an act of love because it means that I'm close enough to you to come to you with this. A lot of people see outreach to their friends and their family as a burden, and it's not. Honesty in friendship is the greatest act of love.

DAN LEVY

My friends have rewired my brain with their generosity. Every single time somebody does something generous for me, something shifts in my head that says: *Okay, you can receive that. You can actually be a recipient of somebody's love in that way.*

LUVVIE AJAYI JONES

Love is so amazing and terrifying
because it has this opposite, which is loss.

Expressing yourself has this opposite,
which is criticism.

Grow up,
but there's this thing called nostalgia.

Look for friendship and belonging,
but there's also left-outness and disconnection.

GLENNON

There are so many cliques in every environment. Some of them you're in, and most of them you're not. But if you just don't abandon *yourself,* you will find someone else who isn't going to abandon you. That's going to be the person who makes you feel good about yourself, who doesn't make you feel like you have to change or warp into something that isn't true to you. You just have to wait for a real match and never settle for a fake one.

ABBY

To make and keep real friends

I focus on the relationships I have instead of the ones I don't.

—

AMANDA: Being left out is universal. It happens every day. I don't think we'll ever arrive to a day where it doesn't happen to us anymore. And it never stops feeling horrible. The part of the brain that's triggered when we get left out is the exact same place we experience physical pain. We shame ourselves for feeling so devastated when we're left out. But our body doesn't know the difference—it is very, very real pain.

GLENNON: Yes. As people who crave belonging and connection, there are going to be moments of beauty and there are going to be moments of heartbreak. But that's not a problem; it's just being a human who is made for love and connection. If we didn't learn to avoid these feelings of left-outness like the plague when we were little, maybe it wouldn't be something that felt so devastating as adults.

AMANDA: Yes. If we could accept that this pain of being left out is inevitable, and it sucks but we have to endure it, then we would probably be less likely to try so desperately to save our kids from it. Instead of rushing in to try to fix it, which just makes them feel more ashamed, we can say, "You are feeling these awful feelings because you are a human. There's nothing wrong with you. I feel the same way when I'm left out. It happened to me just last week."

ABBY: I also think that when you're feeling left out, that could be a unique opportunity for you or your kid to look around and find somebody that you normally wouldn't sit and have lunch with or talk to. Strike up a conversation.

AMANDA: Yes. Research shows that, when you're feeling left out, you can do things to find your people: Instead of a family tree, you can make a friend tree. Write down the friends you've had for a long time, friends in the neighborhood, even potential friends. Then you see that there are actually a lot of folks on other branches. You don't need to focus your attention just on this one branch that is not sturdy right now. Because really, connection is what we need, and more often than not, it's already there. We're just not looking at the right branches because the branch that is activating the pain center of our brain is getting all of our attention.

ABBY: Yup. Also, buy a chain saw and lop off the leaving-out branch.

—

When I met Abby, I was starstruck and also super intimidated. She started just saying these things like "You're going to score more goals than I'll ever score. You're going to have way more success than I ever will. You're the next one."

She would always uplift me and give me so much confidence. It was so amazing to have someone so selfless because when you're playing a team sport, of course you want the team first, but every person has selfish, competitive feelings deep down inside. We all want to be as successful as possible. We all want to have the glory.

So for Abby to show up in a way that I had never experienced before from a teammate, I was just floored. It drew me toward her as a great friend and mentor.

ALEX MORGAN

To make and keep real friends

I cheer for my friends relentlessly and I'm always in their corner.

The "mean girls" trope makes me bananas. Sure, internalized misogyny manifests in girls and women being extra competitive with each other, but that's not inborn. If we end up more competitive than, say, men are, that is because we've been born into a world in which at every table, there are twelve seats—ten of them for men, two for women. Scarcity is our reality. For women, life is a frantic game of musical chairs. Don't hate the players; change the game.

GLENNON

Envy is just unexpressed admiration. Envy is respect and desire holding their breath.

GLENNON

People who address issues with their friends have more intimacy and closeness. Psychoanalyst Virginia Goldner talks about how you can have flaccid safety in your relationships, which is "We're close because we pretend there's no problems." Or you can have dynamic safety, which is "We're close because we rupture and we repair and we rupture and we repair."

DR. MARISA FRANCO

My son was having an issue with one of his friends. His buddy's family came to us to share that it was not going well with the boys. We talked to our son, our family went over and talked to his family, and we came up with a plan, including how they could handle it if things started going downhill again. It could have gone very differently: The other family could have written our son off and ended the friendship. Or, after they told us, we could have been defensive and written them off as too sensitive and meddling. I am thankful we did the harder, riskier thing. I'm grateful every time I'm part of what another friend calls a *carefrontation*, taking on the risk of awkwardness and conflict to keep the relationship moving forward.

AMANDA

At the beginning of our friendship, I said to you, "Just don't leave without talking to me first." There is infinite space for you in this friendship, and that includes stepping away from it if you need to. The one thing I ask is that you advocate for yourself and say, "This doesn't feel good for me anymore" or "My life is too busy and I don't have the space." What I didn't want you to do was not bring yourself into the relationship and slowly divest until you disappeared or not stress the relationship by saying, "I really have a hard time when you do this," and instead just leave. Don't just leave.

ALEX HEDISON

To make and keep real friends

I say and hear the hard things.

I used to think that friendship is what you need in the foxhole; that the shining moment for friendship is in a crisis—that's when you need friends, and that's when you find out what kind of friend you have and what kind of friend you are.

A few years ago, my beloved lifetime friend Lauren called me, upset and hurt, saying basically, "I've been going through something for the past six months that you don't even know about. You don't know what's going on in my life because you're not in touch with me, you're not with me."

She helped me see that my trope of being too busy to keep in touch was tired. She came from a place of such love, but she was clear: You're missing out on the gold of being with me in life. And at some point you're going to have to choose whether to be in relationship with people—with me—or not.

It turns out that friendship *is* what you need in the foxhole; it's just that all of life is a foxhole. It's not that we pay the price of being in connection with our friends so that when life is unbearable they'll show up; it's that the connection we're making with our friends *is* the showing up in each other's lives—and *that* is what makes life bearable.

AMANDA

I was having a conversation with one of my really good friends the other day, and she was reflecting on friendship. And she explained how now, more than ever, she understands the importance of the word *friend* and what it means as we're all getting older. We're going to be losing parents soon. Friends have to show up.

A friend is not the person who just casually tells you on social media, "Oh, my God, I'm so sorry." Your friend is a person who says, "Have you eaten today?" A friend might be the person who says, "Do you need their obituary written? Do you need me to help you write it?" Actions that are substantive. That's why I'm very careful who I call a friend. Will I show up for you in the moment of crisis? If you are not somebody who I would show up for, I can't call you a friend.

My friends are people I'm accountable to and people I'm accountable for. I have to vouch for you. I have to show up for you. Even when I'm not in the room, you represent me and I represent you. So who I call a friend has to be aligned with my values.

Friendship is care, love, sharing joy with each other, and serving as a soft place to land for each other. I know I can never truly fail in this world because my friends would be my soft place to land. They won't let me hit concrete. They'll catch me right before I do. So it also feels like safety.

LUVVIE AJAYI JONES

To make and keep real friends

I show up through it all.

My friend's husband was talking about his friend who lived in his neighborhood who he can never get in touch with and who never reaches out to him. And I was thinking to myself: *That is not a good friend. That is maybe good company.* Good company is someone whose company you enjoy and you like them as a person. But a good friend is: *I'm committed to you. I'm invested in you. I try to follow through with what I say, to show up in your times of need, to show up in your times of joy.* It's intentional, and it requires effort.

DR. MARISA G. FRANCO

There was no predicting who was going to be on my side after the trial. There were people on my side, so that was good, I wasn't alone. But other people I care about a lot were not with me. When we go through these most challenging things in our life, it's never the people we *think* would pick us up at two in the morning who actually do. But then there are people who *do* step up, and you think: *Wow, I've been overlooking how valuable that friend is. What a good friend that they would stand up for me and come to me to try to help.* I think there's something beautiful in the fact that we can't predict which people will be the ones who really show up. We can only know that while some people might not be able to help us during certain phases of our life, there are other people who will—and we can do that for other people, too.

DR. CHRISTINE BLASEY FORD

—

GLENNON: I have this feeling when I reconnect with friends of being tethered to the earth. I don't know how else to describe it, except that I constantly feel like a hot air balloon just floating out in space, completely untethered from the earth. But when I make the time to sit and talk and be seen by and connect with human beings outside of my family, I feel like I've created a tether. Like I'm being held down, a little bit grounded.

AMANDA: The opposite of tethered is untethered, and there's a lot of freedom and there's a lot of control in being untethered. You are unaccountable to anyone. You are living your life, floating around. People can see you from afar, but no one can see you up close. But when you are tethered to someone, there is accountability there. There's a responsibility there. They can see you up close. That's the good news and the bad news.

GLENNON: That's beautiful and so true. I think in my friendships I have been free as a bird, but not held. I think I'm ready to be seen up close.

—

My friend Samira coined the idea of being a barnacle to our friends. Barnacles make a home at the bottom of a boat, and they shackle to each other. They are determined to live there forever. And really, it's just the best metaphor. We've been through all these journeys, me and my friends, and I want to be stuck to them.

TRACEE ELLIS ROSS

It's a delight to me every time my friend Alex comes over. I hear her knock and the dogs go crazy, and when I open the door, she's just standing there on the door-step looking at me. She tilts her head to one side and puts this face on her face that makes it seem like we haven't seen each other for thirty years and that she's been on a long journey and she has finally made it. She has finally made it home. She lives in my town; we see each other once a week. But every time it's like she's come a thousand miles and as if we have been on a long journey and have finally found our way back to each other. I take her bag, and we walk straight to the couch. It's a true delight.

GLENNON

The beauty of getting older is that you have the experience to be able to look around and know: *Hey, that looks like a person and a relationship that could be for me. Not that one, or that one, but* that *one.*

I now have enough confidence and self-knowledge to put myself out there and say, "I know who I am and what I bring. I'm looking at you, and I'm beginning to see who you are and what you bring. I propose that we see what we could be together."

AMANDA

Twelve

How do I love my person?

Going hard has always been easier for me than staying soft. Whether it's flirting with strangers or traveling solo to other countries, I'm more comfortable being anonymous than being known. Adventures are less scary than intimacy. The divorce cemented all of that. The foolish part of me soft enough to get crushed threatened to harden forever.

Years later, on the day I married John, Glennon gave me a necklace with the Joan of Arc battle cry "I am not afraid. I was born to do this."

Trying like hell to stay soft has been the hardest battle of my life. My most difficult, transformational journey has been staying right where I am: showing myself, allowing him to see how much help I need, allowing him to help me, uncovering all my fears.

I am afraid. I was born to do this.

AMANDA

The challenge and beauty of being in relationship is the challenge and beauty of dealing with *otherness.* This thing we do—we reach out toward the world, fall in love, and want to connect with someone else—means we are inviting otherness into our lives. That is important. It is the thorn that will make you grow, it will make you heal and go beyond yourself. That's the journey.

DR. ORNA GURALNIK

If you choose love or connection, you're not choosing safety. It's a risk to give your heart to someone— to give someone else the power to ruin you. But I learned from Pema Chödrön that we are alive only to the degree to which we are willing to be annihilated. That is love. That is life. It's the risk. And it's still the right thing for me: living open to annihilation.

GLENNON

When you're in the falling in love phase, you're really not in a relationship yet. You're just in giddy enmeshment. That's why they call it falling or getting swept off your feet: because you're not on solid ground. You're just gone.

I love that part so much, because I've always loved feeling gone. During the falling in love part, I wasn't even Glennon anymore, which I've always found it so difficult to be. I was just swept away in this swirly beautiful obsession. It was like I no longer had to exist. Love obliteration.

With Abby, the falling stage ended when I started coming to and remembering that I was still Glennon—a whole person with needs to tend to and interests to honor. I remembered my *I*-ness that existed before the *We*-ness. As I began to see myself clearly again, I started to see her clearly for the first time. We were just two complicated, individual, flawed people after all. We had to decide if we were really going to do this—really try to make a life together—without our brains flooded with chemicals, without the rush of it all. Sober love.

When the fall is over, you land with a thud. That's the beginning.
Falling in love is dumb luck. *Rising* in love together is the miracle.

GLENNON

To love my person

I don't just fall in love, I rise in love.

I could see Glennon's high wearing off during the comedown from our initial phase of love. I worried she'd panic and leave. I started trying to prepare her by telling her that phase one of love was ending and phase two was going to begin. I told her that in phase two, our love wouldn't cover up our little idiosyncrasies anymore; small things would start to annoy us. I said, "Falling in love is a trance, and it's going to wear off, and we're going to be in a new place." She got scared at first. I was killing her buzz. She said, "I feel like you're saying it's over, like soon we're going to love each other less." I said, "No, soon we're going to have to love each other *more* than we do now, because our brains aren't going to be artificially lit up with serotonin. But the magic isn't going away; it's just going to get *realer*." Glennon was still scared, but I was excited. I'd fallen in love a million times before, but I'd never had phase two, the landing in love part. I'd never had the real part, and I wanted it so badly with her.

ABBY

I'm so glad that the honeymoon phase does not last forever, because it's impossible. You want to be with this person all the time. You completely meld together. And at some point, there's this click of: *Oh, I have friends! Remember, I used to be on the soccer team?* And once you recognize that, you can start to get back to yourself.

NEDRA GLOVER TAWWAB

We often get the message that there is this hierarchy of love and that the best, rarest, most precious kind of love is the *there-she-is* love, the lightning-strike love, and that every other kind of love is, by definition, settling.

I've been lucky enough to have experienced lightning love. So I get it. But do you know what else lightning does? Lightning occasionally burns down your freaking house along with everything you love and treasure inside. That's what my lightning love did to me.

We do harm when we paint that as the highest form of romantic love. Because it's not the *best* kind; it's just *one* of the kinds. And it implies those of us who've chosen partners for other reasons as settling for lesser love.

The love I have now is a comforting summer shower. It's a light, warm rain. It's a cozy sunny day. You're sitting on your front porch. You're cuddling with your people. You're playing cards. And you have this certainty of knowing that every most important thing in your life is within your arm's reach, and that this ordinary thing is the most precious part of life. I chose coziness and comfort and warm summer rain for myself and my kids. And that love is not settling. It is magical.

I'm being healed under that light, warm rain. I love him so much.

AMANDA

To love my person

I let go of how love *should* be so I can embrace the love I have.

Before Abby came into my life, it was like everything was at 70 percent. Every moment, every dinner, every conversation. Then Abby showed up, and everything is just 100 percent now. It's like life was black and white and now it's color. She leaves the house to go away for two days, and the kids and dogs look at me like: *What the hell do we do now? Where's the fun?* No amount of dancing or turning on the music makes up for her absence. When my son was fourteen, he wrote, "Abby, before you came, Mom never turned the volume up past 11." That was literal, but also not. Abby came into our lives, and she turned the music up.

GLENNON

Karen and I had been together for twenty years, and then Rowan came in and we all three fell in love, and we were like: *This is bizarre.* It is not something I set out to do, but there it was. That's how we felt. It was not optional. Like there was no option to not sit on the couch together, to not be together. In the years since we all got together, I've changed for the better, more than ever before in my life. Because I'm outnumbered. We're all outnumbered. When you've got two people telling their absolute best truth to you, it shows you what you were not able to see alone. It makes you think more, and it makes you change more. And we're like: *Oh, my God, how do people do this with just two people?*

MARTHA BECK

My partner listens a lot. Different people like to receive comfort differently, but I do like that he gives me a lot of advice. I feel safe coming to him to ask, "Am I crazy about this? What should I do about that?" And he always drops everything, and he's like "Alright, yeah, let's work through this together. We're going to dissect it. We'll figure it out." He just makes it clear that me and my happiness and my safety are priorities.

STEPHANIE FOO

John and I have learned that what helps me in moments of hypervigilance and dissociation—when my brain is spiraling off into old stories or future anxieties—is for him to hold on to my arms, look me in the eyes, and say, "I'm here. I'm with you. We've got this." That physical touch and concrete reminder of presence and support are what I need to drop out of my head and into my body, and into right now, where, it turns out, things are actually okay.

AMANDA

My wife, Catherine, is so cool. There have been some times when I sit down to write music at the piano. I don't do it very often. But if I do, I end up glossy-eyed and I'll look around twenty minutes later, and every light in the house will be off. There'll be a candle, a glass of wine, and she'll be gone. And so will the kids. Her love shows up in protecting and honoring my creative joy.

BRANDI CARLILE

My favorite family moments are when our youngest says something that is so ridiculous and adorable and I know with certainty that when I look over at Abby, she's going to be looking at me, too. Since she's paying such close attention to our family and to all the things we're working out with each kid, and since she has such a connection to each of their insides and to my insides, we are always having the exact same experience inside a family moment. That is love to me—our hearts exploding or breaking together inside shared moments. My version of love is deep, mutual noticing.

GLENNON

To love my person

I pay close attention.

Glennon is the one who does the laundry in our family. A little thing I do—I don't know if she even knows this—is that before I throw my clothes in the hamper, I turn all of them right side out. I take my socks off from the toe so that the socks don't need to be turned right side out. I don't want her to have to waste her time on little things like that. I want to give her time back.

ABBY

When somebody wants you to take up so much space and be a full person with all of your sadness and all of your fear, and they want to witness all of it, all your ugly things, it's such a beautiful and healing thing.

STEPHANIE FOO

The most important resource we give and receive in relationships is turning toward each other's difficult feelings.

EMILY NAGOSKI

To love my person

I let my person show
me all of who they are.

—

AMANDA: Sara, I heard you say something beautiful about your relationship with Joe. You said that being loved by him feels like "he can exist next to me in my pain." And that love is "allowing someone the dignity of their own discomfort." What do you mean?

SARA BAREILLES: That's actually something my therapist used to say. Because I'm a fixer, it's a real practice for me to just be next to someone in pain because it's uncomfortable for me. It's uncomfortable not only because you don't want to see this person you love in pain, but it's also ego, it's thinking: *I know better. Here's what you should do, do what I did.* But real love, a real relationship, is allowing someone to move at the pace they're at.

GLENNON: Right, because pain, sadness, melancholy, darkness—they are part of our process, not a diversion from our process. It's like we go into our chrysalis and everyone is like "Hey, it's gotta be too dark and uncomfortable in there. Come on out now!" Everybody tries to break us out of there. But we're *becoming* in there. If we come out too early, we don't transform. The kind of love you're describing—love that allows you the dignity of discomfort—frees you to enter your chrysalis and not emerge until you've become.

—

We must change our definition of what good love means. Love does not require us to disappear, ever. In fact, good love insists that we show up as our complete selves. If we do not find ourselves rising and emerging fully, we are not in good love.

GLENNON

In my past toxic relationship, I wasn't given the space or ability to individuate. The other person told me who I was, and I became conditioned to believe it.

In my relationship with my partner now, I'm in the process of counteracting all of that—of asking myself: *Who am I? What do I like? What do I find funny? What do I want to eat? What do I want to wear? Where do I want to go?*

It's such a relief to be in a relationship where I feel so celebrated and encouraged to find even *more* of my identity through discovery and adventure and failure.

LILY COLLINS

*To love my person **I let my person show me all of who they are.***

GLENNON: When Abby and I got together, my body was absolutely certain that I was going to be cheated on again, so I was constantly preparing myself. I knew I couldn't control the cheating, but I felt like I could control my vulnerability to it. I just didn't want to get annihilated again. One day I found myself going through Abby's phone, and she caught me. I was mortified. But she looked at me and said, "Oh, honey, what else do you need? Do you want my email password? Tell me what else you need to feel safe." It was the most incredible moment for me. She had every right to be angry and shame me, but instead she saw my fear and chose to love me through it.

ABBY: I understand that for some people that's an invasion of privacy. But based on your wounds, based on my wounds, that felt like such an easy thing to do. I think so many partners could benefit from just being like "What do you want to know? What do you need to feel safe?"

Love is holding your partner's fears gently, even when they don't make perfect sense to you. Love is doing whatever it takes to heal together.

—

For me, love is allowing your person to be both *held* & *free*. It is a miracle to find a relationship where you are both absolutely held in who you are and absolutely free to grow.

GLENNON

—

TOBIN HEATH: Honestly, one of the most beautiful things that Christen's ever given to me in my relationship is just complete freedom, even in my crazy ideas. This idea that I'm independent; I'm my own person. And what's exciting to me is that I get to choose her every single day. So I had this crazy idea for us to make a seven-year contract. It's like in sports where we ask, "How many years do you want?" And then at the end of the contract we come back together and we say, "Is this something you want to sign up for again? Okay, great, how many years?" And you sign another contract or you just go your separate ways and you say, "That was really fun."

ABBY: Christen, how did you wrap your mind around this when Tobin brought this to you?

CHRISTEN PRESS: I try to function from the best version of me, and the best version of me is confident enough to believe that one, she'll want to be with me. And two, if she doesn't, who would ever want to be with a partner that didn't want to be with them? So there's really no loss here. We have to give each other the feeling of freedom to be totally who we are.

—

To love my person

I give my person the freedom to be who they are.

If you ask a spider, "How do you feel about flies?," the spider will say, "I love flies." And it will be telling the truth. "I love the way flies crunch, I love the way they taste. And the way I express my love is that I wrap flies up alive, and then when I want a little hit of life force, I go suck some juice out of them. I love flies."

This is spider love, and that is how people often define love in this culture, whether it's "I love my parents and I want them to always give to me" or "I love my child and she can never leave my web."

Here's how you can recognize true love: True love always has, as its first priority, the freedom of the beloved.

MARTHA BECK

Behind criticism, there is often a wish, a longing; behind anger, there is often hurt. When we criticize our partners, we express unmet needs or unfulfilled desires. It's a common way of asking for something, but criticism will typically result in the opposite of what we really want, which is: to be told we are loved. To ask for what you want may be much more productive than to complain about what the other is doing wrong. But when you sense a strained connection with your partner, that conversation can feel too vulnerable. And still, you don't want to approach it by saying, "You don't respond to my needs. There is no spark." You want to focus on the longing, not the criticism. To work on this together, I think deliberate letter writing can be very useful; it lessens reactivity and gets people's attention. You can write a note and say:

> *I was looking at us today, and I saw this beautiful field. Our relationship gives us both a stable anchor and ongoing consistency. But there is an empty space between us. I suffer from that empty space and I don't know if you do too. When we met, we used to be able to talk for hours, there was a real sense of curiosity about each other. I sometimes feel like I don't really know what's inside of you and what makes you tick, and I don't feel that you know what happens inside of me. Maybe this is the marriage that you know. Maybe that's what you grew up with. Maybe that's how you saw your parents. I saw my parents that way too. But I promised myself that I would have better; I would have more. I hope you don't just hear this as my criticism. I want you to feel my longing. I miss you. I miss us. I'm lonely and I can't imagine that if I feel this way, you think we're having the best of times. Shall we meet somewhere?*

ESTHER PEREL

To love my person

I communicate the longing beneath my criticism.

I want couples to know that when you face struggles in relationships, you're not broken. This is the hardest thing you're doing. Marrying another individual, melding two lives and two different ways of being, and then maybe even adding more life into that mix, it's truly the hardest thing.

FORMER FIRST LADY MICHELLE OBAMA

GLENNON: I am pro-conflict. What we're trying to do in relationship is understand each other better and get to the root of things. And I have always understood conflict to be one vehicle we use to do that.

AMANDA: The willingness to bring conflict to the table, to make yourself vulnerable, shows a faith in your relationship, an investment in a relationship, a belief that your relationship could be better than it is. For me, when someone is *not* bringing up conflict, that is being unfaithful to the relationship. It's an abdication of your role in the relationship, and you are actually dumping all of the responsibility on your partner to make things better and to resolve your conflicts—burdening them with the sole responsibility to speak those things out loud. When I catch myself not bringing up conflict, I am like: *Oh, red flag.* Because that's an apathy that atrophies the relationship, whereas working through conflict is an investment that shows faith in the relationship.

Also, I don't think that there are some people who are comfortable with conflict and other people who aren't. Abby always says she's not comfortable with conflict, but she's actually comfortable with inner conflict—not outer conflict. And Glennon, when you say you are pro-conflict, I think what you mean is that you are comfortable with outer conflict, but definitely not fine with inner conflict. We're all just choosing which kind of conflict we're comfortable with: inner conflict or outer conflict.

GLENNON: Yes. There is a price to pay for saying the thing. But there is also a price to pay for not saying the thing. And that price is never being known. That price is slowly dying inside. That price is: no real relationship. So since there's a price to pay either way, which price do you want to pay?

—

To love my person

I welcome conflict as a way to get closer.

ABBY: The other day I was taking a nap on the couch, and I woke up to Glennon putting away the dishes in the kitchen quite loudly and aggressively. I said, "Honey, are you fighting with me without me again?"

GLENNON: And I was! I always win when I fight with you without you. I just crush those fights.

—

People who try to live without any conflict, who never argue or mourn, tend to implode sooner or later—as any psychologist will tell you. Living without conflict is like living without love: cold and eventually unbearable.

AMANDA RIPLEY

—

ABBY: I'm starting to understand that conflict is like a pothole in the road: We can go through it and come out okay. For so long, I was scared that the pothole was going to give our car a flat tire.

GLENNON: Right. And we only have a conflict when we already have a flat tire. Conflict is proof of a flat tire, and the conversation is repairing the tire so we can keep going.

—

When talking about how to share difficult emotions with your partner, I like to use this very ridiculous metaphor of the sleepy hedgehog. When you have a difficult feeling, imagine that it's like a sleepy hedgehog that's just sitting in the bed and you've got to do something about it before you can sleep.

So what do you do? You can't yell at it. You can't just throw it against a wall. Somebody's going to get hurt if you do that. So what you do is, you gently turn toward it, you find out its name. Its name in this case might be Loneliness. It might be Insecurity. It might be Distrust. ⌒

⁓ And then you ask: What does it need in order to move out of your bed and free itself?

When it tells you some things, you take it in your palms, and you go to your partner, and you say, "Hello. When you have a moment, I want to introduce you to Loneliness, which is this difficult feeling I'm having. What it needs is _____. Do you think that might be something you can help me with so that we can get this hedgehog out of our bed?"

EMILY NAGOSKI

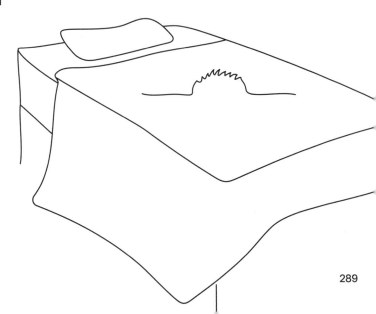

In conflict, sometimes Glennon and I can get lost arguing the facts. I try to keep us out of the facts and into feelings by getting as simple and vulnerable as possible. I can say, "My feelings are really hurt. Period." Or "I feel abandoned." That just cuts straight through it. It's hard to argue with a feeling.

ABBY

What is conflict really about? It's almost never about the dishes or the kids' LEGOs. It almost always has an understory. The dishes represent something else. If we can figure out what the understory of our conflict is, we can get closer to resolution. The good news is, there are really only four understories:

1. Care and concern

2. Respect and recognition

3. Power and control

4. Stress and overwhelm

I just had an argument with my husband about whether we should hire someone to help us with home repairs, because my husband had been busy and things weren't getting fixed. It got really heated. For me, the understory was about care and concern. Because, really, what I was saying was "You're working too much, and I feel like you're not here, and you don't love us." For him, the argument was about respect and recognition. He felt like it was his job to fix something, and he felt bad that he hadn't done it. So until we get to those understories, we're just going to keep fighting forever.

AMANDA RIPLEY

To love my person **I welcome conflict as a way to get closer.**

———

GLENNON: I am really good at apologizing to the kids. I do it all the time, and I do it easily. I have a very hard time apologizing to Abby. I wonder about that a lot, and I think it might be because I have so much confidence in my identity as a good mom. But I don't have a lot of confidence yet about my identity as a good partner. I've never felt like I'm good at partnering.

ABBY: Whoa. That's fascinating because as you know, I have no problem apologizing to you, but it's hard for me to apologize to the kids. And I definitely feel more insecure about my parenting abilities, while I'm pretty confident in my role as partner to you.

GLENNON: It's like: Is it so hard for me to apologize to you because I'm so sure I'm right? Or is it actually so hard for me because I'm sure I'm doing this all wrong and I don't want you to discover that? I think it's hardest to be sorry in the moments and relationships in which we're the least secure. Apologizing takes strength, security, and confidence.

———

We have to think of these imperfect moments as pages in each person's life. With repair, I get to reopen the book and go back to that point in the chapter. And instead of that imperfect moment being the ending, we use repair and it's like magic: I get to rewrite a very different ending to the story. I can go back to that moment and offer connection and coherence and love on top of what was pain.

DR. BECKY KENNEDY

I look like I have my shit together. I'm getting it done. But my brain is a frenetic 24/7 CNN ticker—incessantly *tick tick ticking* with all of my life's latest breaking news, incoming disasters, and nonstop emergency alerts: *Here's all the things you should be doing right now. While you're at it, have you booked that summer camp before it fills up? What about asking the neighbor to get your kid onto that one team? Don't forget the birthday party gifts for Saturday. It's teacher appreciation week. You owe your dad a phone call. And we haven't even gotten to your full-time job yet* . . . And God forbid one thing inevitably takes twenty seconds longer than it should, because the ticker stops for no man. I'm always and will never not be behind.

But the ticker is not an equal opportunity tormentor. My husband, who is deeply good and wants to help, used to always ask, "How can I help?" Which made me rageful and made me realize: *If you're asking how you can help, it means you don't have the ticker. Because I never have to ask what's on the to-do list; I'm the one spending a hundred hours of invisible labor figuring out the ten steps required before an item even makes it on the to-do list.* If you are in the privileged position of just taking items off the to-do list, it means you are not a cocreator, architect, and carrier of the ticker. And you need to be.

If one person lives with a screaming ticker all day and one person does not, they are having an unequal quality of life, and that leads to crushing resentment. It means you look out at the beautiful life you've created and you can't even enjoy it because you're so bitter that you're the only one who made it happen.

I have never felt more cared for than when John and I sat down and decided: We're going to divide up this mental load. We are going to let all the spinning plates crash to the ground so we pick the pieces up, and reallocate them so each of us is carrying an equal weight. When you do this, you can take a deep breath and truly appreciate your person and your life. Because you know you're both holding up the sky.

AMANDA

To love my person

I share the mental load equally.

My partner, Sue, wants a partner who will *partner.* I used to always ask her, "How can I help?" Which proved how totally out of the loop I was about what needed to be done. So I have started telling myself: *You know what? You figure it out, Megan— you figure out a way you can help.*

MEGAN RAPINOE

Doing cognitive labor is like spinning plates at the circus: You're keeping the plates spinning all the time, and you go to sleep at night thinking about what you have to do first thing in the morning so that your plates don't fall. It's exhausting. If one person in the partnership is spinning twenty plates and the other person is spinning ten, there's a huge power imbalance of free time, cognitive space, and balance of how you spend your life.

A partner asking, "How can I help?," is part of the problem, too. Giving some-one a task like a manager in a workplace takes more work. You have to think about what to delegate and then track it. It's still in your cognitive load. In a partnership, both people need to find a way to do physical labor, and both need to also do cognitive labor, so that both have the same number of plates spinning. Life might still be exhausting for both of you, but at least you'll be in it together—a team working to get through something with mutual love as opposed to one person doing more and feeling bitter.

It's also important to note that in heteronormative relationships, it's not just women who lose by carrying the mental load of the family. Men are losing, too. When our second child was born, I said to my husband, "I see you leaning in to work, and I see you pulling away from the family space. Eventually the kids are going to grow up and I'm going to recover and I'm going to be okay. But you've got one shot at little kids, at being a dad, at connecting with them and being authentic and having this life of a parent. So we need to make changes right now, not for me but for both of us. And it's not your fault, this is how society and gender norms have shaped us, but it's our job to change it."

DR. KATE MANGINO

I've tried to break up with Joe so many times. It's this coping mechanism I've developed: If I feel scared, I separate. Early on when I was scared, I said to him, "I really, really liked you, and now I don't. It just went away, and I don't like you anymore. It feels like the lights went out, and that's what's true."

I remember we were on a street corner. He was like "If the lights go out, you go into the basement and you check the fuse box. If we're not compatible or whatever, that's fine. But I'm not falling for this 'I don't know, it's just gone, the feeling's gone.'" He was passionate, and it was the first time I heard him really advocate for himself. I thought it was so sexy. It was this little moment for us to really see each other.

SARA BAREILLES

We move away from each other when hard things happen because we're afraid that we'll be hurt. There's a threat there. And we move toward isolation because we're like: *I'm safer on my own. I'm safer away from you, on my own.* And, yes, in some scenarios, that makes sense. At times, that's the right choice to make. But with those people who we are trying to be on the same team with, who we're trying to go in the same direction with, we have to practice togetherness. We have to practice how to experience something hard, find ourselves again, find the purpose for connection, and turn and reach for each other again.

PRENTIS HEMPHILL

To love my person

I'm brave enough to stay and I'm brave enough to leave.

One of the reasons that I can trust Abby so deeply now is that I finally trust myself. I know now that I have my own back. The second I start to feel something is off, I am going to honor that. I am not going to gaslight myself ever again. Maybe the only people who can actually trust other people are those who can deeply trust themselves. You can never be sure your partner won't abandon you. But you can make damn sure *you* never abandon you.

GLENNON

Even after this very hard breakup, I feel optimistic about the future. I've changed so much, and my love was so big that it just blew me open. And as painful as the ending of something like that is, I'm well versed in the idea that every door shutting is a new beginning. And I do believe it. I don't think that's BS. When you have the grounding and the courage to say, "This isn't working," you're saying a lot more than that to the whole world. You're inviting in things that are going to be more suited to your needs and what you're available for. I'm really happy to be handling a breakup in an honest way for the first time in my life. I'm not distracting, deflecting, or insisting, "I'm fine. I'm fine. I'm fine."

CHELSEA HANDLER

One of our mutual friends was going through a divorce, and Abby said, "That's so sad. I feel so bad for her." And I thought: *Wait. Are we sure that's the vibe?* What if we rethink our compulsory reaction to divorce? What if divorce isn't always just sad? What if divorce often marks the victorious end of a long, suffering road? What if divorce is often the most hopeful, creative triumph that a person ever had? What if it's the brave, new beginning of two lives?

GLENNON

Early on, the point of dating is to try to get to know someone. Long into your relationship, the point of dating is to try to *unknow* them. There is no point in going on a date if you already know exactly what's going to happen, exactly what each of you is going to say, exactly how you're going to feel. There's no surprise. There's no risk. In fact, it can be a vicious cycle. If you feel like you have nothing to talk about in your relationship, you might think: *We aren't connecting, we need to start reconnecting over date nights.* But if you go on dates and you still have nothing to talk about, you'll feel like maybe there's no hope.

Dr. Arthur Aron found that the circuits in our brain that activate in puppy love are the same ones that activate when we do something new. He and his colleagues did a study of middle-aged couples where they had one group spend ninety minutes a week doing familiar, pleasant activities they normally do in their life, like going out to dinner. And they had the other group spend the same amount of time doing new, unfamiliar activities, like throwing a ball back and forth or even crawling across a room with their wrists tied together. After ten weeks, the people doing the new, unfamiliar things had a significantly greater increase in their marital satisfaction than the people doing the pleasant, familiar activities. The novelty, excitement, and surprise allowed partners to see and appreciate each other in a fresh way.

This is why people are attracted to strangers—because they're new, because we *don't know them.* When we don't know someone, our mind can be curious and fill in the blanks with every good thing; whereas with the people we've been with forever, there are no blanks. We've already colored in that whole page and have been looking at it for a long time. We have all our data, so there is nothing to be curious about. We need to do new things in order to open our minds to the possibility that we don't know everything about our person and that our person doesn't know everything about us.

AMANDA

To love my person

I try to unknow my person every day.

After I got my cancer diagnosis, it was as if I was seeing my partner, Meg, like she was a new person. I remember being overwhelmed with just watching her walk through the house and thinking: *Who is this person? Who is this mystery walking around in here?*

Years ago, I heard a poem by Mary Oliver called "The Whistler," about her partner, Molly. They'd been together for decades. And then one day Mary walks downstairs and hears Molly whistling for the first time—she had never heard her whistle before. It makes you realize there is so much to uncover in the people we love. Even decades later, we only know a fraction of them. And that's how I felt seeing Meg after my diagnosis: It just felt like she was *new*. That energy creates an opportunity for the person to do something different, to be who they really are. And I think that's what's kept our love feeling so vibrant.

ANDREA GIBSON

Instead of vowing to our person, "I will always know you," maybe we should say, "I promise I will always unknow you."

GLENNON

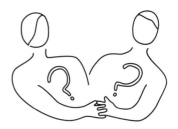

The Light at the End of the Tunnel Is Green

MEGAN FALLEY

The love of my life
has pissed themselves
upon our tandem bicycle
exactly two times,
both while crossing
a major intersection
and leaving me to haul
the clunky metal beast
between my legs
like a dying horse
across the glaring traffic
alone, while they
sit on the curb, laughing
like a stalled engine
and a wet spot blooms
on their tiny, perfect ass,
all the while they're shouting,
I'm having a panic attack!
I'm having a panic attack!
as if they were the one
left for roadkill. Earlier,
we were debating the clock
of love: how one's heart
becomes a flat tire once someone has seen you
for the lemon you are, or no longer peels
their eyes from their book
when you undress.
All day I've been thinking
I'm a lousy poet, so I'm looking
for the metaphor here. Is love
a tandem bicycle—both people
with one destination in mind,
but someone always a little
ahead? I'd prefer to think of love
as a sociable bike, side-by-side.
But love is more honestly,
the swatch of urine on the pants:
born from a blushing, a bliss,
a surprise, sometimes uncomfortable,
often embarrassing, but how,
when it comes, you know
you are going
home.

Thirteen

Sex.
Am I doing
this right?

This culture is obsessed with women's bodies and sex. Everywhere you look there's some company capitalizing off of women's bodies and sex.

But us women? We find ourselves feeling very alone. I think it's because we don't talk about sex enough with each other.

So here we are. Here we go, ready or not. We're doing it.

ABBY

I don't think examining your sexuality just means answering the question "Am I straight or not?" It isn't simply about finding your labels or deciding where you are on the sexuality spectrum.

For all of us, it's about: *What does it mean to identify my desire, to listen to my body, to feel my sexual hungers, to think about what I might actually like, what I might actually not like— to be brave enough and embodied enough to reconcile all of that?*

It reminds me of when Glennon went to a Van Gogh exhibit that was supposed to be a spectacular 360-degree projection of breathtaking art. After she went, I called her to ask how it was, and she said, "It was nice." I thought: *Okay. That's interesting. It's supposed to be incredible.* Later, she realized she'd been sitting in the fancy waiting room the entire time. She never even went inside to experience the real show.

That's what I don't want for my sexuality. I don't want to find out that there was a whole other room just steps away that would've taken my breath away. I don't want to be unreconciled. It's scary because you have to be brave and vulnerable enough to ask the questions you've never asked and try the things you've never tried.

AMANDA

GLENNON: You remind us that sexuality is for everybody, not just queer people. You say that gender preferences are the least important part of sexuality; there are a lot of other parts.

MAE MARTIN: Yes, that's been my experience. Regardless of how you identify, you're rarely attracted to an entire gender. It has to do with pheromones or the way people laugh. I have very specific criteria. I love when people wink. I'm attracted to confidence. I like being in the passenger seat when someone's driving. I think people often forget that it's not just queer people that have a sexuality. Because queer people are asked to communicate about it a lot more, to defend it, to explain it, it feels like a much bigger part of our identity when really, it should be just one small part.

—

I never really wrestled with my sexuality. From a young age, I was like: *Attracted to boys, check. Analysis complete. Moving on to other things.* Because I was straight, I sort of assumed I was exempt from anxiety and struggle over my sexuality. And now I think that has been a disservice to my life. Because if sexuality is an exploration, I didn't really trek out and forge my own path. I didn't think about the questions that a lot of people who were forced to think hard about this did, like: *How do you experience your sexual identity, who do you want to be sexually, what are your specific sexual preferences and values, what feels most true to you?* Because I checked a box early on and never had to define anything for myself, I never did. I'm so grateful to understand this now, while I still have time to explore.

AMANDA

Sexuality is a lifelong exploration for everyone.

We know that the second we label something, our curiosity turns off and our awe fades. This is why Buddhists teach the importance of using beginner's mind to perceive anything fully.

Take a rose, for example. For a second, when I encounter one, I have this moment of awe about it. My mind is not there yet, and my eyes go wide. But then, almost immediately, my mind says: *Rose.* That label replaces the fresh image of the flower, and bye-bye, curiosity and awe. It's old news now. It's just a rose. Maybe something like this happens when we label our sexuality.

About my faith, about my gender, about my sexuality, I like to live in the: I don't know. How could I? How could any of us possibly know all that we are?

GLENNON

For me, sex is a wide thing. It's not just the singular act of "having sex."

When Glennon hands me coffee in the morning, that is the beginning of sex. For her to be in tune with what I love—what is really important to me—and to deliver those things without me asking creates a feeling of love and connection.

To me, I can't get into bed unless the connection has been developed. I don't do it just for the orgasm. I want the full experience—and sometimes it takes a while before I feel that real drive, that real connection that creates the desire.

ABBY

Sex is about much more than sex.

GLENNON: Abby and I often talk about sex as something bigger. It doesn't always have to lead to the act of sex. It's when we are experiencing joy or playfulness together. It's reading a poem. It's a place we go that is sex, even when it's not sex. And it's better when we decide that it doesn't have to lead anywhere in particular, because that's pressure.

ESTHER PEREL: Sex is not just something you do, it's a place you go, within yourself and with another. You can have sex and feel absolutely nothing. Women have been doing it for centuries.

Or you can do very little and feel a lot. And when you describe it as you just did, you touch that broader dimension I call the erotic. I am talking about the quality of aliveness—that energy, vitality, and vibrancy—a sense of curiosity and playfulness and imagination, an encounter with serendipity and the unknown. Those are the key ingredients of the erotic. It doesn't have to be sex.

—

Audre Lorde is the patron saint of pleasure activism. She talked about painting a fence or lying in bed with her lover or writing a poem as all these experiences that give her this erotic aliveness. So now I'll be like: *Oh, I'm sitting on my porch watching the geese fly across the water.* And, God, that satisfies me every time. Just the rhythm of them and the sounds of them and the formation that they get into and the beautiful divine design of it all. I'm like: *This is very satisfying.*

ADRIENNE MAREE BROWN

GLENNON: Living in a disabled body, you had to figure sex out for yourself. Nobody was talking about disabled queer sex. You had no models, no representation. Was that liberating in a sense, because you weren't mimicking something that someone else was telling you to re-create in the bedroom? Is that sexual freedom?

CARSON TUELLER: I never had sex as an abled person, so I never experienced knowing what sex was supposed to look and feel like. I also never consumed any pornography, because I was such a good Mormon, so I came into sex without any ideas about sex. And on top of all that, I was now in this new disabled body, and I didn't know what it could do or how it would respond. I had heard that sex could be very pleasurable in a paralyzed body, but mostly from straight people, so I thought: *Okay, I've heard that there are some possibilities here, but I've got to figure this out.* I started by setting up situations with people that I trusted, where we could start trying things out. It was this slow experimentation, starting very small, with kissing and with touching and a lot of foreplay-esque kind of things. I started to have moments of discovery, finding new erogenous zones that made me think: *Oh, whoa, that felt very special. That was a treat. Let's go there.*

And my hypothesis is this: Because there were no rules, no expectations, I found really incredible ways to experience pleasure. It also required a lot of communication. When I'm telling you what feels good and doesn't, we're going to get a better result.

GLENNON: It's coming to sex with a beginner's mind. I wish we all approached it that way with our partners; that's how every single one of us could have truer sexual experiences.

CARSON: You have to drop the role. You've got to actually show up and say, "So this is actually what I want." And then it's new levels of connection and pleasure.

—

Sex is about creating something new.

The big irony is that one of the best ways to screw up your sex life is to compare your sex life and judge it as inferior to what we think it's "supposed to be."

EMILY NAGOSKI

For many of us, our sex is choreographed by culture—by porn, by movies. We watch things and think: *I'm supposed to arch my back like this, move like that. Make these noises. This is what a woman does. This is what a man does.* I'm constantly trying to detox and untame myself from anything choreographed, and it turns out there's a different way to approach sex. To be like: *What does my body want to do? What noise am I naturally making here?* The goal for me is to not know what to do and instead allow complete surrender. That is ideal sex to me: not tapping into anything that's been conditioned and just letting my body do whatever the hell it wants to do. No script, all improv.

GLENNON

I move other people's voices out of my mind about what should feel good, and I start to notice what does feel good in my own body.

ADRIENNE MAREE BROWN

ABBY: Sometimes when Glennon and I go through little droughts, my mind starts worrying that the lack of sex means that we are struggling, even if that's not how I feel inside my body and my heart. Even when I feel like our life is perfect, I can think: *But are we having as much sex as we should be? Are we normal?*

DR. LORI BROTTO: That's a *shoulding,* right? I *should* feel horny all the time because our life is perfect and because I'm so in love with my partner. That's the underlying worldview that we take on: Relationships *should* look this way. You *should* have sex a certain number of times per week. It's worth asking yourself: *Am I shoulding? And is this manifesting in my life and relationship and in the bedroom?*

GLENNON: We are trained to focus on frequency as the barometer of whether or not our relationships are sexually okay. But if we're not supposed to be using frequency to measure the vitality and health and fullness of our sex lives, what should we be using?

DR. BROTTO: Pleasure. Pleasure has been missing in the conversation for the last hundred years of women's sexuality. No one investigated women's pleasure or how to improve it. And we're finally starting to say: Pleasure is the missing link. It's the next frontier. We know that when women talk about really satisfying sexuality, the moments when they're so present and so in sync and nothing else matters, they're talking about pleasure.

GLENNON: So we stop asking, "Are we doing it enough?" The question is "Am I experiencing pleasure?"

—

Pleasure is the point.

As children we're naturally in touch with what brings us pleasure and joy in our bodies. There's a simplicity to it: If it feels good, I like it, it's fun.

But as we get older, we get the message that pleasure isn't safe or acceptable. "That's not okay. Don't do that. Don't touch yourself there." We start believing that we're not allowed to have joy and delight in our bodies, and we shut ourselves down.

Most women feel deeply uncomfortable with the idea of masturbating. Many have never even tried it. We were taught to feel shame. We were taught that our pleasure wasn't important or necessary. We were robbed of the opportunity to have a joyful relationship with our own bodies.

Being connected with your own body, understanding what your body needs to feel good, to feel pleasure, to have orgasms—what experience can you have that's more powerful than that? Masturbation can be a deeply spiritual act.

For me, masturbation is a reclamation. This is my body. I deserve to touch my body with love and curiosity and openness and excitement. I deserve to explore what brings me pleasure, what brings me to orgasm. I deserve that intimate knowledge of myself.

VANESSA MARIN

Suddenly, I was able to drop into the millions of ways I had given my body away as an apology. Sexuality is one of those places where we can see, if we really just sit and look, how we've given our bodies away as an apology.

We've asked: *Am I worthy now? Am I enough now?* We barter around sexuality and desirability to obtain our worthiness.

Your body is not an apology.

SONYA RENEE TAYLOR

Freedom is the goal.

—

AMANDA: For so many survivors, the same bodies that are our portals through which we access pleasure and sexuality are also the bodies poisoned by our assaulters with shame and hypervigilance. It's like being told to run and have fun on a playground full of land mines. How do we explore safely in the midst of trauma?

TARANA BURKE: It was so important to me to find out how to explore sexuality safely. And I found ways to do this that didn't involve sex at all. I met a friend named Rob. I'm Caribbean. I love reggae. I love to move my body. So we danced together. We went through our whole freshman year of college and did not kiss. We didn't date. We didn't touch outside of the way that we danced on that dance floor, and it allowed me to understand my body and myself as a person who can feel pleasure. It was a form of liberation. It was so beautiful.

AMANDA: So beautiful. You wrote, "They never played the music for long, maybe two songs. But whenever they did, we found each other and let out whatever pent-up sexual energy we were both trying to ignore. We danced like no one else was there, like it was a mating ritual, and we had fire in our bellies. I loved every minute of it. It was the first time in my life that I got to safely explore my sexuality with no demands on my body."

—

It's not just a simple "sex drive." Your sexual mind has a dual control structure made up of accelerators and brakes regulating your desire. Usually when people are struggling, it's not because there's not enough stimulation to the accelerator, it's because there's too much stimulation to the brakes. Getting rid of stuff that's hitting the brakes is more important than activating the accelerator.

ACCELERATORS are all the sex-coded information in the environment that sends a turn-on signal to your brain—everything you see, hear, smell, touch, taste, think, believe, or imagine that your brain codes as something related to sex.

Accelerators can include seeing your partner naked, watching a sexy movie, wearing or seeing lingerie, being shown nondemanding affection, feeling confident in your body, and having a memory of a great sexual experience.

BRAKES are all the good reasons *not* to be turned on right now that send a turn-off signal to your brain—everything you see, hear, smell, touch, taste, think, believe, or imagine that your brain perceives as a potential threat.

Brakes can include stress, anxiety, loneliness, distracting noises, body shame, trauma history, repressed rage, your to-do list, your risk of pregnancy, a lack of privacy or safety, performance anxiety, and relationship struggles.

EMILY NAGOSKI

I need to be able to turn off in order to turn on.

Stress is one of the main culprits for a lot of sexual concerns. When we're feeling that stress on a chronic level, our brain can't turn that response off. High cortisol levels, our main stress hormone, interfere with some of the hormones involved in sexual response, and it makes it a lot harder to get sexually aroused and reach orgasm.

DR. LORI BROTTO

If I were to ask you to finish the sentence *I turn myself on by* . . . Or *You turn me on when* . . . which is not the same as *What turns me on is* . . . you're going to most likely include: When I take care of myself. When I go and spend time with friends. When I go dancing. When I listen to music. When I sing in the shower. When I take time in nature. When I'm in touch with my aliveness and with my inner beauty. These are the things that make you feel alive and energized and radiant. So my next question is: *When is the last time you did this?* Because if you don't have any of that aliveness or receptive energy inside of you, your tank is empty. There needs to be a full tank or at least a half tank inside to go.

ESTHER PEREL

Hotel sex is the best sex. Why? Because there's nothing around to remind you of your crushing mental load: no piles of laundry, no lunches to pack, no bathrooms to clean. So in a hotel your brakes are more likely to be turned off, and you can be more responsive to your accelerators. We need to bring hotel sex home by sharing the mental load. There is so much pain for people everywhere who feel like they are the only one thinking about and worrying about their family at all times. It creates resentment and loneliness. And then you're expected to get into bed at the end of the day and want sex, which creates even more resentment. But when you can work together on balancing that mental load, and when someone pulls their weight in cognitive labor, it is incredibly sexy.

AMANDA

Your sexual desire manifests in one of two ways: spontaneous or responsive. With spontaneous desire, arousal starts in the mind; with responsive desire, arousal starts in the body. What gets you to the place of basic arousal?

Spontaneous desire emerges in *anticipation* of pleasure.
You're walking down the street and you have a stray thought or see a random person, and that's enough for your brain to feel: *Kaboom!* It happens spontaneously in anticipation of pleasure.

Responsive desire emerges in *response* to pleasure.
You're sitting next to someone on the couch, and they touch you and say nice things. You start kissing, and your brain gets input from your body and thinks: *How about kaboom?* It happens in response to an accumulation of pleasure.

EMILY NAGOSKI

Desire awakens differently in each of us.

I am rarely the initiator of sex. But afterward I'm always like "That was a good idea—we should do that more!"

Which I thought was weird until I learned that 75 percent of men have primary spontaneous desire. So they're thinking about it, then they get the physical desire, and that's when they're like "Hey, want to make out?" But 85 percent of women have primary responsive desire, meaning they need some physical pleasure to even get them to the mental space where they have desire.

Before I learned about my responsive desire, I thought there was something wrong with me because I didn't have that kind of spontaneous "Oh, I can't wait to jump in the sack" thing. But it's completely normal. And if neither you or your partner is spontaneously craving sex, maybe you both have responsive desire, and that's totally normal, too.

AMANDA

A big part of sexuality is just our basic biology. When things are new, there's a particular part of our brain, the reward center, that lights up. It shoots out dopamine. And when things become less novel, there's less lighting up of that area. So when we look at it through that lens, we realize: *Well, of course love doesn't equal desire.* They're not synonymous with each other. In fact, we have a lot of examples where we crave someone sexually and we don't love them. And we accept that. So, then, why is it when we're deeply in love and decades go by, we think that the loss of desire means that we don't love our person anymore? It makes no sense whatsoever.

DR. LORI BROTTO

The brilliant sex therapist and researcher
Peggy Kleinplatz's radical idea:
It is normal not to want sex you don't like.

EMILY NAGOSKI

Before you beat yourself up for having low libido, ask yourself if the sex you're having is worth craving. Do you ever find yourself craving a bowl of overly steamed mushy broccoli? Of course not. Do you judge yourself for that or feel like something's wrong with you for not wanting it? No, of course not. But let's be honest: Many of us are having sex that's the equivalent of overly steamed mushy broccoli and feeling like we're broken for not wanting it! If the sex you're having isn't pleasurable, it makes zero sense for you to crave it.

VANESSA MARIN

Of course you don't want sex if it feels bad. One-third of women experience pain during sex. Actual pain. Why don't you crave stubbing your toe? Because it hurts, that's why. And we don't think there's anything wrong with us because we don't crave stubbing our toes. So if one in three women is in pain during sex, they shouldn't be berating themselves for not waking up in the morning being like: *Damn, can't wait to get that paper cut!*

AMANDA

I thought it was just me, but I've learned that dissociation is common for people who are having unsatisfying sex for any reason. It's this thing we do called spectatoring—we leave our bodies and either watch ourselves from above or we engage our minds in an entirely different activity. I used to make grocery lists during sex. Good times.

GLENNON

It is normal to not want bad sex.

A study published in 2018 showed that more than one in seven married people in the United States hadn't had sex in the prior year, and more than one in eight hadn't had sex in the past five years. We don't talk about that much.

Most of the conversations I hear among married women are along the lines of "I'm always too tired to have sex and he always wants to, how do I deal?" That seems socially acceptable to talk about. But no one ever seems to talk about the opposite problem: when your husband does not want to have sex with you. This happened to me in my first marriage. When you are a woman, it is expected that you will be pursued, that your partner will always want to have sex with you, and that your job will be to decide when to reciprocate. So it is a doubly lonely place—in a world in which everyone else is talking about how much of a hassle it is to have to navigate their husband's desire for them—to admit that your husband has no desire for you.

If you are in that place, so was I, and I know it feels like there must be something very, very wrong with you. It's a special slice of hell to be in a marriage with a person who does not want you. Please know that there is nothing wrong with you and there are many, many people in that lonely place with you.

AMANDA

If Glennon asks, "Do you think we're having enough sex? Shouldn't we be having it more?" I immediately go into: *Oh, no, I'm not craving it enough. I'm not initiating enough. What if she's not craving me enough? She has a problem with me. This is my fault.* I just spiral. But if she brings up a fun memory of a specific time we had sex, then I'm immediately tender and blushy and like "Oh, my gosh. Yes." I am out of my head and in my body.

ABBY

Talking about sex helps.

We're taught to believe that we shouldn't have to talk about sex, and so we don't—*until* things are really bad. Which just makes sex an even scarier, more intimidating topic. So here are some tips for those conversations:

(1) Focus on the positive.

If you immediately launch into criticism or complaints, your partner is going to get defensive and you're going to get into a fight. Instead of focusing on what's *not* working, start with discussing what you *like* and what you want *more* of. Pretty much any complaint can be reframed into a positive request. For example, instead of complaining, "You're always rushing past foreplay!" you can say, "It turns me on so much when you go nice and slow with me and get me to the point where I'm practically begging you for more."

(2) Have a postgame conversation.

Start with talking about sex outside of the bedroom *first*. Then start talking about sex closer to the act itself. The best starting point is right after you've just had sex, since it's fresh in your mind. It can be something as simple as "That was really fun. I liked that position that we did."

(3) Provide options.

Instead of asking, "What do you want?" which puts all the mental load and effort on someone else, give options. If I ask you, "What do you want for dinner?" it's a little annoying. But if I ask, "Do you want Mexican, or do you want sushi?" it's easier to pick.

(4) Lower the bar.

Rather than thinking: *What's going to make me orgasm?* I like to think: *What's something that I'm curious about experiencing right now?* So maybe it's just "I would love for you to kiss me a little bit softer" or "I would love for us to pick up the pace a little bit." So it's not about: What's going to bring you the maximum level of pleasure in this moment? It's just: What's something that sounds kind of good right now?

VANESSA MARIN

Make space for physical intimacy.

I'm a fan of scheduled sex! We all lead really busy lives, and we have to be intentional about making space for connection. I prefer to schedule quality time rather than sex. You're not putting pressure on yourselves to have sex, but you're creating the space for it if you do wind up wanting to connect physically.

VANESSA MARIN

Start with things you'll never do.

Fantasy doesn't have to be what you actually want to do or what you are doing in your life. It's just creating a scene in your mind. I often talk about fantasy as a tool. Ask yourself: *What would you like to do together?* We can start with what we actually will do, but then we can get fun and playful and talk about some of the really "out there" things that we know we'll never do. It's a fun exercise; it kindles interest and desire.

DR. LORI BROTTO

Create a sex menu.

Vanessa Marin talks about how, when our partner asks, "Do you want to have sex?," it's confusing, because it's like asking someone to go on a trip with you. You need more details first: How long is the trip? Where are we going? What do I need to pack? So she suggests making a sex menu: What are you ordering up right now? Do you want fast food—a quick-and-dirty five-minute drive-through? Or are we sitting down for a five-course meal here? The sex menu can include things as simple as "Dance with me."

GLENNON

Sex is about small experiments.

Tap into curiosity.

I don't like the question "What's your fantasy?" because it makes it feel like the only acceptable answer is an elaborate scenario. Instead, I like "What's something you're curious about trying?" It lowers the bar. You can be curious about something as simple as making out more passionately or listening to music during sex.

VANESSA MARIN

Practice tuning in and communicating.

Sensate focus is a classic sex therapy practice. Person number one touches person number two head to toe for about fifteen minutes. Person two is relaxing into the touch and is giving some gentle feedback, either verbally or non-verbally. Now the giver of the touch becomes the receiver, then the receiver becomes the giver, and it's repeated a number of times. The next stage includes breast and genital touch, but the goal is not to create arousal or orgasm; the goal is relaxing, tuning in, and communicating. We know that sensate focus is useful for most sexual problems or struggles in a couple. We can *always* stand to learn something about how the other person wants to be touched.

DR. LORI BROTTO

Let things go wrong.

Some of my favorite experiences with my partner have been "fails." We tried a weird sex tip that we saw online. It went horribly wrong, and we laughed so hard with each other. I'm not interested in having perfect sex; what I really want is authentic and vulnerable sex.

VANESSA MARIN

You deserve the dignity
Of sitting at the table
With a quiet cup of coffee.

Take it.
Take it for yourself.

Once you have the dignity,
You'll have the worthiness.

Once you have the worthiness,
You'll find yourself worthy of pleasure.

Once you're worthy of pleasure,
You'll figure out what the
Hell kind of pleasure
You want and
You'll go get more of it.

AMANDA

Fourteen

Parenting. Am I doing this right?

Parenting is a roller coaster. The early years are so slow; every day you're just climbing that hill, *tick . . . tick . . . tick*. Then the kids turn eight or nine and you hit the top of the hill, the crest. After that it's a blur. The next decade or so flies by, and then the car suddenly jerks to a screeching stop in the station and you're looking around, trying to get your bearings. They're unbuckling themselves, climbing out of your car, walking away from you, and all you can see is their backs. You panic and think: *Wait! Stop! Come back! I thought there would be more time for me to get this right!*

The whole ride is just a gorgeous, terrifying, lucky heartbreak.

GLENNON

After reading like seventeen thousand parenting books, I finally decided: I'm going to stop trying to be a better parent; I'm just going to start trying to be a better *person* and let my kids watch me.

One way to try to be better is to stop trying to be perfect. We try so hard to make our kids think we're perfect. We hide from them our mistakes, our fear, our uncertainty, our anger.

How will we ever teach our kids how to be human if we never let them see us being human? Mama elephants aren't spending all day trying to hide their elephantness from their calves, are they?

One day our kids are going to wake up and realize that *they're* fully human. They're going to have anger, they're going to have fear, they're going to have doubt, they're going to get tired, they're going to screw up. If we haven't shown them how to do all that out loud, they're going to feel ashamed and alone. If they've never seen full humanity in us, they might assume they're doing it all wrong.

I think a "perfect" parent can really do a number on a kid. Maybe what kids need most is exactly what we need most: to see brave, honest, kind people making mistakes and repairing and carrying on and forgiving each other. Repeat forever.

GLENNON

I used to think that my kids were balls of clay and my job as a parent was to mold them according to a societal checklist of expectations. But after a while, I realized that that's not the gig at all. Just not at all.

Kids aren't clay, and parents aren't sculptors. It is not our job to make our kids into our idea of who they should be.

Maybe we're more like gardeners. Who our kids are meant to become is already there in the seed of them, after all. So maybe our sacred duty is to carefully nurture the kind of loving, healthy, open soil that allows them to slowly grow. And we—in reverence and awe—get to watch them bloom and protect them from storms as they grow stronger and stronger and more beautifully, perfectly themselves.

GLENNON

I see my child for who they actually are.

It's picture day. I pick out Alice's clothes, braid her hair, put her into a dress. She gets home from picture day and says she wants to tell me something important. She goes, "Mom, I'm actually really not a dressy person. I'm more of a casual person. Is it okay if I don't wear a dress for picture day anymore? Will that make you sad?" A picture is supposed to document a person, but I wasn't documenting *her*; I was imagining the picture I wanted and then making her look like that. I told her, "No more dresses. I don't want to make you look like a picture. I want a picture that looks like *you*."

AMANDA

We create these stories in our mind about who our children are: "Tish is the artistic one, Amma the sporty one." But what I've learned is that my story of who I've decided they are is always what blocks me from seeing who they *actually* are. At the end of the day, parenting is just about seeing your kids clearly. In order to do that, you have to let go of the stories you have about them so that when they walk into a room, you can think: *Oh, there you are, fresh to me in this moment. Look at you!*

GLENNON

When kids are acting out, they can tell whether they're being looked at as a good kid having a hard time or a bad kid doing bad things. The reason we insert such badness into our kids is because we take their behavior as a sign of who they are, rather than assuming that who they are is a good person and that their behavior is a sign of something they're struggling with or a set of skills they don't yet have.

DR. BECKY KENNEDY

Don't become so concerned with raising a good kid that you forget you already have one.

GLENNON

Watching my son, who has ADHD, navigate a system that is incompatible with his executive functioning and his attentional biology crushed me—a perfect storm of all my internal biases and fears and achievement addiction.

I was plagued with future-casting anxieties like: *What does this mean he won't be able to do? How will his choices be limited?* At the end of the day, it came down to my primal fear: *Will he be okay? Will he be okay in a world that demands so much of us and can be so cruel?*

I was trying so desperately to protect him from the shame and judgment of the world. But my fears for him were made of the same shame and judgment that I was trying to protect him from—which meant that he would feel the shame and judgment either way. ⌒

⌒ Slowly, painfully, I realized that the only thing I could do to help him be okay was to truly believe he was. Not to *tell* him he'd be okay but to *believe* in the deepest parts of me that he already was okay. That he was already perfect—miraculous, even.

So now I get the joy of just radically loving him exactly as he is. Instead of trying to make him okay in the world, whatever the hell that means, I am doing my best to make sure he's okay in himself. Now when I look at him, I actually see the best version of him and reflect that back to him.

Which means I have the deep, sweet relief of no longer asking the world to tell me whether my kid is okay. I'm not asking that of the world anymore. It's no longer a question. He is already perfect— miraculous, even.

AMANDA

I want my girls to release the idea that they need to be validated by outside forces, including their parents, to receive their power.

ALEX ELLE

It's really hard as parents to get out of your kid's way. But it goes back to the idea of trust. One of the most amazing things about being a parent and raising a child is I have to trust him and get out of his way and know that he is wise enough and beautiful enough and sensitive enough to live and make decisions for his life.

CHLOÉ COOPER JONES

Tish came home one day a few years ago and said, "My school counselor wants me to join all of these clubs, and I don't want to. I'm not a club person." I said, "Okay, so don't join the clubs." And she said, "Well, I don't want to disappoint him." I said to her, "Oh, honey, your job throughout your entire life is to disappoint as many people as it takes to avoid disappointing yourself." She said, "Even you?" And I said, "Oh, *especially* me."

GLENNON

I teach my child not to abandon themself.

I have friends who are fierce leaders and activists, but at the end of the day, they're really living their lives to avoid disappointing their parents. In some cases their parents aren't even alive anymore. That is the ultimate taming—the idea that we have to live not to disappoint our parents—that we have to live their lives, their ideas, their values, instead of discovering and living our own. I was talking to Liz about this awhile back, and she told me to think hard about the word *disappoint*. If you're scared of disappointing your parent, that means you've already "appointed" them the guide of your life. So to disappoint is actually dis-appointing them and re-appointing yourself.

That's what I want my kids to do. I don't want them to live with me as their guide; I want to teach them to trust themselves to be their own guides. I want them to wake up each morning and ask, *Who do I need to disappoint today so I can reappoint myself as the guide of my own life?*

GLENNON

The world is ready to judge and shame our babies for any number of things: their bodies, their brains, their skin, their sexuality. One parenting approach attempts to change the child for the world. We don't want our child to feel the pain of the world's rejection, so we try to change them to make them fit more inside this narrow window of acceptability.

But when I was a teacher, I noticed that kids seemed to be able to recover from the whole world telling them that they were weird and different as long as their adult at home said, in word and body, "I love you exactly as you are. You're alright. You're just exactly right."

I know that even if the entire world disapproves of my baby, she'll still be alright if she knows that her mother approves of her. So I'll use all of that nervous mama energy to go out and change the entire world before I'll attempt to change one hair on her perfect little head.

GLENNON

When I came out as gay, there was so much fear from my family. It scared me. Now, being a parent, I understand that my mother was not afraid *of* me, she was afraid *for* me. But her fear of the world rejecting me caused her to bring that rejection energy to me first. We're afraid of how the world will receive our kids. But we forget that we *are* the world to our kids.

ABBY

I don't change my kid to earn the world's acceptance.

The hardest thing about raising a middle schooler is that it triggers the unhealed, sweaty seventh grader inside of us who's got the tray in their hand and doesn't smell quite right and doesn't know where they're going to sit. We so desperately don't want that for our own children. That feeling is still so raw that we almost can't take it if we have to watch it unfold again. But helping our kids feel like they belong is as simple as "I see you, I love you, and you will always belong here." It's as simple and hard as doing your own work so you're not working your stuff out on your kids.

BRENÉ BROWN

One day, Zaya comes home, and she is shaking. Bawling. She says, "I'm gay." I say, "Oh, my gosh, this is wonderful. We're going to celebrate. I'm so happy that you told us." I asked her, "Do you think you can tell Dad?" When she shared that she didn't know, I told her I thought her dad might surprise her. When she told him, he said, "I'm so happy for you. I'm so proud of you." She was so surprised that she was being embraced with love and understanding and joy. We made it clear that our home and anything that we touch is a sanctuary. If you can't get right by how we are living and embrace all of our family members, you are not welcome here.

GABRIELLE UNION

My mother blew my mind when she said, "I regret that I raised you as if you were straight. I shouldn't have assumed. And I wasn't your friend, and I should have been. I wanted you to change because I knew the world wouldn't." That meant so much to me.

HANNAH GADSBY

As we get older, resilience really comes from having felt like someone was there for you in your hard moments. Picture your kid wandering around a garden that has hundreds of benches. The garden is life, and every bench is just an experience or a feeling: *I was left out, I wasn't invited, I didn't make the soccer team.* Happy ones, too: *I was valedictorian.*

When we find our kid on an unhappy bench, our instinct is to yank them off and bring them to some sunnier or happier bench. "It's not that big of a deal. You were invited last year. It's one night. We'll have our own slumber party that night with all the other friends."

When we do that, what we're really doing is setting them up so that the next time they're on the bench, they think: *Oh, let me get off. This bench is so bad, my mom wouldn't even sit on it with me.* Often, resilience building is just you, as their parent, sitting next to them.

When your kid is upset, there are three lines you can say to sit with them on the bench:

1. "I'm so glad you're talking to me about this. This is so important."

2. "I believe you."

3. "Tell me more."

And then what ends up happening is, your kid gets off the bench before you. They'll move on when they're ready. You'll find them at the next spot they need you.

DR. BECKY KENNEDY

I let my kid feel hard feelings.

It's not our job to protect our kids from their pain. It's our job to let them sit in it, sit beside them through it, and just say to them over and over again, "I see your fear and it's big, and I see your courage and it's bigger. We can do hard things." You don't want them to learn to avoid every fire. You want to help them bravely walk through enough flames to learn that they're fireproof.

GLENNON

We learn as adults that we have to disconnect from our feelings about the devastating things happening in the world. But if we truly want to prepare our kids for the world, we need to look at all of it together. They're witnessing it already. Don't leave them alone in it.

PRENTIS HEMPHILL

My mom's favorite phrase growing up was "Crying doesn't solve problems." That wasn't helpful. Now I cry in front of my kids. I don't hide my tears. I tell them, "Go ahead and cry. Can I give you a hug?" Sometimes they say, "No," and I honor that. I try to make sure my children know they're loved and that I'm here for them when they are ready. Inviting people to feel safe enough to shed their tears is such a sacred act.

ALEX ELLE

For parents, one of the greatest things you can do is to ask your kid how they are. To be like "But *really*, how are you? On a scale from one to ten, zero being the worst, ten being the best, how are you?" This way, they're encouraged to actually think about where they really are. Kids automatically want to say, "Fine" to please their parents or get away from them. Usually both, if they're teenagers.

JENNY LAWSON

DR. BECKY KENNEDY: Imagine you're the pilot of the plane. There's extreme turbulence and everyone's screaming. In that situation, three pilots could come on.

One pilot says, "Stop screaming, it's no big deal, nothing's going on." If that's my pilot, I would not feel good.

The second pilot says, "I'm going to open this door, and if anybody wants to fly this plane and knows what to do, just come, because I'm not feeling so sure." Any one of us would be like: *It's not the turbulence that's scaring me, it's this pilot that's scaring me.* That's a real lack of boundaries.

The third pilot says, "You guys are screaming back there. It is really, really turbulent, yes, it is. I believe you that it feels bad. I know what I'm doing. I've done this before. We're still landing in Los Angeles at the same time. I'm going to go off the loudspeaker so I can do my thing. If screaming continues to be your thing, do it. And I'll see you when you're on the ground." I want that pilot every time. Our kids want that pilot. Embodying your authority while also validating their experience is what makes that pilot feel so sturdy and safe.

GLENNON: I love that. Since I know there's so little I can control, I've always thought of my kids as the passengers and myself as the flight attendant. When planes hit turbulence, the passengers look at the flight attendant's face to know if it's time to panic. So when my family hits turbulence, I tell myself: *Glennon, just stay calm and keep serving the tiny freaking pretzels.*

—

I keep serving the tiny pretzels.

ABBY: I keep thinking about a time that we took the girls to a swimming lesson. They were clearly struggling. Glennon was dying; she absolutely hates to see them struggling. The girls know this about their mama. Halfway through the lesson, Tish gets out of the pool while Amma stays there at the edge, hoping that her big sister could talk us into letting them get out of the water. I squeezed Glennon's hand under the table and said to Tish, "You have to get back in the pool and finish. You're going to be okay. You can do this, and you will." She was stunned. Glennon bit her lip so she wouldn't start crying. I usually think back on this moment as good and important for all of us. But sometimes I think: *Oh, God, did that mess them up?*

DR. BECKY: Abby, you did not mess them up. There is a way to honor your child's feelings *and* set a boundary. You can say to a kid, "You really don't want to finish your swim lesson. I believe the water is cold and that you're really tired. We also paid for this lesson, and I know you can finish it. Let's reassess lessons going forward." We can hold two truths at once: We can see, name, and validate a kid's experience as real, and still hold a decision that feels right as a parent, as a leader.

—

Parenting is a daily spiritual, centering practice because kids find different ways of testing the limits. My work with my child is to not scare her into submission. With her, I'm really lucky that I can do a lot of explaining of *why*. And even if she doesn't understand the words, she feels respected by my explaining. I'm like: *You don't even understand these words I'm saying.* But she nods, and she's learned to say, "Okay, okay." Sometimes she doesn't. Sometimes she's like "I'm going to fall out on this floor, and I don't *believe* you that you can't give me a cookie right now for breakfast." And I have to explain to her that that's not going to happen. "I'm here for you if you're going to have this fit, but it's not going to change the reality, which is that you're not going to have a cookie."

PRENTIS HEMPHILL

GLENNON: Memory is the thing that happened, plus every time you've thought about it since then. So let's say I'm eight and a conflict happens between my parents and me. They come back to me a week later, sit me down, and say, "Okay, we're thinking about that moment where we lost connection, and we want to talk about it. This is what we could have done differently." That actually changes the memory, instead of me having to wait until I'm forty-seven to change the memory with a therapist. Repair is like photoshopping life. It's like magic. It's actually changing the memory for our kids as they go forward.

AMANDA: Yes. And we are not doing that to make our kids feel better about us. We are doing it to make our kids feel better about themselves. We are changing the memory in order to snatch away the self-blame that our kids are putting on themselves because of what we did. We are adding accountability and closeness to the memory. So repair is essential. But what's really cool is: The original misalignments are as essential as the repairs. Studies show that if you're aligned with your kid 100 percent of the time, it's worse for your kid. They learn to expect that love looks like perfection, which is a fiction they'll never be able to replicate. But if you are misaligned 70 percent of the time, and you are coming back to repair, they learn that love looks like imperfect people who screw up—and when they do screw up, they come back and say, "Hey, that wasn't about you. That was about me."

ABBY: Years ago, I made a parenting mistake. Glennon said, "It's okay. Why don't you just talk to Amma about it? Just apologize." I was forty years old, and this was the first time I've ever heard somebody tell me that a parent can apologize to a child. So I did it. I gathered up all my courage and went to Amma's room and apologized. And she was like "Okay! No problem. I understand." It gave me this experience of being able to reparent the little kid in me that never got apologized to. I think that there's this beautiful reparenting healing that can happen when we give our children what we never got but really needed.

—

I repair.

Repair is the number one relationship strategy. Period.

DR. BECKY KENNEDY

Children need their parents to see them, help them understand what feelings are, and help them understand themselves. But emotionally immature parents struggle to self-reflect. They tend to be defensive and self-centered, interact very superficially, and they aren't capable of empathizing. They won't go back and attempt repair by apologizing or sharing empathy for something they did that was hurtful. And that ability to repair is so crucial to any kind of relationship, especially the parent-child relationship. Kids of emotionally immature parents learn that they have to supply the empathy to the parent, so they stretch to develop a level of empathy that they're not prepared for. They become vigilant. They feel emotionally lonely.

LINDSAY C. GIBSON

The opposite of raising a child who's full of shame is normalizing, normalizing, normalizing. We have to normalize hard things.

BRENÉ BROWN

If your kid has ADHD, there's about a 50 percent chance that you or the other parent has ADHD. My husband has it. Doing that testing—and talking about it—is such a gift you can give your kid. We are able to say, "Your brain works the way your dad's brain works," so that our child doesn't feel othered or like there's something wrong with him. The two of them can share experiences and strategies. And most important, he's able to look at his amazing dad and say, "You figured life out. I can, too."

AMANDA

I show my kid my full self.

—

GLENNON: We're raising three teenagers, and I don't know what to say about anything, ever. Especially sex. But I have learned that when I come to conversations with a little bit of uncertainty and vulnerability, they seem more capable of sharing their vulnerability.

CHERYL STRAYED: Part of what happens in adolescence, and certainly when our teenagers do become sexually active, is that we as parents are *not* part of that scenario. We need to let them go. As somebody who has had sex with people I didn't care about and who didn't care about me, and sex with people I've cared an awful lot about and who have cared an awful lot about me—all of those experiences are part of what taught me what I needed to know about my body and about sex and helped me figure out relationships along the path. Sometimes our kids find their way by walking down paths that we never walked, and that's really scary.

ABBY: I grew up in a family in which we *never* talked about it. I had to go out into the world and figure it out myself. Even if you don't have any answers for your kid, having those conversations, even if it feels a little uncomfortable, opens the doorway and makes the whole subject less terrifying.

GLENNON: I think of sex talks with kids the same way I think about faith talks. Nobody has any answers. If you're bringing rigid answers to conversations with kids about faith or sex, you've already lost. It's fake and dangerous to come to kids with a bunch of pretend certainty when the truth is we haven't really even worked it all out for ourselves. We have to normalize not knowing and talking about things anyway. If we're not ready to be vulnerable and honest about our confusion and questions around sex, then we can't expect our kids to. We don't have to have any of the answers before we talk to our children; we can just explore the questions together forever.

—

GLENNON: Some of the women in my life who I consider to be the best mothers—who just have the most pristine, nurturing, mothering energy—are you, Liz Gilbert, Alex Hedison, Oprah, Megan Falley, Andrea Gibson, adrienne maree brown, the list goes on. What you all have in common is that you didn't birth kids. I also know plenty of women who have biological children who don't emanate mothering energy at all. I have come to think of mothering less as an identity that people are or not and more as an energy that we can share or not.

TRACEE ELLIS ROSS: Thank you. I say this to people all the time: "I'm a wonderful mother." And it's been hard for me to claim that. I was just writing in my journal, "I can feel my body's ability to make a child draining out of me." Sometimes I find it hilarious, as if there's a fire sale going on in my uterus and someone's in there screaming, "All things must go!" Is it my fertility that is leaving me? Is it my womanhood? Or is it really neither? I have to fight to hold my truth, because I have been programmed so successfully by the water we all swim in. But I don't agree that that's what fertile means, I don't agree that that's what woman means. I feel fertile with creativity, full of power—more and more a woman than I've ever been. ⌒

I embrace my unique form of mothering.

AMANDA: It would be so different if that was how our fertility was presented to us. If when we were young, we were asked, "What are you going to do with this vast, creative fertility that you have, only one aspect of which is making babies?" It's heartbreaking to realize there are countless generations of fallow ground because we were never empowered to grasp the full scope of our own creative, ambitious, beautiful fertility.

TRACEE: It's a heartbreaking thought. And I'm grateful to be able to look at it with curiosity instead of heartbreak. The heartbreak does come up, and I get to hold that gently and lovingly and remind myself: *I woke up every morning of my life and tried to do my best, so I must be where I'm supposed to be.* The idea that there is one pathway of fertility that is informed by this random construct that somebody came up with around gender is an unbelievable injustice. When I pull back from it, I'm like: *That's a joke. Who did that? You've just limited so much life. You've limited so much life.*

AMANDA: It's almost like that was the point.

ABBY: I've never thought of it that way. And as a person who won't have my own biological children, you just gave me a road map of work I need to do. I'm really grateful.

I always knew that motherhood was not the path for me. But because I was raised to believe, as all girl children are, that women are biologically wired to not only procreate but to *desire* to procreate, I always felt like: *I'm the only one. I am an anomaly, there must be something wrong with me.*

Those of us for whom having kids is an affirmative *No, this is not for me* are often seen as selfish, career obsessed, narcissistic, uncaring, unfeeling, unloving, and potentially defective in some way, whether it be emotionally or otherwise—projections that truly led me to believe that perhaps there was something biologically wrong with me: *I must just not be wired right.* Which is a heavy belief to carry around about oneself. Living with this has also given me a huge amount of empathy for queer people, who have also been told: *There is something wrong with you for experiencing your body and your desire in the way that you do.*

Some of the well-meaning but thoughtless comments women who choose not to have kids get are things like "Have you really thought about this?"—the implication being that you're ignorant or deluded or you don't know yourself. Honestly, for most women in my position, it's one of the things that we have thought about *incessantly* since we started getting our period. Yes, you can rest assured we've thought about this deeply.

Huge swaths of the population find deep purpose and fulfillment in parenthood and could not imagine life without that dimension to it. But as humans, we need multiple expressions of our creativity and our love and our generativity. The more women who are able to pour not just our love but our time, our energy, our resources, and our intelligence into pursuits other than motherhood that might impact public life, the better.

RUBY WARRINGTON

I embrace my unique form of mothering.

Abby wasn't *added* to our family. She was *missing* from our family.

GLENNON

When I entered Glennon's family, now my family, I'd feel this pang in my stomach when the kids talked about their childhoods. I wasn't there. Actually, to this day, that pang still happens.

In the early days, I tried to buy their love. Once at a coffee shop, the girls asked for a cake pop. Glennon is not a "Sure, you can have a cake pop!" kind of mom. But I was like "Yes!" When the barista asked how many we wanted, I said, "All of them." The girls' eyes went wide, and so did Glennon's. I learned after a while that you actually can't buy love. That sucked. Love to kids is not: *I'll give you whatever you want.* It's: *I'm here and I'm not going anywhere, no matter what you throw at me.* Bonus parenting is a long, selfless act of faith.

Recently, we were playing a game and Tish's question was "Who has taught you the most about love?" Tish looked around the room and said, "Abby. My mom and dad have to love me. Abby wakes up and chooses to love me." It was the best moment of my life. Tish was the hardest to win over, because loyalty is everything to her. But those kids—once you earn your place in their life—the bond is unbreakable.

Over the holidays, Amma told a childhood story, and I was in it. I turned to Glennon with tears in my eyes. I was just like: *I'm in her memory bank now. I've made it. I'm a part of her past!*

For somebody who joins a family, there's such a huge gap. It takes so much time, and it's so hard. It's hard to sit at the first Christmas family dinner and hear about all of the past Christmases. But you just have to stay long enough to become part of the record. It's the most important thing I've ever done, becoming part of those three kids' memories.

ABBY

One of the most important elements of our coparenting is that we have guiding principles—but we always put people before principles. We have structures that mostly work, but we also have enough freedom and kindness to break those structures when needed. I'll never forget when Covid started and my anxiety was through the roof. Craig was supposed to have the kids, and I called him and was like "They can't leave the house. I have to keep them. I cannot let them out of the house." And he immediately said, "Okay. Yes. That's fine. I understand." He didn't say, "Nope, that's not the schedule." He heard the fear in my voice, and he understood. It was just grace and tenderness and a deep kindness. When we began coparenting, I read this book about forest systems and I learned that even though trees in a forest are separate from one another, the roots underneath are all connected. So if one tree is unhealthy, that makes the next tree unhealthy because their roots are intermingled. Craig knew that if he demanded that we stick to our structure, I wouldn't be mentally healthy. And he knew if I wasn't mentally healthy, the kids would suffer. He'd done enough work to see that. I think that we coparent well because Craig, Abby, and I are separately so committed to our own individual growth and work. When we come to each other, we're actually trying hard to be the best versions of ourselves.

GLENNON

When I first started dating Dwyane, I knew he had children. But all of a sudden, he got custody over them, and they needed guidance and parenting. So I became an extra adult in their lives. I knew that when I married him I was marrying them. I realized very quickly that it was not my job to replace their other parent. My job was to be consistent; to not be sometimey; to be a loving, compassionate adult in their life that they can always count on. To be a sanctuary in the storm.

GABRIELLE UNION

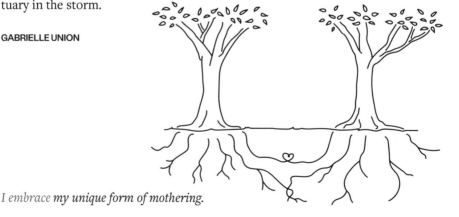

I embrace my unique form of mothering.

I have a friend who's trying to coparent with a narcissist. In a situation like this, the goal has to change. She's no longer trying to actually coparent. Nor is she trying to fix him or influence him or help him be a better parent. She's no longer trying desperately to protect her children from the emotional damage of having him as a father, because she can't.

She knows her children's task will eventually be the same as hers: to somehow find peace and freedom, even with this person in their life. So she's decided that she has two jobs: to keep her side of the street clean, and to model for her children how to stay sane and healthy while having to be forever connected to this person.

My friend broke the cycle. Her kids have a safe, stable place with their mother—and that's enough. The reason they have a safe, stable place with their mother is because *their mother is safe and stable*. And she is safe and stable because she left, and now she maintains strong boundaries without shame or apology.

My friend's kids are watching their mom and learning what self-respect is and what love is and what love is not. Her courage has become deep roots of peace and hope for her children.

GLENNON

Watching my kids grow into beautiful adults has been the best feeling in the world. They like me, they like us, they like being around us, but they don't need us. And that was our job all along as parents—to get them to a place of not needing us. When I see them building community with each other, staying connected to their friends, and creating their own rituals, I don't doubt that they can handle what comes. I see that in them, and that gives me a great sense of relief. I taught my kids to be competent and independent early, and we practiced it for a long time. We can't wait until our kids are twenty-three and out of the house to teach them that they can get themselves up in the morning, that they can handle their homework, that they can deal with disputes at school and with their friends. Let them practice. Let them fail. Let them get hurt, because that's waiting for them. We can hold on and try to fix the world for our kids, but if we do that, we're going to be doing that for the rest of our lives.

FORMER FIRST LADY MICHELLE OBAMA

A teen's job is to find independence and to find themselves, to step into their own identity. A lot of parents during this era of kids' lives go through that, too. *Who am I without my kids? Can I be happy if my kids aren't?* Those are questions I've been asking myself a lot. It's been humbling for me to remember that there are happy times and there are sad times and there are hard times and there are easy times and they're going to come and go and come and go and come and go again. I'm really trying to find my way—to figure out how to be the best mother to my kids and also how to be stable and balanced in my own life when they're struggling. I just try to keep putting one foot in front of the other.

CHERYL STRAYED

I accept that sometimes love is letting go.

Transitioning into parenting older kids really scrambled my ideas of purpose, worthiness, identity, and belonging. So pretty much *all* my ideas.

It feels like going from being a director of your kid's life to being a consultant. But the thing is, in order to be a consultant, you must be *consulted*. I've recently learned that unsolicited advice is actually just criticism. So if I am *not* being consulted but I'm consulting anyway, then I'm failing at this parenting stage.

There's usually a period in an adult child's life where they do not ask for consultation because they have to individuate to gain confidence. This is a necessary stage but such a hard one for me. The only way I survive these times is to shift my center of worthiness to my own life and wait for them to come to me. When they see me living my own beautiful life with peace and joy and wisdom, they start asking for consultation again, because they see me as having what they want and need.

And when I miss them deeply, instead of putting my missing on them, I start loving them during meditation. I'll sit and send all the loving-kindness that I can from my little bedroom out to them—wherever they are. I know that sounds weird, but it's worked for me. It makes me feel close to them when we can't be physically close. And sometimes it really seems like they magically feel the love I send.

GLENNON

So many people are trying to answer the questions: Can I parent well when I was not parented well? Can I give what I've never gotten?

GLENNON

We may never get what we need from the people who raised us. And that is a tough pill to swallow. But we have to remember what our work is. Our work isn't to change people by forcing it and trying to get them to understand. Our work is to lead by example. Everything else is a bonus. Focusing on our healing is all we can do.

We must be healed separate from the person who hurt us. Because if we are not, we are going to continuously be in these cycles of external validation and wanting the person to say, "Sorry." We can want those things. I'm not saying I don't want those things. But there has to be acceptance when you don't get those things. That's the hard part. A big part of my healing was accepting that hard work—still working through it but changing my behavior with how I raise my children and how I raise myself. As I parent my children, I am reparenting myself.

ALEX ELLE

I can give what I never received.

—

INA GARTEN: We're stuck with the voices that were put in our heads when we were small. When I was about thirteen or fourteen, my father said, "Nobody will ever love you." And now I walk up Madison Avenue, and somebody just leans in and says, "I love you." It happens all the time, which is so lovely. And I always say to myself: *He was wrong.* Even when my parents' voices still tell me it's going to turn out badly, everything I've done has turned out better than I could have imagined. I have this little cosmic joke with myself: Whenever something good happens, I'll just say, "Wrong."

GLENNON: And your father used to tell you that you'd never be satisfied, right?

INA: Yes. And I think what he was talking about was that I wasn't satisfied with the things that he wanted for me. I'm always satisfied with doing what I want to do. How about I have bigger ideas than you do? I want to use my creativity and ambition to do what I want to do.

GLENNON: It seems like we were all little girls whose parents sensed in us a bigness of spirit that frightened them. They sensed a voraciousness, an appetite, a desire to take up more space than they thought would be available to us in the world. Thinking about it that way almost makes you understand them a little bit. If you're a rigid person looking at the world and seeing only a handful of things available to your daughter and you're raising a little Ina with this mighty life force, you might spend all of your time telling her, "You will never be loved if you stay like this." You might try to squash the bigness right out of her. I don't know that any of that is conscious. But maybe parents who shut us down noticed our powerful spirit and were afraid the world would reject it, so they tried to squelch it first.

—

With intergenerational trauma, we tend to see codependent qualities, people pleasing, lack of trust in self and in others, or self-hatred. There's chronic shame. Then we start peeling back, and the next set of stories comes out in the conversations in the therapy room, like "Oh, your mother was codependent. There were family secrets that were making everyone sick because no one was actually taking them out of the shadows to sort through. Oh, that zoning out that you do is, in essence, dissociation—that's something that your father would also do. Oh, it's really hard for you to accept love, just in the same ways that it was for your mother and your grandmother. No one really ever said 'I love you' in this family because 'I love you' was never really modeled for generations."

When we see some of those patterns, we start healing. The first step is to go into the body to help you befriend your body, help you to understand how your body responds to triggers, and then help you to engage in relaxation practices so that your body can default more to a state of calm and ease rather than a state of alarm. Because if you go into a conversation with a parent who is perpetually triggering you, you'll go with your entire body—every cell in your body feeling like it needs to protect you. And what's going to come out of your mouth is something that's reflective of that need to protect. If you have actually helped your body to absorb stress and triggers and learned to down-regulate your emotions, you're going to go into the conversation coming from a place of calm and ease, not survival mode.

DR. MARIEL BUQUÉ

I can do things differently.

A woman
becomes a
responsible
parent when
she stops being
an obedient
daughter.
When she
finally
understands
that she is
creating
something
different
than what
her parents
created.

GLENNON

I keep thinking of this idea that all the water in the world can't sink a ship unless it gets inside—and that it takes a very, very brave parent to seal the ship.

The world doesn't deserve our kids, but our kids deserve a parent who will see and celebrate them as the tender treasures that they are; a parent who refuses to pass along the world's cruel, incessant messaging, who teaches them every day, in a million different ways, that the world is wrong and who they are is exactly right, exactly as they are.

If your fear about the world is making you doubt your belief that your kid is deeply okay and worthy of every good thing—exactly as they are—they will sense that. So your only job is to truly *believe* that your kid is worthy of love and acceptance and celebration every day, exactly as they are.

AMANDA

Fifteen

Why can't I be happy?

Sometimes when I'm really stressed and overwhelmed, it's tempting to fantasize about letting it all go— moving my family to some gorgeous tropical island and just tending a garden.

As if gardener me would be a different me.

But the truth is, tropical island or not, I am going to find a way to project manage my life into a whirlwind. I am going to be the most productive, maximizing, stressed-out gardener in the history of gardeners.

You can bring an overachiever to the island, but you can't make her chill.

AMANDA

My life came to life when I stopped trying to escape pain. Everything I used to "take the edge off" turned out to be a lifeforce blocker.

I used alcohol to take the edge off. Makes sense. By the end of the day, we feel edgy and uncomfortable—itchy, almost. Just a couple glasses a night, what could be the harm? It's like a boundary we draw with the wine. It's our signal to ourselves and the world: *I'm done now. I'm done.* After a glass or two, all the discomfort, angst, and stress fades. That edge is gone, and it's such a relief.

But I think it's also why so many of us live half lives. It's why we stay where we shouldn't stay and don't try what we could have tried. Because the edge we're numbing every night is the very edge that—had we sat with it and investigated it long enough—would have been the catalyst to make real changes in our life.

If we touch a hot stove, the discomfort makes us move our hand away. If that discomfort was numbed, we'd get badly burned. I think the reason people end up feeling badly burned about their lives is that they numbed the pain that would have gotten them moving. Every night they numbed the discomfort that was trying to tell them to leave the bad relationship, move toward their dream, heal that friendship, really figure out their problem. Every night, they numbed the edge, so they lost their edge. The edge was speaking to them, but they silenced it their entire lives.

At the end of the day, when I finally slow down, edginess sets in. Instead of silencing it, I investigate it. Am I edgy because of my job? Then let's look at what changes we can make there. Am I edgy because of my marriage? Okay, we better dig in there. Sitting in the pain, in the daily discomfort, listening to it and responding to what it's telling me—that's my secret. Suffering a little bit every day is how I avoid big life suffering. For me, that's the right kind of hard. I don't ever want to take the edge off, because the edge is pointing me toward a happier, freer life with less regret.

GLENNON

There's this perpetual desire to reach the mountaintop. It feels grand and triumphant to look out from above everything and everyone else—to be on top, having conquered the mountain. But I want to ask people: What is it in you that feels like you need to conquer something to access beauty? Why do we feel the need to achieve ownership over beauty as opposed to bearing witness? What would happen if we started believing that whatever is on the mountaintop is also in the face of our neighbor, the sunlight flickering through our kitchen window, the hands of the old woman selling roses on the sidewalk? It is liberating to know that we can witness beauty everywhere—not just from the mountaintop.

COLE ARTHUR RILEY

I was at a table with a bunch of "successful" people recently, and everybody seemed stressed and exhausted, yet all they were talking about was what's next, what's bigger. I asked, "How do you know when you've done it—when you've done the thing you set out to do? How will you know it's time to stop and enjoy your life?" It was just crickets, like no one had ever heard or considered that question before. It really got to me.

I don't want to live as if happiness or success is one great project or accomplishment away. I want to stop this frantic climb to nowhere. The pursuit of greatness keeps us from greatness. The pursuit of happiness keeps us from happiness. The pursuit of love keeps us from love. Because those are things we don't have to chase or earn; they're right here in the everyday. But I don't think we can see any of it until we intentionally decide:

What does *enough* mean to me?

GLENNON

I'm happier when

I find joy right here, right now.

I have known for a long time that I live this kind of horizon living. I'm always looking beyond, always planning, always excited about the life that is next, but never arriving there. Never living now.

I understood my tendency more clearly when I read Kate Bowler talking about "possible futures." She said her problem was "failing to love what is present and deciding to love what is possible instead."

That's what I'm doing in my horizon living: loving the version of my life I can imagine in the future, the life I can work toward, but not loving the life that is here in front of me right now.

AMANDA

I was in a somatics class, and my teacher turned and asked me, in front of everyone, "Are you satisfiable?" It was one of those stop-me-in-my-tracks questions. I realized: *No, I'm definitely not satisfiable. There's nothing in my entire life that has cultivated satisfiability in me.*

I think it is fundamentally an anticapitalist thing to be satisfiable. We live in a culture that is constantly telling us: *You don't have enough, you are not enough. You are not pretty enough. You're not skinny enough. You need better skin, you need better hair. You need a better car, you need a better house. You're just not there yet.*

A trick to satisfaction is asking yourself: *What if it wasn't something I could purchase? What if it wasn't something money could ever buy? Then what would satisfy me?* The clue to our future is in there somewhere. If our species is going to survive right now, we have to really let go of having too much.

The people who have too much are not satisfied. So that clearly is not a winning strategy. So we have to let go of that, and we have to materially redistribute things, because some people don't have enough to even get to think about what would satisfy them. But if I can recognize, *Oh, the simpler things satisfy me,* I don't have to keep hoarding and accumulating and aiming for millions and billions when I can live a good life without any of it.

ADRIENNE MAREE BROWN

I'm happier when I find joy right here, right now.

Every message I was getting from the world was saying: *Joy is right out there somewhere if you can just use your coins to get it. It's right beyond your reach.*

And I was like: *So what about people who can't afford it? We just don't get joy?* That can't be right. There's no way that God set us up in a world where joy is for the rich or the privileged. So in my early twenties, I started keeping a joy journal, because I wanted to document what joy looked like in my life. I thought: *If I can quantify it, then I don't have to afford what they're selling, because I already got it.*

I used to pick up Kaia from daycare, wearing my bracelets that you can hear from a mile away. Every single day, I'd hear Kaia say, "My mommy is here!" and then start running. So I would write that moment down. Or I would get on the phone with my girls and laugh until my stomach hurt and I had tears coming out my eyes. You can't pay for that. I would write that all down. And once I started to document that, I was like:

Okay. You can't sell me anything anymore. I'm not buying any of it.

TARANA BURKE

I'm the child of immigrants, and I was raised with a striving ethos. Now I'm just trying to recognize that what I do is not a reflection of my worth, which is a hard lesson to learn when you have been very ambitious your whole life and you have substituted self-esteem for ambition. I'm trying to recognize that it's enough. It's just enough. And that I never just rest. I win an award, and literally five minutes later after I'm notified, I'm on to the next thing. I have not enjoyed it. I haven't acknowledged it. It's just a blip in my day. And once I started noticing that, I was like: *Oh, no, we're going to have to work on this.*

ROXANE GAY

It is so powerful to decide, inside of this system, that maybe satisfiability and enoughness are something we *can* access. So much of joy and satisfaction and enoughness is just sitting and considering those questions: *Could you be enough? Could you consider that you're already enough and that there's nothing to fix about you?*

ADRIENNE MAREE BROWN

I say, "You are enough" so many times. I do that for a reason. I believe our brainwashing calls for that. I believe our deprogramming calls for repetition. It will become like a lullaby, this incantation over you: *I am enough now. I don't have to do another thing. That was already given to me by birth, so I'm going to rest.*

TRICIA HERSEY

I'm happier when
I decide what is enough.

There's this belief that you want success so badly and that's what motivates you. But what if that's not what motivates you? What if it's not the trophy? What if it's something much bigger than that? Because you get the trophy, you get the medal, and you feel empty inside. I actively work toward a flow state, where playing soccer feels like the most blissful and joyous thing that I ever did. I believe that if I love it, if I'm laughing, if I'm smiling, that's when I'm at my best.

CHRISTEN PRESS

The week of Glennon and Abby's wedding, I flew down and they had a place to get married and some outfits and a restaurant—and not much else. And I was like: *Oh my. Okay. We don't have place cards. We don't know who's speaking. And where's the schedule? Oh, my God.* And Glennon said something that I will never forget. She said,

"It's not: *Everything will be perfect, so we will be happy.* It's: *We will be happy, so everything will be perfect.*"

It wasn't a belief that being happy would make things perfect. It was a belief that they didn't need things to be perfect to be happy. Instead of holding their breath to see if everything turned out perfect so that they could be happy, they just decided to be happy—and damned if that didn't make them experience things as pretty close to perfect.

AMANDA

At one point in my life, I was a fiery person.

But you need heat and oxygen to turn fuel into fire. I have fuel in me—fuel for fun and joy and desire and curiosity. We all do. But because our lives are endless to-dos, we don't give those things heat and air—we don't give them space, time, attention—so our fire burns out. Even though our lives are full to overflowing, we don't actually have life running through our lives.

Fire's out. So we're either going to spend our lives smoldering with resentment and be all smoke and no fire, or we're going to have to allow some heat and air around our fuel to reignite the fire we were born with.

If we have no room or time in our lives to live, we just won't. Not a damn person is going to require it of us. Because the world is fine with women not living; in fact, the world profits from it. Which means that *we* have to decide whether we are going to live.

No one else has the heat and air to light up my life; I have to do that for myself. But I don't have to *add* anything to my to-do list. *I* am the fuel. *I* am the heat. *I* am the air. It's in my fun self, my joy self, my desire self, my true self. All I have to do is leave room for the spark to catch and burn.

My fire is my birthright. I know I have it in me, and I don't want to live without it.

AMANDA

I'm happier when

I make room for joy to emerge.

We need to make more space for fun in our lives, and one of the ways we can do that is by learning how to say no. I used to volunteer on my daughter's preschool board, and at some point I realized that I wasn't enjoying it and my contributions weren't essential. And so I did something I don't normally do: I quit. That opened up several hours a month in my schedule, and I use some of that time now to take drum lessons. Drumming is now one of my biggest fun magnets; I love it, and my lessons are a highlight of my week. That would not have been possible if I hadn't made space by saying no.

CATHERINE PRICE

We could all learn to infuse more fun into our lives, even if it's for five seconds. Fun doesn't have to be something separate from the mundane. I laugh at my own thoughts sometimes. When I'm doing bills, I get a little timer and I turn the timer on and it's so fun because I'm trying to beat that timer. I'm having fun, and I'm also paying the bills. Fun is a muscle that you have to exercise.

ABBY

We have a rule in our family that it's insulting to God if you don't dance in an elevator. Every time we're in one, I have to dance. If the elevator is full, my kids look at me mortified, and I'm like "Sorry, no dice. It's your embarrassment or God's fury." It's a joke, obviously. But it's ridiculous and fun. It's a way of opening up a mundane part of life and bringing in a surprise shot of joy.

AMANDA

My husband is out of town, and the responsibilities of being everywhere all at once are on me for the four-day sprint. I manage to get myself to the school pickup line to retrieve the children with the hope of getting my son to his violin lesson that, because we are overscheduled suburban masochists, is scheduled twenty minutes from the dismissal bell and located twenty minutes from the school. But I do it. I get there right on time to find my kids so famished that, they strongly insist, they cannot possibly wait until after the thirty-minute lesson ends to eat.

To my shock and delight, I do not freak out. I pull into the doughnut shop, surprising myself by caving to an indulgence that would not have been granted to me when I was their age, since my parents' household was as full of practicality and efficiency as it was of love.

We get back into the car, noting that we are now four minutes late as projected by the GPS. I proceed to make up each and every one of those four minutes on the drive. I should be embarrassed to admit, but I'm not, that besting the GPS projection by one or even three minutes is my most fail-safe daily delight. We pull in triumphantly to violin at precisely the appointed time, only to learn that there is, in fact, no lesson today.

To all of our collective astonishment, I do not freak out. Instead, I take them to the Italian store around the corner, where we pick up spaghetti and meatballs. ⌇

At the checkout line, I notice a tall, red tin of amaretto cookies. And now I am seven years old in my Aunt Peggy's house. Aunt Peggy, whose home was full of deliciously frivolous things, like the amaretto cookies she'd smuggle into that one side table where she knew I'd look first; like the most divine Queen of Hearts costume she made the time to sew for my fifth-grade Halloween; like the echoing, unapologetic full-bodied laughter that defied her two divorces; like the piles of logs chronicling her flights around the world until she was eighty-five in her own plane—a plane she piloted for me as a kid so I could see the world from the breathtakingly expansive, thrillingly selfish perspective of a woman who does what she wants.

I told the lady at the checkout how much I used to love those amaretto cookies. She said, "You still love them." So I bought a few, admiring their parchment-paper wrapping, squeezed at the edges like a bow. Later, at home with an unexpected boon of fifteen frivolous minutes, minutes I didn't even need to steal from the GPS, I sent Aunt Peggy a message about the cookies and about every fanciful, delicious treat and inspiration I found in her home and in her life. And about how the lady at the checkout said that aunt's houses are the best houses, and how I had agreed—and knew that I had the best of those houses and the best of those aunts. Then I ate all of the amaretto cookies. And I still love them.

I wonder what else I still love.

AMANDA

The magic of being a photographer, a writer, a joy seeker, a gratitude journaler is not in the hour she sits down to write or paint or journal. The magic is in the way she experiences the rest of the hours in her day. If you are a photographer and you're out there looking for beauty to snap, then your morning, noon, night, everything becomes a search for beauty. If you are a person who knows you'll end your day recording what made you feel grateful that day, you will spend your day looking for things that light you up. Seek and you shall find. When we seek beauty or joy or gratitude—that's what we find. That is why being an artist is life changing—not because of what the artist creates in her studio but because of the way she sees and experiences the world outside of her studio.

GLENNON

Sometimes I feel like: *Dammit, I went through this whole day and didn't see the joy. I missed it all.* Like that part of Alice Walker's *The Color Purple* where Shug says, "I think it pisses God off when you walk by the color purple in a field somewhere and don't notice it." But the next part of the conversation is so important. Celie asks what God does when God's pissed off about you not noticing the purple. Shug answers something like "Oh, God just makes something else. People think pleasing God is all God cares about. But any fool living in the world can see God's always trying to please us back . . . always making little surprises and springing them on us when we least expect it." How wonderful is that? There's forever tries and a constant supply of delights! It's not: *Shame on you for missing that.* It's: *Catch you in the next round. There's going to be endless more.*

AMANDA

I'm happier when

I notice and name the delights in my life.

Seek Beauty

AMANDA: I am a person heavily steeped in hustle culture. Sometimes I think about the lack of peace in my life, and I'm like: *I'm screwing up. I don't have enough peace. I don't have enough exercise. I don't have enough quality time with my family. I'm screwing it all up.* Listening to you talk about practicing peace and presence and joy by picking up sticks and hearing Glennon talk about picking up purple rocks, all I'm thinking is: *Well, add this to the list of my abject failures.* Because never in one million years am I going out into the woods to pick up sticks.

MORGAN HARPER NICHOLS: There are so many ways to find delight and presence. It's the person who's planning a dinner party and remembers that someone has an allergy, so they go out of their way to prepare something separate. It's the person who's writing an email and backspaces a few words because they're thinking about how to be more sensitive to someone. That's the same thing as going outside and looking at the sky. There are so many different ways that we can access and nurture presence and peace.

GLENNON: Sister, I see you coaching on the sidelines of the basketball court. The intensity and encouragement that you are beaming in to these girls—that is your sticks and rocks. I don't think you need to do anything new; maybe you just need to notice with fresh eyes all the sticks and rocks you're already picking up.

MORGAN: I used to think: *Okay, we all got to get out in nature to be happy.* But you know what's a huge part of nature? People. Humans. We need other humans to be present to humans. Not everybody can go outside and pick up sticks off the ground. It's not about adding some new activity to find peace and presence. It's about noticing the ways you're *already* doing that.

People who are able to recognize and protect their own humanity, their own preciousness, their own individual divinity are much more likely to be moved to protect others when their divinity, preciousness, and humanity are denied.

AMANDA

Growing up in activist communities, there was sometimes the feeling that if you weren't devastated, if you weren't despairing, if you weren't enraged, then there was something about you that was heartless. For me, I am much better and I have far more to offer the world when I am joyful. But I had to learn how to open that up.

ANDREA GIBSON

Joy is about having a real clear sense of one's purpose: that you have a place, that you matter in the fight, and that there is a shared thing that we can do together. And that shared thing for me is that we want a baseline of democracy in this country where people's voices matter, where people's experiences matter, where people feel seen.

BRITTNEY COOPER

I'm happier when

I stop being a martyr.

We have been conditioned to prove our love by slowly ceasing to exist. What a terrible burden for children to bear—to know that they are the reason their mother stopped living. What a terrible burden for our daughters to bear—to know that if they choose to become mothers, this will be their fate, too. Because if we show them that being a martyr is the highest form of love, that is what they will become. They will feel obligated to love as well as their mothers loved, after all. They will believe they have permission to live only as fully as their mothers allowed themselves to live. When we model martyrdom as love, we teach our children that when love begins, life ends. That is why Carl Jung suggested: *There is no greater burden on a child than the unlived life of a parent.* Maybe we need to stop dying for our children and start living for them.

GLENNON

I always just thought joy was about how it made *me* feel—like the joy was mine alone. I never have considered the idea that it was actually about people and the earth. It's all about connection. Now I consider not just how much joy I am feeling but how much joy I'm offering to other people. I used to think that my joy was only beneficial to me. But now I know that joy is contagious—and the happier I am, the happier everyone around me is. So now I consider nurturing my own joy as the greatest act of parenting and friendship I can do—because what I have, they will have also.

ABBY

Joy is not frivolous. We all wonder: *How is there time for fun? We have to be fighting for the earth. We have to be fighting for each other.* But these moments of purpose, joy, and flow are when we remember what we're fighting for. If all we're doing is living like robots, we lose all our fight because we forget why it even matters so much to live. Delight and fun *are* our why. They're why the earth is worth fighting for and love is worth fighting for and life is worth fighting for.

Because of that: Joy and delight are what will save us.

GLENNON

Sixteen

Why am I so angry?

For decades I was a dormant volcano in lip gloss, just constantly simmering right beneath the surface. Letting any of it out, letting anybody see or feel my anger, would have torched and changed my outer landscape in ways I couldn't fathom. That felt like too high a price to pay. What I never considered was that there was also a price to pay for holding it all in. That price was that I slowly burned myself up. That price was: Inside of me, I slowly died, and outside of me, nothing changed at all.

GLENNON

Everyone gets so angry about an angry woman.

I read a quote that said, "Behind every angry woman is something to be a lot angrier about than her."

We all focus on the angry woman. But there's a reason she's angry. We should focus on the reasons instead of her.

SARAH SPAIN

Glennon: Abby and I were on a little vacation in the desert. While we were out walking, we approached a cactus. I looked at it for a while and started thinking about how that cactus was exactly like people. People who do not have enough protection and nourishment in the soil of their lives end up having to grow rough and prickly. Then everyone thinks they're mean and hard, without understanding their *why*: that they had to grow this skin and these spikes in order to survive.

Abby: I'll never forget when you turned to me and said that you'd been thinking all that. I'd just been thinking: *Cool. A cactus.*

I'll see people behaving badly out in the world and online, and I almost always assume there's pain there. I don't think there are many weapons that are more dangerous than our wounds, and we live in a really wounded world.

ANDREA GIBSON

I hated my younger self because I couldn't allow myself to be angry at the people who actually failed me and the systems that purposefully oppressed me, that oppressed my family, that oppressed my community. I couldn't be angry at them. That felt wrong. That felt like pointing the finger and not taking personal responsibility. The anger had to go somewhere, so it was with me.

ASHLEY C. FORD

Anger can be a form of self-protection. John Bowlby observed a child who didn't have any primary caretakers and was living in the hospital. One of the nurses, Marianne, went away to get married and then came back to the hospital. Instead of saying, "I missed you, Marianne, where were you?," the child yelled that he hated her. The child had no hope that if he expressed his needs, someone would actually fulfill them. So his only way of protecting himself was through vengeance—to make him feel less weak and less vulnerable.

DR. MARISA G. FRANCO

I have always valued loyalty above all else. I used to think of anger and loyalty as opposites, so it was very hard for me to allow myself to feel anger. I'd feel disloyal when I had thoughts like: *My mom did the best she could, but it just wasn't good enough.* But now I know that acknowledging the truth is not disloyal. In fact, it's self-loyalty. Sometimes the truth is that I'm angry, and that's okay.

ABBY

Anger is telling me

There is something wrong, not something wrong with me.

After performing "good girl" for so long, anger and rage felt really, really good. Anger and rage became a coping mechanism for me. We don't realize what brings people to their coping mechanisms; we just look at the end result. Like: *Oh that's an alcoholic, that's a drug addict, that's a bad girl.*

So I'm a teenager who will bite your head off, who will fight anybody that steps toward me and says anything crazy, but not a single adult says, "What happened to your heart? How did you get here?" I'm still a child, but I don't get seen as one. I'm held accountable for the consequences of things that happened to me, but no one is accountable for the root cause of them. Nobody is digging into the root cause.

TARANA BURKE

When we enter into conflict with someone we love, we feel vulnerable. We've gotten into the conflict because we feel hurt or sad or fearful. But hurt, sadness, fear—those are very soft, vulnerable emotions. So we throw on our armor, some sort of stronger emotion or way of being that makes us feel less vulnerable. My armor is always anger and rightness.

GLENNON

When I jump off a cliff of anger, I am learning to—very slowly and terribly—ask myself if there is any iota of chance that there might be something else going on inside me that I'm not recognizing. Let's say my husband doesn't respond to a text with an important request that I have about the kids. I will immediately go straight to anger. His lack of response triggers in me certainty that I am alone in this, that it's up to me to figure it out, that my kids need things that we're not giving them, and so they're going to be ill-equipped for life. Now I'm completely gone, dog-paddling through a sea of cortisol. In learning to see what is generally underneath my rage, I've realized that, instead of relying on anger, which I am very comfortable with, I need to learn to express to him what is less comfortable to me: my anxiety and fear.

AMANDA

Glennon: What's the thing about yourself that you find most challenging?

Brené Brown: When I'm afraid, I get angry. I can be scary when I'm scared.

Anger is telling me

There is something I must express.

I've been learning how to say, even when I'm angry, even through a mad face, "I really am afraid right now that you don't love me, and I'm mad about it. It's making me mad."

PRENTIS HEMPHILL

When I was grieving my mom, I didn't think about anger or being mad at her. Then I was in a therapy session. And I noticed this feeling of heaviness, kind of like exhaustion. But I knew I wasn't tired. I couldn't figure it out. My therapist was like "We're going to keep going. What does it really feel like?" I was like "It's heavy, but it's also hot." And then I realized: *Oh! Maybe I'm angry. Is this possible? That doesn't sound like me.* As we went deeper, I realized I was *pissed.* I wasn't just a little bit angry; I was overwhelmed with rage that I didn't think was there. I realized I was mad at my mom for dying and for leaving me with my dad and my sister, both of whom I felt some responsibility to care for. I was mad that she wasn't there when we lost our pregnancy. I was mad that we lost our pregnancy. I was so, so mad. Then I was guilt ridden. How could I be mad at my perfect mom, this woman who loved so deeply? How could I be mad at her? I felt like a terrible person. Then I learned that anger is a very, very normal response for bereaved children. I realized that the people who we love the most are also the people who we are most often called to forgive and who we most often need to forgive us.

MARISA RENEE LEE

I heard about a study where people put their hand in icy cold water and scientists timed it and tried to figure out people's pain threshold based on whether they were allowed to swear while doing it. And it was the people who were screaming curse words who were able to keep their hands submerged for longer. And I thought: *Yes, of course. We need a big vocabulary to manage the wide spectrum of reality.*

KATE BOWLER

AMANDA: We're made to think rage, especially as moms, is a deficiency that proves we don't have what it takes. But it's just proof of human limit. There is a limit to one's capacity to respond to constant demands, overload of physical touch, incessant problem solving, overwhelming mental load—even if it's for tiny humans you love. The fact that there is a limit should be unsurprising, but it isn't, because we have this myth that if a mom loves her kids enough, there will be no limit and she will find a never-ending well of patience to draw upon.

DR. BECKY KENNEDY: What moms do, metaphorically, with our emotions is feed everybody. We put things on the calendar. We show up for them. We do all of the things. And if you think about that as food, you're constantly feeding your kids and family members. At the end of day, you've fed everyone else and you're left hungry.

Your body gives you signals that you need to eat, but women have become expert at avoiding and pushing away those signals; we learned that acknowledging and taking care of our own needs was threatening to our earliest attachments. So we ignore and we ignore and we ignore. Okay, well, what would happen if you went a week without eating? Think about how loud the signal would be in your body to get you to eat. It would be like: *I have tried to alert you, and I'm actually going to scream out and take over your entire body to protect you, because anything at a lower level has not been heard.* At the end of the day, anger is just a feeling that tells you what you need. And by the time it converts to rage, we're starving.

—

Anger is telling me
I have unmet needs.

My favorite little sentence ever is "How can we best get the need met that's nestled in our anger?"

DR. MARISA G. FRANCO

Anger is the quality that is under boundaries. For many of us who have a hard time with boundaries, we actually probably don't know how to feel anger in our body. And anger is not violence or destruction or oppression. Anger is a little bit of heat, usually in our chest and jaw and hands. It's literally just nerve activation, a nervous system response. And it is because of that anger that we get a sense of clarity about what doesn't work for us and what we need to do.

DR. HILLARY MCBRIDE

The way I know I have to stop something—a relationship, a project, an activity—is: First, I get really bitter and angry and defensive and nasty and mad at everybody else for making me do it, whatever it is. This is stage one, in which I forget that I am an adult and responsible for my own life and that no one else is responsible for my life. Then, if I don't handle my business, stage two is that my body starts shutting down. I become totally exhausted. That's how I know something's not serving me anymore and that it's time to handle my own business by leaving or stopping. But it always takes me a while to stop blaming other people and remember that I'm the one who is responsible for taking care of me.

GLENNON

We resist our anger. We shame ourselves for feeling it. But then it becomes two forces pushing against each other: our anger and our shame about our anger. That tension is what feels exhausting and insufferable. It's often not the actual anger that feels so painful, it's the resistance.

Not resisting is better. More helpful, too. We can turn toward our anger and loosen up about it and ask, "Okay, so what is that, actually?" It's just energy in motion in my body. What does it feel like? It feels like my chest clenching up a little bit. My hands are sweating a little bit. That's all. That's often all that anger feels like.

And actually, you do not want that anger energy to be shamed away or repressed. You need it. It's a message. It's a part of you that has activated to keep you safe—to give you important information about what is not right for you.

GLENNON

Anger is telling me
I need to get curious about what's bothering me.

Sometimes you are mad at somebody, and then something happens to them, and you're still angry at that person. Even though I lost my spouse to cancer, and he's gone, I'm still pissed off. But that's okay. I have to figure out how to continue to live my life and be celebratory of him with my child *and* make sure that she understands that he was human and not just this big saint that everyone has wrapped in rose-colored glasses. All of us have experienced something like that—trying to reconcile our feelings over someone we lost.

BOZOMA SAINT JOHN

My whole life, I've been very afraid to touch anger because I thought it would threaten my connection to the people I loved. So I suppressed all of my anger; I learned to assimilate, to not rock the boat. Because of that, I was never able to experience the feeling of anger and still be okay. So I started to equate anger with not-okayness. But now I am able to feel anger, and in the same breath I'm able to feel okay. I realize: *I'm okay with this.* I realized that the people I love won't leave if I show them my angry self. And that helps me release some of the shame I felt about it.

ABBY

After I got my cancer diagnosis, I started to feel like everyone would've been fine if I just died very politely, just sort of quietly absented myself. But I love that moment in a television show or a novel where the character is just like "Screw it!" and flips the table and says all of the unscripted things. I was just so enraged. I was enraged about everything. Rage really helped me feel like I wasn't living in this world of precious moments with little delicate figurines and doilies. I was like: *You know what? We're going to be brutally honest regardless of whether or not it feels acceptable anymore.*

KATE BOWLER

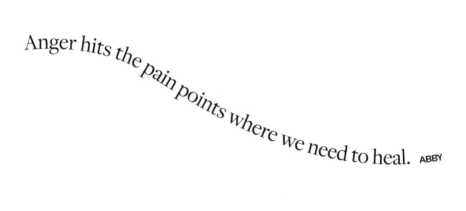

Anger hits the pain points where we need to heal. ABBY

Heat and anger are so wonderful because they move us into action. When we don't understand the source of the anger and aren't able to contextualize it, then we get into trouble and we might burn things down. But maybe things need to be burned down. When we can channel it and try to understand it, that's when we can really move people and inspire people to action.

CHANI NICHOLAS

Anger is telling me

I can use anger as the fuel
I need to make change.

Isn't it interesting that anger is what tells us what we need and that anger is so systematically shamed out of women?

If women start listening to anger as a signal pointing us toward what we need, and then we start demanding it and taking it, our culture would be rearranged.

That's why they teach us to be so afraid of our anger, because it's the ultimate change agent.

GLENNON

Resentment and anger
are your best friends,
because they sharply
point you to the places
where your freedom
is most constrained.

MARTHA

BECK

Seventeen

How do I forgive?

What the hell is forgiveness? I'm desperate to know what it really means. I ask everyone. I'll say to my waiter, "I'll have the burger, please, and also can you tell me what forgiveness means to you? Have you ever actually done it? What does it feel like in your body?"

Everybody's just throwing forgiveness around as if it's this magical prescription. But nobody can tell me what it really is or how to do it. What does it *mean*? How is it supposed to feel afterward? Does it mean saying to the other person, *Everything's okay now*? Because that's not gonna happen. Does forgiveness mean somehow not feeling angry or hurt anymore? I'd love to magically not feel hurt anymore—but *how*? People should quit telling us to forgive until they can also explain *how*.

GLENNON

After the infidelity in my first marriage, I desperately wanted to stop feeling so angry. I just wanted relief for both of us. I worked so hard to forgive, did the recommended therapy, date nights, conversations, exercises, retreats—and waited for forgiveness to arrive as a reward for all our efforts. We had some moments where I would look at us and think: *We're doing it. We're still a family.*

But I was a dormant volcano. Inwardly, I was still raging all the time. My anger would be triggered dramatically when there was any suggestion of physical intimacy. My body would just react— I'd cringe and withdraw.

The constant refrain in my head during these years was: *How could he do this to me? How could he do this to me? How could he do this to me?*

Then one morning I woke up and thought: *Wait, how can I do this to me?* How can I keep putting myself in this situation that my body is begging me to understand is not safe? He betrayed me, yes—but my biggest problem is that *I* keep betraying me. He can't change what he did. The only one who can change what's happening right now is me. I need to honor my instincts and establish self-respecting, protective boundaries for myself. I decided to divorce.

We got into an elevator together after our divorce mediation, and I looked at my ex and realized: *I feel soft toward him again.* Much of my rage was gone, because my rage was rage at me for not creating a boundary. That was *my* responsibility. After I'd created the protective boundary of divorce, I started feeling safe and relaxed enough to explore real forgiveness. Divorce was the kindest thing I could do. It is not kind to override your instincts, keep people close, and then rage at them forever. As Prentis Hemphill says, "Boundaries are the distance at which I can love both you and me simultaneously."

GLENNON

For me, forgiveness is giving up on the idea that it was going to be different. It's giving up on the version of my life where it was different, because it's not *ever* going to be different. It is this way, and the past is the past.

ASHLEY C. FORD

When I'm trying so hard to forgive, what I'm really trying to do is make it all make sense. I just want to make the way they treated me make sense so I can understand it. But that's not my job. Understanding the why of their behavior is the other person's job, not mine. I can move on even when—especially when—none of it makes sense.

GLENNON

To forgive

I don't squander my energy on the past.

—

CAMERON ESPOSITO: Forgiveness is an evolving thing for me. I don't think I've hit some finish line here. Because what is forgiveness? Is it *I send you on your way sweetly*? Or is it *You're wrong. Oh, well*? Maybe forgiveness is really just lightness?

GLENNON: Yes, lightness. It's putting something down. It's directional. Forgiveness is *I will no longer live backward toward you. I'm going to move onward.*

CAMERON: During the pandemic, I did a deep dive on forgiveness. I decided: *This is what I need to spend my energy on.* I came across a Buddhist teaching that says running away from something and running toward something is the same thing. So the need to leave and get the hell out—which is how I've felt a lot of my life—or the need to find the solution, which is the other half of how I've felt: It's all just panic. It's utter panic and a lack of acceptance. So I've been working on less running toward and away and more sitting still. Because that's not even a decision. It's accepting that maybe there is no decision to be made.

—

It's helpful when the person who hurt us is genuinely sorry, but forgiveness doesn't require their participation. We don't have to sign off on the same version of what happened. Forgiveness is an inside job. It's just deciding that, by letting somebody else off the hook, I'm really letting myself off the hook. I can just exhale, lay the whole thing down. It's too heavy to keep hoisting up and carrying around every day.

I'm responsible for me. That's it. I'm not responsible for what someone else does, says, thinks, or chooses. I am responsible for my words, my responses, what I decide to believe, what I hang on to, and what I release. That's mine. So it's not true that we're powerless. It's tempting to lean in to a victim model; it plays better. It's easy to be sympathetic toward a victim. It's easy to rally the troops to your side. It's neater. But this approach lacks nuance. Forgiveness is personal. It's mine. It's entirely mine to sort out.

If we don't choose forgiveness, it truncates any further work we're going to do on ourselves. The longer I carry the story—which is: *This is your fault, you have harmed me, and I am pissed*—the longer it prevents me from genuinely and honestly facing my own stuff. I can't do both. It's either all your fault, or I get to also face my responses and patterns. The question is: *Am I ready to move into the work that's going to be required of my own heart and soul?* Forgiveness is the path to that moment.

JEN HATMAKER

To forgive

I know that forgiveness is between me and me.

There's a minute where unforgiveness is my choice and I *want* to choose it. It feels good. It's keeping my adrenaline active. It's keeping me vigilant when I am thinking: *Oh, this lack of vigilance, look where it got you.* And for a minute, that feels self-protective. But unforgiveness is a cousin to resentment, bitterness, and fury. After a minute, it's corrosive to my insides.

JEN HATMAKER

Forgiveness is between me and me. When I forgive, it's not to set the other person free; it's to set *myself* free. Forgiveness is not accepting what they did; it's accepting that they did it. They are responsible for what they did, but I am responsible for the power I give them because of what they did. Instead of saying, "They did this terrible thing to me, so now my life is this way"—which cedes control to them over the course of my life—I can decide to take back responsibility for my life and my future. I can say, "Yes, this happened. And I will decide what happens next."

AMANDA

The way I understand it, forgiveness is releasing a connection between you and someone else.

In my divorce, this person went from being the center of my world to being completely gone. You feel that absence viscerally. And when you can't be connected in love, it can feel like it's better to be connected in any other way than to not be connected at all. Passionate contempt is the second best thing to passionate love. The absolute worst thing is indifference.

That you would have to accept nothingness where everything used to be feels insulting to your soul. At least when you are angry and aggrieved, you're still able to channel the intensity of your emotions toward them—you are still able to have a semblance of connection to them and power over them. There is still *something* between you.

Harboring unforgiveness is the shitty consolation prize to real connection. Forgiveness is releasing the need to have anything left between you.

AMANDA

To forgive

I'm willing to let go of connection.

Forgiveness
is not always
about getting
closer to
another person.

Sometimes
we forgive
in order to
let go.

DR. GALIT ATLAS

How to Apologize

WITH RABBI DANYA RUTTENBERG

In Judaism, we use the word *teshuvah* to talk about repentance, which means "return." It's about coming back to the best version of you, your integrity; it's about coming back to the path that you wanted to be on before you started screwing up and harming out of ignorance, pettiness, laziness, sloppiness—out of all the reasons we hurt people. Do you want to be a harm doer? Probably not. So we need to do work to change that.

① Accept the harm of your action.

RABBI RUTTENBERG: The first step is confession. Own your stuff. We all have a story of ourself as the hero. We have to face the fact that: *Today I caused someone else pain, I was not the good guy in someone else's story, and I have some cleanup work to do.* You have to acknowledge that fact without talking about what you *intended* and what you *meant.* A hurt person doesn't care what your intentions were. Just own what you did.

GLENNON: At this point, the victim is probably gaslighting themself with: *Did that really happen? Are my feelings valid?* The harm doer is giving relief by saying, "Yes, it was real. Yes, I did this." If the harm happened publicly, the ownership taking needs to be done publicly, because the harm was done to more than just the person who was directly offended.

RABBI RUTTENBERG: It has to be at least as public as the harm that was caused, and it is praiseworthy to make it even more public than the harm. It's not a name-and-shame thing. It's asking for accountability. It's saying, "I was not my best self, and I need help getting back on that path of where I want to be."

AMANDA: And the first reconciliation has to be within *you,* or else you're never going to be able to offer the truth of a confession to someone else.

RABBI RUTTENBERG: Yes. For example, in our society, people think: *I'm not racist, so the thing I said can't possibly be racist.* As opposed to: *We are all human beings, and some of our actions are helpful and some of them are harmful.* It's not an indictment of your whole self.

To forgive

I take steps to make it right.

(2) Prevent yourself from doing it again. Change.

RABBI RUTTENBERG: What are you going to do so that you don't keep doing the thing that caused harm? You have to change—but change looks different for everyone. What is at the root of the behavior? Do you need therapy? Do you need to call your sponsor or get into a rehab situation? Do you need to separate from a group of friends because you always behave horrendously when you're with them? Do you need to do some deep education on antiracism or trans liberation? Are there places of ignorance that you need to be working on? What is the thing that needs to happen so that you can start to become different?

(3) Make restitution. Make it right.

RABBI RUTTENBERG: Steps one and two are really victim-centric. You're ending the gaslighting, you are preventing future victims, and then, in step three, there's restitution. What is owed to the person who was harmed? You can't undo what you did. But it's like the Japanese art of *kintsugi*, where you repair broken pottery with gold so you can still see the cracks. It's not unbroken, but repair has happened. Do you owe them money? Are you going to give time, resources, connections? You find out what people need by asking them. Because if you decide *for* them what appropriate amends are, you're not centering their personhood and their needs; you're making them an object. So you have to ask them, and then you have to accept the consequences.

(4) Apologize.

GLENNON: So next, after we've accepted consequences, no matter how sensitive or fragile the other person was, comes the apology. By now the transformation has already happened. You are already someone else. You understand what you did, and you're genuinely sorry.

RABBI RUTTENBERG: Right. It's not about getting off the hook and out of the work of repair. Do the work first. We don't want your words until you've already done the fixing. Then we can have the conversation from a more openhearted place.

(5) Make different choices next time.

RABBI RUTTENBERG: There will always be a next time, with this person or someone else, and if you don't get to the root of the issue—if you don't work the steps to change *you*—you will not make different choices. But if you do steps one through four sincerely, meaningfully, with humility and care, five will happen on its own, naturally and organically. Because you have become transformed through the process of repair, and the different you will make different choices.

The Right Way to Be Wrong

WITH RABBI DANYA RUTTENBERG

You can hurt someone and say, "I'm sorry, I didn't mean to." But more than not having *meant* to, one of the most important things in reparation is the ability to recognize the harm done and understand where the other person is coming from. This process has more than one stage.

The *intellectual* part must recognize: *I understand that you're a different person than me who has a separate experience from my own. I see now that it doesn't matter what I intended; it matters how I impacted you.*

The *emotional* part must acknowledge both: *I understand that I hurt you* and then also look inward and start the work of inner change.

Repair comes from tolerating our own imperfection, from letting go of: *But I'm a good person. I did it because of X reason.* It necessitates getting to a place of: *I did something to you, and you are hurt.*

To forgive

I let go of my need to always be the good guy.

—

GLENNON: The quickest way I know to lose my mind is to try to control other folks' narratives about me. We think of our lives as stories, and we always want to be the good guy in our own story and in other people's story. But there are plenty of times in my life where I was, for sure, the bad guy. I think it's okay to accept that. It's okay to let go of the idea that you are going to turn yourself from a bad guy into a good guy because of the way you justify or apologize or even repair. Sometimes you can do that and you still have to let yourself have been the bad guy in someone's story.

AMANDA: Or, at the very least, you cannot make the person you harmed call you the good guy! It often seems as if "I'm so sorry, can you forgive me?" is shorthand for "Can we agree to pretend like that thing I did never happened?" Which means the person who was harmed has to accept what happened to them—but the harm doer gets to pretend like it never happened. A lot of offers of apology are actually requests for forgiveness, which is no good.

What if we started calling them acknowledgments instead of apologies? Acknowledgments don't require something of the person who was harmed. There is something beautiful in expressing "It's been a lot of years since this happened, and I just want to say . . . I didn't act right." With that kind of acknowledgment, we honor the person in a way we failed to honor them before—without asking them to do anything for us or to absolve us of that.

—

I try to be very forgiving
and kind to myself about
my mistakes. I just don't
know how any real change
happens without pain and
struggle and even some
regret about things you
wish you had done
differently.

CHLOÉ COOPER JONES

To forgive I let go of my need to always be the good guy.

We are so hard on ourselves. You beat yourself up like: *I should have known better. I've seen it before, I should have seen it again.* I constantly have to forgive myself for sometimes making the wrong call for me. It's so much easier to forgive other people. If my daughter makes a mistake, I'm like "Oh, hon. It's fine. It was bad for the moment. You're still an amazing person." I encourage her that she can make mistakes and that she can turn around and do better. Yet for me, I could spend months trying to forgive myself.

I'm learning that how fast I forgive myself for making the wrong decision will determine how quickly I'm able to get out and correct it.

BOZOMA SAINT JOHN

I got to something that is a little texturally different from forgiveness: acceptance. That happened, period. It happened.

I learned from it. Everything is a teacher if you let it be—if you keep your antennae up. I'm not going to pass up the opportunity to gain something from it.

MAGGIE SMITH

Eighteen

How do I get unstuck?

Have you ever noticed that—whether it's silliness with your kid, an unexpected tender exchange with a stranger, an eye-watering belly laugh with a friend— certain moments hum inside of you at a different vibration than all the others? Is it because those moments make us feel human? Is it because these moments make up what it is to be human?

Do the specific types of moments that make each of us hum show us the specific kind of human we are? Is that why we feel most like ourselves when we are humming at our own particular vibration? Could that be a clue to help us know when we're stuck—when our specific hum is gone? Are the moments of connection that make us hum exactly what we need to get unstuck?

AMANDA

We get stuck a hundred times a day, don't we? Stuckness is that moment when you catch yourself thinking something, saying something, doing something that feels familiar but just isn't quite the thing you want to be thinking, saying, or doing. You suddenly feel like you're not in alignment, like you're living on some kind of old autopilot, like you're not in your free will somehow. Maybe you finally lie down to rest but you still have this nagging shame about it, so you can't enjoy the rest. Or you're in a conflict with your partner and you hear yourself say the same old tired things to protect yourself. Or you watch yourself pick up the phone and start scrolling again even though you *know* that's going to make you feel worse.

In order to actually break these patterns, we need to change our underlying beliefs. What we learn as we're growing up becomes our software. When we catch ourselves doing something that doesn't align with our current values, it's because there's an old code in our software that we haven't done the work to update yet.

When I try to change my behaviors without simultaneously investigating the beliefs beneath them, my life becomes all about willpower and discipline because my actions are at war with my beliefs. Being in a civil war with myself never lasts. White-knuckling is always short-lived because I can only act against my programming for so long. The goal is to get out of the war and back into alignment—which is peace.

The tricky thing about changing your programming is this: You can't change your actions without changing your beliefs—but you can't change your beliefs without changing your actions.

It's like: *I'm stuck, I've caught myself ghosting this person I had a conflict with—and I don't want to be doing that anymore. I'm going to start considering that maybe I don't have to ghost people; instead I can speak my mind and listen, and that won't kill me. I'm going to pretend like I believe that, and I'm going to call this person back now.*

We have to live *as if* in order to get our actions to change, and we have to change our actions to believe the *as if.* We have to do it all at the same time.

GLENNON

When my marriage to my ex-husband was crumbling, I was deeply shaken and so afraid because I had no idea what to do. One day, feeling desperate, I went to a yoga class. I sat down in the room, and the yoga teacher walked in. She asked us all to go around and name our intention for the class. I said, "My intention is just to make it through whatever's about to happen here for the next hour without picking up my mat and running out the door."

The yoga instructor looked at me like I had said something revolutionary. Then she said, "Okay, just sit there and stay on your mat." So I sat there without moving for fifty minutes. This was my first experience of deep, deep stillness. I'd been running so fast to stay distracted from the truth of things.

While I was sitting there, I just let it all come up. Every single fear, every single bit of shame, all my anger, all my memories—they all started popping up one at a time like a twisted game of Whac-A-Mole, where you have no mallet and you're certain that all the moles are out to kill you. It really felt like if I kept letting the memories come up, if I let the pain really arise, I would die.

But I stayed on my mat, and I didn't run out. And I didn't die. Sitting in that deep stillness and refusing to run out the door didn't free me from pain, but it freed me from being terrified of pain. I don't have to be afraid of pain anymore. I can allow it all to come up, and I can stay with myself.

The truth of my thirties was:

Stay on your mat, Glennon. Staying is making you.

GLENNON

To get unstuck

I get still and I get moving.

My friend Ashley took her first hot yoga class. She walked into the room, unrolled her mat, sat down, and waited for something to happen. "It was exceptionally hot in there," she told me. When the instructor, young and confident, finally walked into the room, Ashley was already dripping with sweat. The instructor announced, "We'll start soon. You are going to get very hot, but you can't leave this room. No matter how uncomfortable you feel, stay strong. Don't leave. This is the work."

The class got started, and a few minutes in, the walls began to close in on Ashley. She felt lightheaded and sick. Each breath became harder and harder to come by. Twice her vision became spotty; then briefly went black. She looked at the door and felt desperate to run toward it. She spent ninety minutes terrified, close to hyperventilating, holding back tears. But she did not leave that room.

The moment the instructor ended the class and opened the door, Ashley jumped off her mat and ran into the hallway. She kept her hand over her mouth until she found the bathroom. She threw the door open and vomited all over the sink, the wall, the floor. While she was on her hands and knees wiping up her own puke with paper towels, she thought: *What is wrong with me? Why did I stay and suffer? The door wasn't even locked.*

The truth of my forties is:

I'm made. When my body tells me the truth, I'll believe it. I trust myself now, so I will no longer suffer voluntarily or silently or for long. I will not stay, not ever again, in a room or conversation or relationship or institution that requires me to abandon myself.

GLENNON

You can't heal without being still for a minute. I know, it's terrifying. But there's no other way. We can skate across the top of life forever, and most people do, because the consequences aren't that dire or, as with workaholism, they're actually applauded. But I've never met an individual who didn't know that somewhere inside was this little voice giving small, one-word instructions, like: *Stop. No. Yes. Do.* Your soul speaks in very simple statements. You have to be in your body and still for enough time to hear it. It's about getting some kind of quiet. It can be sitting on the subway and putting headphones in and asking: *How do I feel? What do I want?*

LAURA MCKOWEN

The more I practice coming close to my fear and sitting alongside it, the easier it is to do, the less resistant I am, the less I'm trying to do smoke and mirrors on myself and pretend like the fear isn't there. Ten years ago, I would've never asked my wife to hold me while I shook. I would've been like: *That's not who I am. That's weird and kind of weak.* But now I know myself enough and understand my body enough, and I can figure out: What I'm feeling is fear. This tightening and tensing up in my body is because I want to tremble and I don't think I can. So what if I allow myself? Then the fear can be positioned in the right place. If I tense up around it, the less informative it is for me and the more it controls what I do. But if it can drop into my belly, it can become information.

PRENTIS HEMPHILL

Stillness is not about doing nothing. Stillness is the precursor to everything. Stillness is where you gather both the wisdom to know what hard thing you must do and the energy to do it. Stillness is where you stop and collect the potential energy that will become the kinetic energy needed to make change in your life.

GLENNON

Walking has shown me who I am, that I don't have to know where I'm going—and how to put motion to emotion. So when I'm pissed, I go for a walk. When I'm happy, I go for a walk. When I'm walking, I often imagine I'm rocking myself, lulling myself. Walking is the promise to myself to move my body every day. And I deserve to keep the promises I make to myself.

ALEX ELLE

It's hard to know what kind of dread to avoid and what kind of dread to go toward. There's necessary dread that arises when I really don't want to do something but I know I have to do it in order to live my life in integrity. For necessary dread, my strategy is: *Worst Thing, First Thing.* If I have a hard, important thing that I know I have to do—write the important email, make the scary phone call, finish the work project—I tend to put that thing off. But when I put off the hard thing, I spend all my time between waking up and finally doing the hard thing in anticipatory misery. Instead, if I wake up and do the worst thing first thing, I suffer less, simply because I've shortened the dread time. It's just a bit of dread, then the thing is done, then the rest of the day I feel lighter, happier, freer.

GLENNON

> We ask people to be superhuman.
> But do we actually want to be
> superhuman? That sounds like you
> wouldn't be a person anymore.

CELESTE NG

—

GLENNON: It's important to note that it's not pain-free to stop doing the things that your family, community, or culture rewards you for doing. For example, if you're stepping off the wheel of hustle, productivity, visibility, relevance—all these things that we pursue mindlessly if we don't check in with ourselves— we have to withstand the inevitable FOMO. My energy is forever vacillating back and forth between *Please leave me alone!* and *Wait, I feel left out.*

DEVON PRICE: For me, the big decision when I hit burnout was the decision to leave any hope of being a tenure-track professor. But ultimately it didn't feel like a loss. Deciding that I was going to disappoint all of my faculty mentors and have to invent my own path was scary. But it was also necessary. I've talked to many people for whom the decision has been costlier. I know a lot of disabled people who have decided, "Okay, I'm going to just live on disability, $14,000 a year. I'm going to have to live with a relative, but then I'll be present to help raise my niece and nephew. I'll be able to volunteer and make art. I'm never going to have any money or financial independence, but I'll be woven into this interdependent community." People have to make all kinds of sacrifices to break out of this hamster wheel. But if we just get some time to rest and listen to what we are actually called to do, then we get rewarded with so much more connection and authenticity, and it's ultimately worth it.

—

To get unstuck

I stop trying to win a losing game.

Somewhere along the line, I started playing an unwinnable game: I internalized a zero-sum myth that if I dare try to make things better for myself, it will mean making things worse for my people. The loop in my head says that if I am not at a breaking point, then I'm not doing enough, and my work or my family will suffer, and I will lose what I have. Intellectually, I know this is not right, but I'm trying to convince the rest of me. So now I'm asking myself questions like: *Is this working for me? Are my people benefiting from my insistence that this is true? Is it possible that something else is true that will feel more like freedom? Is it possible that my life and my family and my work would benefit from me not being empty? And also, is it possible that I'm worthy of being full of life even if no one else benefits from it?*

AMANDA

I don't buy the idea of always showing up and giving 100 percent. No, thanks. I just want to show up sometimes and then do exactly what feels good and right and tender and loving to me. I don't want to work hard and then play hard; I just want to work medium and then rest. My therapist used to make me repeat "Just because I *can* do something does not mean I *should* do it." It's okay to say no, even if what you're saying no to is something everybody else on earth might want desperately.

GLENNON

I just recently realized that I can focus on making sure I'm happy with my life, or I can focus on trying to make other people happy with my life, but I can't do both.

AMANDA

Dump Truck is my chinchilla.

He is a really great role model for me, because he's never been productive a day in his life. In fact, he's very destructive. He's torn up floorboards, he's wrecked a lot of things. He's not a value-generating force. But I would never judge his life on those terms. Every single day, when I turn around and I see him eating his hay, I think: *Oh, my God, it's so beautiful. He's eating.* Him just being alive is this most exquisitely beautiful, pure thing in the world.

When he's sleeping, I'm in love with him when he's sleeping. When he's just sitting there, staring into space, it's the most beautiful, weird little thing in the world. I think animals can do that for us. Animals can really remind us that we can just be alive, and that's beautiful. If him eating is the most beautiful thing I've seen in the world, maybe there are people who feel that way about me just existing. And maybe I can feel that way about other people. ⌒

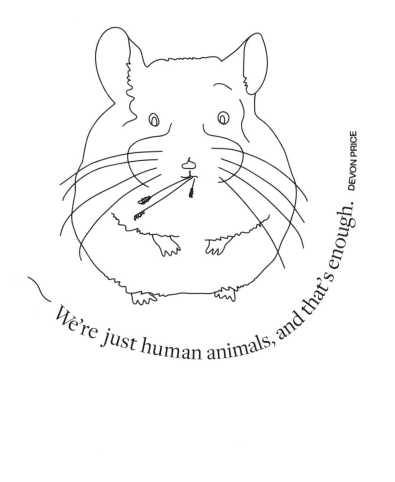

We're just human animals, and that's enough. DEVON PRICE

> When you feel you need more grit, what you need is more help. When you feel you need more discipline, what you need is more kindness.

EMILY NAGOSKI

—

ABBY: One of the best things that I read recently was when someone was asked, "What is your favorite thing you're up to these days?" And they said, "Divesting." That is awesome. We think we need to *invest*—in our work, in our future, in our goals, to create and grow and whatever—but I think we need to make the transition to divesting.

AMANDA: Yes! Extricating yourself from the things that aren't the core of what you care about.

GLENNON: And looking at the things everyone tells us we have to be doing and asking: *Do I?*

—

One of my teachers, Richard Strozzi-Heckler, says, "A relaxed body is the most powerful body that we have." I know it feels counterintuitive, because there's so much to fear and so much that we are facing. But being relaxed doesn't mean I'm not afraid. It means I have a place in me and I have a practice that I do that gives room for that fear. It allows me to recognize what else is inside me, what else I'm made of, what else I long for. And that's what compels me forward. That's what causes me to move.

PRENTIS HEMPHILL

To get unstuck

I do less instead of more.

When a perceived obligation is making me miserable, I like to step back and look harder to make sure it's really an obligation at all. It often isn't. For example, the entire texting system used to stress me out completely. I felt obligated to respond to everyone who texted, so I'd spend all day in reaction mode, just waiting to see who wanted me/needed me/demanded my attention and then dropping whatever I was doing to give it to them. I lost all creativity and peace and intentionality in my life. I always felt jumpy and guilty. Then one day I was like: *Wait a second. Twenty years ago, nobody lived this way, and I don't remember ever agreeing to this way of life. I actually don't have to live this way. I never signed a texting contract vowing to owe my attention to everyone who demanded it at any time.* So I just stopped. Now when someone new texts me, I am careful to say, "I don't use my phone in the way many others do. If we want to communicate, we'll have to negotiate a different way that works for both of us."

GLENNON

There's a saying, "You don't have to attend every argument you're invited to." I've been thinking about how, when I react to every single thing that bothers me, it's exactly like my accepting nonstop assignments from strangers. All day, every day. Which, when you think about it, is an insane way to live. Instead of automatically accepting those assignments, I'd prefer to decide what my own agenda will be. I want to lead my life instead of reacting to it. This is what I'm practicing: When something bothers me, instead of asking: *What should I do about this?* I'm trying to ask: *What part of me is disturbed by this?* So if music is playing too loud, I don't jump to: *What am I going to say to get them to turn it down?* I ask: *What part of me finds this loud music bothersome?* Is it the part of me that's frustrated/jealous that this person doesn't have the courtesy/anxiety I would have if I played loud music in public? Is it the part of me that's nervous because I know this would have been a big problem in my family growing up? Is it the part of me that's trying to control everything around me? Because if any of those is true, then there's actually nothing for me to *do*. I can remind myself that strangers are not the bosses of me, and I don't need to accept this assignment from the world. I don't need to make this situation different. I can just allow it to be. I can take a deep breath of relief and do nothing other than take care of myself.

AMANDA

Once we start realizing: *Okay, I cannot do all those things,* the next step is saying: *And that's okay because I'm not alone in this. I am part of a team.* I have a partner who can pitch in when I am stretched thin. Or I have friends who can support me. Or the teacher at school will make sure my kid does not go hungry even though I forgot to put his lunch in his backpack. It's a way of realizing: *I'm not alone. I am in a community.* Strength does not have to come on an individual basis; it can come as a collective. We can help lift some of the burden off each individual person's shoulders. The world won't end because I can't do it all myself.

CELESTE NG

I'm starting to be able to own my part of a situation. Recently, one morning when I had a thousand things going on, all of which needed to be done in a very compressed period of time, I said to John, "I'm going to be very anxious today. I have to be incredibly efficient, so I want you to know that while you're talking to me, I'm going to be listening to you but walking around doing things." A year ago, I wouldn't have said anything, but the tension would have been obvious, so he'd probably have thought: *She's pissed at me for some unknown reason, and the last thing that I'm going to do is ask her about it. She probably doesn't even know anyway.* Now I'm at the point where I can acknowledge, "This isn't about you, this is about me being really anxious," which gets us to a place where he can offer help and I can actually accept it—which also would not have happened a year ago.

AMANDA

To get unstuck

I do my part and let others do theirs.

If you are struggling to have a conversation with your partner about dividing the mental load, you can start by saying, "This is not just happening to us. This is happening to millions of households across the world. I'm aware of it, and I think it's hurting both of us. So let's talk about the frustration I feel, the frustration you feel, and then let's together think of some ways that we can fix it for us. Maybe you do laundry, you do cooking, I'll do elementary school correspondence and soccer, so that there's something on each of our plates."

And on a deeper level, you can talk to your partner about what you each think makes a "successful" mom. Is that different from a "successful" dad? Can you agree on what a good parent is? And then can you split that stuff up?

DR. KATE MANGINO

A couple of years ago, I was feeling really stuck and was doomscrolling a lot. I noticed that when I was spending time with my daughter, I wasn't present. All of the bad things that could happen to us were invading our time together, so I was missing her. I was missing our connection. So I set constraints like: I won't be consuming this media after this time, or not in the room with her, and also constraints around *what* I was consuming. Now I try to consume deeper, more thoughtful things by people who know what they're talking about, instead of consuming a bunch of comments by people who are in the same kind of terror that I'm in. I had to reorganize everything so that I could get information that I needed but also keep the constraints that would allow me to be in relationship with my people, with my daughter.

PRENTIS HEMPHILL

I do a values exercise with my students where I have them come in and they write a big list of the things they value. They circle all these virtues like "a spirit of adventure" and "learning." And then we do a new exercise where they just write down how they spend a typical day. Then we review and notice how the two match up. Often they have this moment where they realize: *Oh, I'm not putting my time into the things that really matter to me.* It's an important exercise we can all do. What can we do to restructure our lives?

DR. LAURIE SANTOS

To get unstuck

I spend my days the way I want to spend my life.

When I spend time having small moments of connection, it can seem frivolous because it was not on my to-do list. But I've realized it's actually the most productive thing I can do, because it makes me feel more human. Not just human, but a very specific type of human who is most myself when I am *acting like myself.* And doing that is at least as important as getting things done.

AMANDA

I signed up for a narrative illustration class, which is basically comic making. I would take my little Prius over there at night and make comics in this class of seven people, and we would translate what happened in our days into these daily drawings. I'd just go to this comic book class and sit down and be like: *What comes to mind first?* What comes to mind is that my dog peed all over my floor this morning. So I'd spend the evening coloring pee in with highlighter. And that would put me back inside my day, which taught me to notice things that were happening in my present life and to pay attention to the fact that life was moving forward. Because when you're in your past, you feel like you are stuck. You have to know that life is in motion and that it's impossible to get stuck, even if you feel that you are.

CHANEL MILLER

If that idea is true that the definition of insanity is doing the same thing over and over and expecting different results, then sanity must be trying new things and being open to new results. So when I'm stuck—when I feel a certain way and I want to feel a new way—I try something completely new.

When I felt alone and isolated as a young mom, I started telling my truth in writing. It was scary, but people started reading and saying, "Me, too," and the result was: connection. I felt less trapped. New action, new feeling.

When I started feeling dead inside, like a hustling capitalist robot, I tried something completely unproductive: painting. The act of that woke up the sparkly magical artist in me, and I started feeling free and alive again. New action, new feeling.

Sometimes when I'm in conflict with Abby, I feel myself shut down into roly-poly protective mode and I feel so alone, as always. When I get desperate enough for a new feeling, I try staying open. I tell Abby I feel confused and scared, which is so difficult because it's counterintuitive to my old programming. But then a new thing happens—some old spell is broken, and she softens and reaches out. I suddenly feel unalone. ⌒

I try something new to feel something new.

GLENNON

When you think, "Why am I doing this thing that I don't want to do?" or "I keep doing this thing, and it's not aligned with who I am," that's how you know it's an old pattern that you're finally ready to be free from.

Old patterns come up when we're disembodied. The only things we can do when we're disembodied are things that we've done a million times. Changing our patterns is only possible when we are embodied— when we stay in our bodies through discomfort. Like with my disordered eating patterns, there's always a moment before I'm in the bathroom throwing up when I feel uncomfortable.

When I feel uncomfortable, I have a choice: I can either stay in my body and deal with that discomfort in a new way, or I can leave myself by dissociating, by abandoning myself. When I dissociate, I come to and I'm in the destructive behaviors again, or I'm saying those old hurtful things I pull out in conflict, or I'm overworking again.

So what if, instead of leaving my body during those moments, I love myself through them? What if I pay attention, feel the fear and discomfort, and still refuse to abandon myself? What if I use all of my energy to take care of myself? What if I say to me, *This is hard. What do I need to get through it? How do I take tender care of myself right now?*

If you learn to stay with you, over time you realize that your discomfort is the greatest gift, because it points you toward all the tender, hurt places you need to heal—and you heal them. Yourself. And that's how you learn to trust yourself. You become a person who will never leave you. You become a person who will love yourself through it all. *You* become your person.

GLENNON

Nineteen

How do I feel better right now?

I spend most of my day trying to feel better. And somehow I rely most heavily on things that make me feel worse. It used to be booze, and now it's junk food and junk TV and doomscrolling. Why do I do things that make me feel worse when I actually want to feel better? I confuse myself.

ABBY

When I'm in an anxiety spiral,
I know I've accidentally time
traveled again. My anxiety is usually
the result of my mind launching
me into a scary imaginary future.
So the antidote is to return to now,
where I'm usually safe and okay.

Here's a common exercise that helps me: Grab something, an object close to you. Notice how it feels in your hands. Next, notice something you can see. Now what's something you can hear? Are there any smells that you notice?

I return myself to the present moment by deactivating my imagination and activating my senses instead. It works every time.

GLENNON

Wherever you are, see if you can get into a relaxed physical position and, as you breathe in, think: *I can allow everything in the universe to be the way it is right now. I'm okay breathing in.* Now, as you breathe out, think: *I'm going to let go of my resistance to reality.*

You breathe in, and you allow things to be as they are right now; you breathe out, and you stop resisting. You breathe in and you breathe out, and you surrender and allow and surrender and allow. And then this moment becomes the haven that is okay—just this moment. You'll find that moment is always there. It's always there.

MARTHA BECK

Peace is a practice of breathing deep. I mean that in the most literal sense.

MORGAN HARPER NICHOLS

To feel better right now
I take a deep breath.

I have an extra nervous nervous system, so I have learned strategies that calm it. Concentrating on my breathing is a good one. There's one breathing exercise I learned a long time ago that helps get me out of fight or flight. It's called box breathing. I breathe in deeply for five seconds as I envision drawing the top of a box. Then I hold the breath for five seconds and envision drawing down the right side of the box. Then I exhale for five more seconds as I turn the bottom corner and draw the bottom. Last, I hold for five seconds and finish the box. I repeat this until I feel calm again.

GLENNON

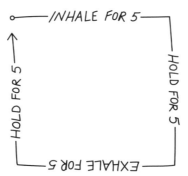

I just learned that I've been breathing wrong for four decades. This was a surprise to me. When you breathe, you are supposed to inhale through your nose and your stomach goes out—because you are expanding your diaphragm, you are letting the air into your lungs. Then when you exhale, your stomach comes in, and if you give it a little extra pinch in, like you are contracting your belly, it expels the bad stuff out of there. Which is a good way to think about breathing: getting rid of the toxic stuff and filling up with the life-giving stuff.

AMANDA

The magic pause is when I remember who I am so I can respond from my truest self instead of my nervous system and conditioning. For me, the difference between war and peace is usually about thirty seconds. If, before reacting, I can pause and allow some space, intentionality, wisdom, and creativity in, I can almost always respond in a way that works better for everybody involved. The magic pause is not just about being kinder; it's also about being more effective.

GLENNON

It is work to learn how to identify shame and how it feels in our bodies—what it actually does to me physically, where my thoughts start going when I'm in a shame spiral. I'm learning to grab that by the tail and say: *Oh, this is instruction. My body is instructing me right now that I am getting pushed into a shame space. Let's take a beat and talk about what's true here.* Shame is always constructed on something that's not true, some sort of lie, whether it's fear based or reality based or both. Something in here is not true, and it's not going to serve me. So let me take a deep breath. Let me go put my feet in the grass. Let me drink some water. And let me pause before I start to respond out of this space and regret it tomorrow morning.

JEN HATMAKER

To feel better right now

I pause.

A lot of times when I'm scrolling, I get that triggered feeling; I suddenly feel my anxiety rise. I'm so trained to just push it down and move on. But when that feeling grabs me, I'm learning that the better practice is to ask my body what it's feeling. Is it fear? Rage? Frustration? Let yourself have the emotion deeply. It lasts forty-five seconds and moves on. Then you can go back to what you were looking at from a more neutral, centered place.

JESSICA YELLIN

Whenever I'm losing it, my friends ask me, "Have you run around the block yet?" I'm forever trying to get better at metaphorically running around the block, which means instead of lurching to action, I try to remember that if I could take a minute, I am less likely to really step in it and more likely to handle things better. After a conflict, people who know me really well will ask, "Did you run around the block?" And I'm like "I did not." Then sometimes if I *do* run around the block, I'm literally like "Guys! I ran the block!" And it's progress . . . until I don't run around the block again.

MELISSA MCCARTHY

I do a body scan.

When I'm doing something that's unpleasant, I do a body scan. For example, if I'm running I'll ask: *Okay, what does my toe feel like?* I'll scan each part of my body, and just that simple shift of awareness away from whatever part of my body is really hurting stops the hurt. It's like a magic trick.

CHRISTEN PRESS

I touch my heart.

The quickest way I return to myself is to put my hand over my heart. Every time I do that, I remember I am a precious being who deserves love and peace.

GLENNON

I feel my feet on the ground.

I put both feet uncrossed on the ground and notice how my feet, toes, and heels feel against the floor, focusing on each point of connection as I press down. This jostles me out of being trapped in the past or caught in the anxiety of the future and grounds me in where my feet are in *this* moment. For me, the past and the future are the dangerous places, but most often, right here, right now is actually safe—as long as I can figure out how to actually *be* here.

AMANDA

I hold a hot cup of tea.

One of my strategies to stay embodied and out of my spinning mind is to carry around a cup of hot tea. When I feel the heat of the tea in the mug, my attention travels from my spinning mind to my hands and I'm back in my body. I'm feeling something. I feel the heat. I exist.

GLENNON

To feel better right now

I return to my senses.

I notice a different kind of time.

The warblers have just shown up, which means that there are birds that I'm seeing that I haven't seen since spring. I'll be in a really big hurry, carrying all these bags, super stressed out, and I'll see this bird in a tree and forget about calendar time for a little bit.

JENNY ODELL

I play the vibe.

When the kids were little, I wanted everything to be playful and cozy and fun, but I was often a smidge miserable and tired and cranky. One day, I turned on some kids' music, and suddenly my house felt so peaceful and vibey. I learned you can use music to just play the vibe you want to be. If you want peace, turn on peaceful music. If you need energy, turn on energetic music.

GLENNON

I show myself that I'm okay.

Sometimes at the end of the night when I'm putting one of my kids to bed, my head won't stop swirling with the forty-seven things I still have to do, and my anxiety and my heartbeat start sprinting. To pull myself out of that, I touch my heart and notice, and actually say to myself: *I am here. I am okay.* I touch my child and say: *My kid is here. My kid is okay.* I touch my dog lying beside us: *My dog is here. My dog is okay.* As I notice that everything I can see and touch is actually okay, I realize that my mind and nervous system are just confused, and I can reassure them of the good news that we are, in fact, okay.

AMANDA

When I was in crisis over my divorce, Brené Brown called, and she said, "You need to take absolute radical care of your body. This is your number one priority. I know you don't think this. But this is it. You're only going to eat good food. You are going to drink this much water a day. You're not going to drink alcohol. You are going to start moving your body every single day. You are going to figure out a way to sleep at night. So if that means you've got to go to your doctor and get help sleeping, whatever it means, you are going to give your body sleep, and you're going to meditate. We're not talking about how to rebuild your finances yet. We're not talking about how to make a new power of attorney. We're talking about breathing and drinking water."

I credit her intervention in my life with giving me some first steps to hang on to and to just survive the tsunami, to find a way to stay on the surface and stabilize my body a little bit—because our body tells us what's going on.

JEN HATMAKER

To feel better right now

I care for my body.

Our bodies are designed to interpret touch as a signal of care. So if your brain is in fight-or-flight mode, drop out of your brain and into your body. Where do you feel pain? Notice: *Oh, I feel it as tension in my throat.* Now put your hands there or just hold yourself and be with that pain in a caring way. Studies have shown that doing this for even twenty seconds a day increases self-compassion and actually changes your physiology. You're reducing cortisol levels. And once our bodies are calmer, it's easier for our heads to follow.

DR. KRISTIN NEFF

Every time I get a massage, it's not just a spa appointment. Healthy, loving, sane touch puts me back in my body. I have been so against my body so much of my life, and massage work is part of my amends to my body to say: *I'm just going to let you be loved and cared for.*

KERRY WASHINGTON

Moving your body makes a huge difference for your well-being. If you look at the countries that are ticking off high on happiness, they are countries that just naturally culturally prioritize that stuff. Like in Denmark, people walk to work, they're moving their bodies, they're out, they're present.

DR. LAURIE SANTOS

DR. KRISTIN NEFF: I was on a transatlantic flight with my son, who is autistic and has sensory issues. They turned the lights off, and my son went into a full-on flailing screaming tantrum on the plane. I started to worry that the people around me were thinking: *We're used to screaming two-year-olds. He's five. He shouldn't be acting like this. What's wrong with that mother? Why can't she control her kid?*

I didn't know what to do. So I decided to take him to the toilets and let him have his tantrum in there. I took him kicking and screaming, flailing down that little aisle, "Excuse me, excuse me, coming through," to the toilet, which, of course, was occupied.

We got down on the floor because I couldn't hold him. I made sure he was safe, and then I flooded myself with compassion. I just sat there and I put my hands on my heart and I started rocking myself and saying to myself: *I'm so sorry, Kristin, this is so hard. I'm here for you. It's going to be okay. I love you.* I just flooded myself with warmth and care and support. I was really there for myself in that moment. And then, instead of my awareness being totally consumed with his tantrum in this horrible situation, my awareness was flooded with the love and the kindness.

The problem was still there, but it wasn't overwhelming me. And my son was very attuned to me in that moment, and he actually started to calm down. I couldn't reach him directly, but when I could calm down and I got filled with this loving presence, he calmed down, too. What we cultivate inside is not only a gift to ourselves, it's a gift to everyone we come in contact with.

GLENNON: Sometimes we can't give those we love peace, but we can give it to ourselves, and hope it spreads.

—

To feel better right now

I am gentle with myself.

> I want to be good at everything: I want to be the best soccer player I can be, the best activist, the best mom, the best sister, the best daughter. But it's not possible to do everything. And in order to give my daughter everything, I need to give myself more time and more grace.
>
> **ALI KRIEGER**

—

DR. KRISTIN NEFF: We are wired for compassion for others. We understand it instinctually with our children, and that communicating with them works much more effectively when the bottom line is unconditional love and fierceness: *Mom is doing this because she loves me, not because she hates me.* That's going to land a lot better, and it's the same thing with self-compassion for ourselves.

AMANDA: It's wild how we can see that clearly for others. We know that telling our kid they are stupid and lazy is not how to motivate them to get their grades up—that they will actually internalize that negative self-talk and self-doubt and do worse in school. But when it comes to ourselves, we somehow think it works the other way. We think the mean voice in our head is what keeps us great, that if we didn't have the incessant self-critic, we would be lazy and complacent and our life would be crap. But your research shows the opposite: that the more self-compassion we give ourselves, the more motivation and self-responsibility we have and the less anxiety we have.

It makes me think of exercise. Instead of struggling to get yourself to the gym with the critical voice berating you as lazy and gross, which is zero percent compassionate and therefore zero percent motivating, what if we were to replace that mean voice with a compassionate voice saying: *I love you so much, I want you to feel good. And if the gym won't make you feel good today, to hell with it. We will check in again tomorrow to see how you feel.*

—

We're affected not just by things that happen but also by our thoughts about things that happen. If you think: *This is the worst thing ever,* your body is naturally going to react to it as though you've experienced a threat. And once you activate your fight or flight, you're releasing stress hormones, putting your cardiac system under stress, literally shutting off your sexual function, your digestive function. You've changed the physiology of your body because of your interpretation of an event.

In the parable of the second arrow, Buddha is talking to his followers and he asks, "If you're walking down the street and you get hit by an arrow, is that bad?" And the followers say, "Yeah, it sucks to get hit by an arrow." And Buddha replies, "Alright, well, if you're walking down the street and you get hit by *two* arrows, is that worse?" His followers are like "Yeah, two arrows suck even more."

Buddha goes on to explain that the first arrow you can't control—that's the circumstances in life—if your partner leaves you or if you get a bad medical diagnosis or if there's a global pandemic. That's just circumstance. But the second arrow is your reaction to it. It's whether you react to the global pandemic by being pissed at your kids for the next six months or you react to the breakup by holing up in your apartment and never seeing a friend. The second arrow is usually our reaction to the suffering.

Try not to jam yourself with extra arrows.

DR. LAURIE SANTOS

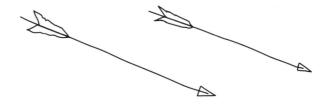

To feel better right now

I tell myself better stories.

My mother would always say, "We aren't poor, because we're rich in love." And at the time, as a kid, I rolled my eyes. But what I realized later is that she raised my siblings and me with a theory of abundance rather than scarcity. At every turn when I would say, "I want this," she would say, "We aren't poor, because we're rich in love." When I became an adult, I started to really think: *What does that mean?* And part of what it means is that we become conscious about those received thoughts we have. If I think: *I need more money*, then I feel stressed out and I feel controlled by it. What if you take a breath and say, *I feel acutely right now the things I don't have because of money. What are the things that I do have?* You actually will feel better if you can say, "I am rich in these things."

CHERYL STRAYED

Some people are wealthy in money and not in friendship, time, love, and health. Some people are wealthy in friendship, time, love, and health but not in money. Money isn't the only resource required to make a life. Time, love, money, friendship, health—there are many ways to be wealthy.

ABBY

Recently someone asked me how my kids dealt with having a broken family. I quickly corrected him. A family's wholeness or brokenness has little to do with its structure. A broken family is a family in which any member must break herself into pieces to fit in. A whole family is any family, regardless of structure, in which each member can bring her full self to the table knowing that she will always be both held and free. My family is not broken; my family is fixed.

GLENNON

My biggest healing practice is friendship. To be able to call people when I am on the floor, whether metaphorically or physically, and be completely transparent is so important to me. Friendship tethers me to what I like best about my life.

TRACEE ELLIS ROSS

When I'm having a hard time, my inclination is to isolate. We feel like we don't want to drag people down because we don't have a happy story to tell. But connection, and the joy others can bring, is so important. If I can push through that, go out and meet my friends for a walk or tea, I always feel better. It doesn't have to be deep stuff we're talking about; it might just be that I laugh.

CHERYL STRAYED

Every available study of happy people suggests that happy people physically spend more time around other people, and they tend to prioritize time with their friends and family members. Happy people do for others and volunteer their time. They're doing self-care through care of others.

DR. LAURIE SANTOS

To feel better right now

I reach for connection.

AMANDA: A twenty-second strong hug is proven to settle your body, and it isn't because of the hug. It's because the physical act of the hug tells your body that you are in a safe place. Twenty seconds is an absurdly awkward amount of time to be hugging someone; I know this because Alice and I do it at home when one of us is dysregulated. But when you hold someone tight for twenty long seconds, it works.

GLENNON: You know what I love about that? An important part of the effectiveness of the long hug is that both people embracing are solidly in their center of gravity. The hug doesn't work to calm us if one person is leaning too much on the other person or one person is holding both people up. Isn't that a beautiful metaphor? What makes us feel safe when hugging someone is what makes us feel safe in most things: that we are both on solid ground. It's not really "I've got you." It's "You've got you and I've got me and we are holding each other." I think about this a lot when I'm hugging a child. We tend to want to grab them, scoop them up, pull them in to us. But the twenty-second hug that will help your child is the one where your kid is on their own two feet, in their own center of gravity, and you are both steady and solid.

AMANDA: Yes. It's the difference between being codependent and interdependent. It's the difference between "I will protect you" and "You are safe inside yourself."

Having a front-row seat to Glennon's therapy—watching her explore herself and dedicate herself to the consistency of therapy week after week—gave me the confidence to even want to *think* about going to therapy. At the time, there were a lot of things in my personal life, professional life, and in our family life that were becoming challenging for me.

Finally, I decided to try it. Therapy helped me realize I wasn't living into the fullness of myself. Therapy has encouraged me to start allowing uncomfortable emotions like anger and sadness. It's given me the responsibility to claim what is mine and to release the ways I've been protecting myself through defense mechanisms.

Therapy is so expensive. I recognize that it's a huge privilege. I'm so grateful that I've had access to it and that it's allowed me to realize my full self for the first time.

ABBY

To feel better right now
I get the help I need.

I started having these anxious episodes very early in my life and was able to manage them through therapy, through meditation, through exercise. It was deeply uncomfortable and also manageable.

But the breaking point for me was in the lockdown of the pandemic—the claustrophobia and the rattling of dread was so loud and oppressive, so I finally decided: *Okay, taking medicine is the one thing I haven't tried.*

I always felt like my sadness was my identity, like this layer of melancholy is why I'm a writer, it's why I think deeply about the pain of other people, why I want to interpret it. I felt like if I abandoned that sadness, somehow I was abandoning my essential self.

But oh, my God, the relief. The relief of returning to myself. I was so scared that medicine was going to make me disconnect and go farther away from my spiritual center, but I actually came back and I was like: *I'm here. Here I am. This person can laugh.*

I still have terrible days and am still very much in touch with my sadness and my anxiety. There's not a blanket of bliss put over anything. I don't feel like another person. But I'm so grateful I took the leap because the relief is as wide as the universe.

SARA BAREILLES

If you are debilitated by anxiety or depression, get to a doctor. If your doctor's not taking you seriously, go to a different doctor. Don't let anybody shame you for wanting help. When I was on my medicine, it wasn't about *escaping* the human experience; it was about *allowing myself to have* the full human experience. Everyone deserves to have the full human experience, so get yourself whatever tools you need for that, and don't let anybody's backward thinking stop you.

GLENNON

To feel better right now I get the help I need.

You need to make sure that you're safe. You need to talk to a therapist or talk to a friend. If you, right now, are feeling depressed and numb and like you're never going to feel well again, you just have to trust that you will come out of it.

If you are in any way thinking about suicide, at all, I can tell you: You need to reach out. You need to get help, because there are so many people who would miss you. You do not know the ripples that you make.

I've called the crisis hotline so many times, and it's wonderful. Sometimes I'll get somebody and I'm like "Mm, nope. I'll talk to you later." And then I'll call right back and ask, "Can I talk to somebody else?" Sometimes you get people who want to fix you, and I don't really want somebody to fix me, I just want somebody to say, "That sucks. I'm so sorry. You're going to get through this." And that's what I continue to remind myself. Every single time I'm in a depression, I have to go back and read my own stuff to be like: *Okay, the past Jenny said I'll come out again, and past Jenny must know.*

It doesn't feel like it's possible, and then it does and you can breathe again.

JENNY LAWSON

IF YOU ARE EXPERIENCING HOPELESSNESS,
DIAL 988 FOR THE SUICIDE AND CRISIS HOTLINE
OR TEXT "HELPLINE" TO 62640 FOR THE NATIONAL
ALLIANCE ON MENTAL ILLNESS SUPPORT LINE.

I want people to take a deep breath, slow down, and understand that this rest work is a meticulous love practice. Resting is a generative state. You generate ideas, you are connecting with your body. You are participating in the spiritual practice. It connects you. Napping allows you to have a portal that opens and allows you to see things differently—to have a moment outside of grind culture, to connect with something deeper outside of yourself, connect with your ancestors, connect with what you want to be, connect with the dreams.

TRICIA HERSEY

For twenty-five years I've been doing a practice where I ask Love what it would have me know or do in this moment. So many times, it has said to me, "Go get a glass of water, take off your bra, lie down, and stop. That's enough for today."

ELIZABETH GILBERT

I've realized that the reason I'm not getting it all done is *not* because I'm not good enough or I just haven't learned some trick to do things faster or better. It's because our modern lives are set up so we'll never be without one thousand things we should be doing. So relief can't be on the other side of getting it all done. Relief has to be found, if at all, while things are undone. I'm working to get more comfortable with the discomfort of leaving things undone. I'm trying to trust that if I show up and do what I can every day, that is *enough,* even if it's not. I tell myself: *I have done what I can do today. Tomorrow I will do what I can do again. It's okay that there are things undone. Life is always undone. I trust that there is enough time.*

AMANDA

Part of the rhythm of creation is rest. You work and you work and you work, and then you stop and you rest and you call it good. You stop and rest and call it good because it's part of the creative process. The potential for the next thing is all in the stillness and the quiet and the enjoyment of this moment right now.

GLENNON

To feel better right now

I rest.

On the subway or at the park, I remind myself that my skull is a tiny, tiny acorn and it's full of these swirling thoughts that I think are so big and devastating—but it's really just a little acorn in this huge landscape of ginormous silver buildings. So I'll go out into the city, and I'll notice things—people inside their lives. It saved me when I realized that there are so many different types of lives unfolding.

Recently, I saw a little girl dressed as a mermaid on a swing. Her conundrum was that she was sitting on the baby swing and she had to fit both of her legs in her mermaid tail through one swing hole. I thought: *This is her biggest problem today.* And if I were in her life, that would be my consuming issue of the day.

In the subway, there were two friends sitting, eating grapes. One friend had this smiley face patch on his sweatpants, and his friend took a grape, pressed it to the smiley face, and went, "Yum, yum, yum, yum." His friend was laughing so hard he couldn't breathe. And their little game became pressing the little grape to the mouth and then the other one would just lose it. That was the whole ride.

Seeing that puts my brain in relief. My brain is inside their game. The world is full of that stuff, and it's free and it's happening all the time. If you are stuck focusing internally, redirect your focus to those outward small moments. I swear, if you string them along, you come out somewhere different.

CHANEL MILLER

To feel better right now

I delight.

There's a feeling of freedom and release that comes when you're having fun. You're not thinking about your laundry, you're not thinking about your mental load. That's one of the reasons that fun boosts our resilience: It's a release. It gives us the emotional strength and energy that we need to weather life's hard things and to be the best version of ourselves. And that's why it's so essential that we prioritize fun and focus on filling our lives with more of fun's ingredients: playfulness, connection, and flow.

Start with recognizing the fun that you're already having. Get a piece of paper and think back on your day. When did you have a moment of playfulness? When did you have a moment of connection? When did you have a moment of flow? Write it all down. Allow yourself to tap back in to what it felt like physically and emotionally to be in those states. Then ask yourself: What are some of your own memories of experiences from your life that stand out to you as having been *so fun*? Write a few of those down, too.

It's okay if it feels hard at first; once you open the gates, it'll be easier. The goal is to try to amass a collection that you can then mine for details and to use your stories to start to identify your personal fun magnets—that's my term for the activities, people, and settings that tend to generate fun for you *personally*—so that you can carve out time for them and prioritize them. Playing music with friends is a fun magnet for me, so I make it a point to make space for it in my schedule.

Most of all, having fun requires being present. So put down your phone and look up. Notice things, notice people, notice the world around you. Present yourself as someone who's open to a passing joke or a little conversation. There are opportunities for fun floating around us all the time. We just have to learn how to reach out and grab them.

CATHERINE PRICE

To feel better right now I delight.

CHERYL STRAYED: It has not been the easiest time in my life the past few years, but I've had this experience lately: I laugh with abandon and I actually feel it in my body as a good thing. It's a wave of something really positive. Seeking out laughter is one of the most healing acts of love we can give ourselves.

ABBY: I've been doing that exercise with smiling. Even if it's a fake smile, I actually feel better. There's something chemical happening. I know it for sure in my bones, so just go out there and laugh. Find laughter, and also just smile to yourself.

I love to throw a loud, aggressive compliment. I yell things at people a bunch, like "You're doing great!" or "You look terrific!" I'll roll down the window in my car and yell, "I'm in love with that scarf!" I really encourage it—it's the best, and I feel better for doing it. I think it's that wonderful ripple effect of *I'm so glad I did it*, and then I bet that person, within the hour, is going to say something nice to another person, and then it's going to keep ping-ponging. We need more of that ripple effect.

MELISSA MCCARTHY

We have moments of playful connected flow in our regular lives all the time. When I played with my dog a little this morning, I had a moment of playfulness. When I laughed with my daughter, I had a moment of connection. Those little moments count. But if we don't call them out and give them names and acknowledge them, they will just pass us by.

CATHERINE PRICE

My mother would always say to me, "Put yourself in the way of beauty. No matter how hard things are, no matter how miserable or ugly things seem in your life on any given day, you always have the opportunity to put yourself in the way of beauty. There's always a sunrise and there's always a sunset, and it's up to you to be there for it or not."

It wasn't until later that I realized she had given me the tools I needed to save myself. It was so simple: Seek beauty, and you will be better for it.

CHERYL STRAYED

Twenty

What is the *point?*

I feel grateful that I had kids before I was old enough and wise enough to look hard and critically at the world I'll one day leave them in. Sometimes I feel like I have brought my dearest friends to a terrible toxic party. I feel responsible for their experience and utterly panicked about leaving them here without me to block for them. I keep asking myself lately: *Did I do the right thing bringing you here? Overall, is this experience of being human—with all this pain and loss—worth it? Does it net out positive?* I don't feel certain, which scares me. But I do wonder if maybe life itself is not an objective experience I can measure from a distance. Maybe how I live it changes its measurements? Maybe there are ways I can live—ways I can model for my children—that actually make life worth living?

GLENNON

There's no formula for being human. If there were a solution to the problem of being a person, we would've found it. We wouldn't be stuck endlessly managing our beautiful stupid gorgeous lives. So you can fight that; you can spend forever searching for the answer, clinging to everything. Or you can try to acknowledge that everything dissolves in your hands so you just have to live openhanded.

People are magic, and moments are magic. Magic moments come and go; we don't know when there will be that moment where everything is alive and bright in each of our days. It's all just fireflies, blinking on and off. We want so much to control it, and we want so much to predict it. It would be nice if we could just count them and line them up and make sure there would always be more of them. But that's the perpetual human condition: wanting more. We will feel that until we die. And I think that is okay. It means we are alive and we know what love is, and we know that there is never enough.

KATE BOWLER

Glennon: I remember sensing the inextricability of joy and pain, love and loss, very young. When my mom would lean in to hug me and I'd smell her lotion, it felt so wonderful and so horrible to me. I would experience a wave of tenderness and then immediately the second wave of horror: *Whatever I love, I'm going to lose.* I still feel this double wave every single day. When I look at my kids in a moment of pure beauty, like when they're on the beach and they're running free, what I feel is not pure joy. It's joy matched with dread. C. S. Lewis called this a *stab of joy.* It's such a constant deep ache to live with: to love so much and to know we will lose each other. I think that this is the ultimate ache so many of us are trying to run from. ⌒

⌒ Susan Cain: Whether we know it consciously or not, we know that a child is going to grow up. We know that we may or may not be there to see it, but we won't be there to see something in that child's life when they're grown up. The child won't be a child forever. They won't be alive forever. We know all of that when we're seeing these moments of beauty. So we're holding these two truths at the same time: this amazing, precious child and the fact of impermanence. And that's what makes us cry. But it's possible, when you totally immerse in these feelings, to feel less tormented by it and more just deeply appreciative of it. We can get into a mysterious state where we're aware of the tragedy of life but also that life is so incredibly beautiful and that it's all wrapped together. The tragedy and the beauty is happening simultaneously at every moment.

That universal human ache inside of us is because everything is so unbearably brutal and unbearably beautiful at the exact same time. It's so tempting to numb the ache. But I've learned the hard way that numbing doesn't just change the brutal one bit. Reality is still there. All numbing does is make the beautiful inaccessible.

If there's any secret to life, it's that being human is not about feeling happy—it's about feeling everything. All of our feelings are for feeling. Even the uncomfortable ones, even the hard ones—they are all for our becoming. They are the furnace inside of which we become what we're meant to be next.

Since I got sober and quit numbing myself, I have never been fine again. Not for a single moment. I have been exhausted and terrified and angry. I have been overwhelmed and underwhelmed and debilitatingly depressed and anxious. I have been amazed and awed and delighted and overjoyed to bursting.

I'll tell you what I've been: I've been alive.

GLENNON

To be a human is to be deeply connected. To be aware of that connection is the most beautiful thing. And it's also the most terrifying thing. It's loving someone so deeply that you cannot live without them—and it's having no control over whether you will have to. To love someone that much is only terrifying because it's beautiful. And it's only beautiful because it's terrifying.

AMANDA

The brutal and the beauty of the world, of life, are neck and neck. But for me, the beauty always wins. Brutal = 49 percent. Beauty = 51 percent. It's a tiny margin, but it's also everything. Life is brutiful. But life and love win.

GLENNON

When you get a cancer diagnosis and you're lucky enough that it's caught early or that it's treatable—both of which were true with my breast cancer diagnosis—people will say things that they think are encouraging. Many of these things enraged me. Things like "The vast majority of folks live up to ten years after this diagnosis!" Like that was a good thing. Like I would be satisfied with that, even celebratory of that. I am not. I don't think it's a win if this thing doesn't kill me. I think it's a win only if I get to live as many years as I was going to live without this diagnosis. I know this is greedy, that there are so many folks who would be overjoyed to have even one more year. I understand, and own, that I am deeply, unapologetically greedy when it comes to having all of life, all of my time. I don't want to be shortchanged. I don't want anyone congratulating me that I get another few years. I want all of them.

AMANDA

We all go through pain. Some people very unfairly go through more than others in a way that we will never be able to understand. Some people go through pain beyond measure. And what we see is that some people take that pain and, for a thousand reasons, might not be able to integrate it. They take that pain out on other people. And the cycle continues. But there is this other pathway, where people transform that pain into something different, something beautiful.

In 1992, there was a war in the city of Sarajevo. And one bombing in particular happened right next to the apartment of Vedran Smailović, the principal cellist of the Sarajevo Philharmonic Orchestra. So he left his apartment. First he went and helped the people who had been wounded. And then, a few hours later, he came back and sat in the middle of the rubble with his cello and played Tomaso Albinoni's *Adagio in G minor*. It's the most incredibly haunting and exquisite music you can imagine. He could have played something cheerful to rouse people's spirits. He could have played something more neutral. But he played the adagio, which is this aching music. And I think that something about that sad music is expressing our longing for the heavens. It's our recognition that there's a world that we wish we could live in and we don't live in right now, but we're all deeply united in the fervor of our wish to live in a more perfect and more beautiful world. It's the beauty that we feel we're banished from but want desperately to get back to.

SUSAN CAIN

My friend Ethel told me that when a butterfly is trying to make its way out of a cocoon, it's really hard for that butterfly and it can look bad. And so humans, when they witness it, often try to go and peel open the cocoon to help the butterfly out. But if a human does this, the butterfly has far less chance of thriving because the struggle was crucial to its thriving. So we have to figure out the balance of when to really show up for each other and when to teach strength. When we do that, we're saying, "You can get out of that cocoon. I know you can. And you'll be more beautiful for it."

ANDREA GIBSON

When you feel like everything in the world is breaking apart, it's like you're looking at life, but it's a shirt that's inside out and you see all the seams. Then, all of a sudden, in all the jagged seams, there's just so much beauty in the world. You notice your pain, but then you notice everybody else's: the person struggling to reach something and the person who helps them; someone in the cancer clinic smoothing their mom's hair. And you just get flooded by how fragile, gorgeous, and ridiculous life is. I just kept feeling like: *Man, I really hope I don't unlearn this.* I wouldn't have known it if my life hadn't felt so unbelievably fragile and somehow crystalline in those moments.

KATE BOWLER

Birthdays bring us very close to the ache. That day pushes us dangerously close to the cliff that separates us from the swirly purple-and-black abyss we're living right next to—the abyss of the reality that we're all going to die and be taken from each other and that all we really have is just this one brief moment of life. On our birthday, we are right there with the truth of mortality, so we want people around us to block us from the ache, to keep us tethered in this dimension. Maybe that's the reason for all the parties—because when we're alone, we feel the ache too acutely. Birthdays are a lot.

GLENNON

My oncologist said to me, "You have to live every day as if it's your last day." Which is a thing that a lot of people say, and with good intentions. But what does that even mean? Do I empty my bank account and go on vacation and possibly declare bankruptcy later? Do I eat ungodly amounts of ice cream for every meal?

I realized that I don't want to live every day as if it's my *last*. I want to live every day as if it's my *first*. To wake up with the awe and curiosity and wonder of a newborn baby.

And that doesn't look like crossing off bucket-list items. It often looks like the simple things. It looks like play. It looks like taking my dogs for a long walk in the woods. It looks like curling up with a good book and allowing myself the luxury of unstructured time, where I can tap into my curiosity just for the hell of it, not with any sort of end goal or expectation associated with it. And that's how I've been navigating the uncertainty, by taking the pressure off, following the threads of my curiosity, and cultivating the things that bring me joy.

SULEIKA JAOUAD

I've always had a pull toward the extraordinary and a fear of the ordinary. Ordinary is the life where you already know what's going to happen: the spouse, the two kids, the job, the thirty-year mortgage. Extraordinary is chasing what's next and never knowing what's ahead.

While John and I were dating, I remember one night sharing all of my agonized strivings: *If we're going to have a life together, it's going to have to look like this, we're going to have to do this, we are going to have to be like this.* When he asked why I wanted those things, I explained it was because I knew I was meant to have an extraordinary life and those were the ways to have one.

He looked at me and asked, "What's wrong with ordinary? Because I really, really want ordinary." He told me he very much wanted the kids and the job, and the boring predictability of getting out the door on Wednesday mornings, and the monotony of stories you've heard six hundred times, and the frustration of having the same fight with each other for a decade, and the comfort of seeing the same face at the dinner table for the next fifty years. He told me that his dream was ordinary.

I realized that ordinary isn't the lack of extraordinary. Ordinary is a whole other thing with a beautiful cadence and rhythm and purpose and bond and magic. And here was this lovely man putting a very high value on ordinary—not as a thing that lacks whatever extraordinary has—but as a thing that has something that extraordinary doesn't have. And he wanted that with me.

The more I've thought about it since then, the more I've realized that maybe I don't really have a fear of being ordinary. Maybe it's actually a fear of accepting who I am, where I am, and who I'm with—and trusting that it's good enough. Maybe I don't think I can be ordinary and still be worthy. Who am I to be okay with where I am and who I am? Do I have the audacity to give myself that much peace—to stop chasing a better life and just settle into *this* life?

Chasing and finding the prize has been easy for me. Staying and finding the prize has been harder. I am very lucky to be married to a man who loves the ordinary and who loves the staying.

AMANDA

The most wonderful life might be brushing your teeth next to a person you love. Or it might be singing with six hundred people. Or it might be having a good conversation with your homie. This is being alive. We're all right here. That is what life is actually all about.

There's something really revolutionary about what happens when people are fully in their bodies and they come together and galvanize. I just went to see a Stevie Nicks concert, and I was watching this witch and watching the scale. I was like: *This whole room just believes in a fricking landslide right now.* Everything is connected. I can feel everyone feeling togetherness right now: the love, the aliveness, and the hope of all these people and their ancestors and their future.

So now I'm like: *Okay, how do I right size that for daily life?* Here's what I've been playing with: *Can I touch into that connectedness doing something mundane? Doing the dishes? Taking care of one of the kids in my life?* One of my babies who's almost two just visited and is one of my goddess friends' kids, and we're playing, we're making art together, drawing on this box, and I was like: *How connected can we be just drawing on this box right now? How much can we just be one being? I'm here. She's mine. She's now a part of me.*

ADRIENNE MAREE BROWN

—

AMANDA: My life has been changed by helping walk my dear friend Wendy to the end of her life. Her generosity—inviting us into her life in that time—resulted in some of the most profound peace, wisdom, and connection that I have experienced. She gave us gifts that aren't possible to find in other places.

We stepped into a reality that we don't have access to in the regular street-level experience of daily life. When you're invited into something like that, you're on a higher plane. From that perspective, you can actually see that we are all connected to each other. So you act like it. But on the street-level plane, we can't see that we're connected, so we act like we're not.

Having the privilege to tap into that bigger reality makes the world feel safer. And it's not just the person who's "being helped" who feels safer; I feel safer because I was able to operate momentarily in that reality.

We can't see that we're all connected, we can't see that I'm dependent on you and you're dependent on me, until we show up for each other during these sacred times. *That* showing up is what makes the invisible visible—that is what allows us to see reality.

GLENNON: It's like there's this invisible web of connection beneath us all the time. When we help someone or allow ourselves to be helped, we're not creating the web. We're just throwing ink on the web that is already there so that we get to see it. We're just remembering the web that's always been there.

AMANDA: Yes. No one is creating anything. We're just having the privilege of seeing, and experiencing, what's already there.

—

Ultimately, what I want to do on this earth is leave it a little happier, a little safer. You can think really macro and be like: *Okay, then, I have to change this policy.* But you can also make someone feel safe in a moment: *I believe that my well-being is tied to your well-being. The more well I am, the more well you are.* It's so life giving to know that even a smile or warmth can be contagious; it can lift somebody, and that person can then spread it on. And in that way, simple moments can have massive impact.

CHRISTEN PRESS

When I'm on my deathbed, I want to be able to say, *I did everything I possibly could so that this incredible planet and all its magical, wondrous creatures are saved.* I want young people to know and enjoy the wild parts and critters of the world that I've experienced. I'm an activist, so I'm hopeful.

JANE FONDA

So many of the oppressive forces in the world are just waiting for us to give up. But if I just keep showing up and speaking up, even if I have a hoarse voice, I'm always going to be here.

CHANEL MILLER

You're not alone, you're part of a community
that cares about you. You're going to be lifted up.
So get out of that chair. Shoulders back, chin up.

FORMER VICE PRESIDENT KAMALA HARRIS

With any kind of matter—it could be DNA, it could be water, it could be anything—you add a molecule into the matter and the whole matter changes. If you have a glass of water and you drop some red dye into it, regardless of how small that drop is, it changes. If I walk into a corporate culture, I am the molecule. The matter has to change. It's not even a choice. It *has* to change. Then why would I consider myself insignificant?

BOZOMA SAINT JOHN

Faith is the distance between what we believe is possible and what we can prove is possible. Black people have put their blood, sweat, and tears into the best vision of what this country can be. I think that's part of my own political inheritance to have and to claim and to work for. There's a particular kind of cynicism, and rooted in that cynicism is a kind of cowardice that is about a desire to not be wrong. When folks say that they're going to bow out, it is about a desire to not be made a fool of, but all of us have to be a fool for something, and I'm going to be a fool for the side that says that the people can fight toward the future they want to have. And if I get made a fool of because that is what I choose to believe in, then that's a risk I'm willing to take.

BRITTNEY COOPER

Faith is the hunch that it was all supposed to be more beautiful than this. Action is stretching toward the beautiful and making it so. Our son loves plants. At one point he had maybe thirty plants growing in his room. He once taught me that the magic of a monstera plant is that it lives in a rainforest, so it has learned to grow through darkness. Other plants grow only toward the light, but a monstera knows how to grow first through the darkness—reaching, reaching—because it senses what it cannot yet see. It knows the light is out there somewhere—if it just grows long and strong enough in the dark.

GLENNON

The problem with opening the door to hope—to light—is that you don't forget what it looked like. You always remember. When you open a window in a room, you don't forget what that room looks like when the sun pours in. Even if you decide to keep the shade drawn.

At some point you're going to want to pull that shade up again because you're going to remember what it felt like to have the sunlight on your skin and you're going to crave it. You're going to want it. You're going to keep reaching for it.

That's what hope is for me, remembering what the open window looked like even when I'm sitting in the dark.

ASHLEY C. FORD

—

GLENNON: I love your paintings so much. I was stunned to learn you just started painting two years ago. In an interview back then you said, "I do home design, but lately when I go to museums and look at paintings, I feel tingly." Is tingling the life force that guides you toward what to try next? Is following the tingle how you make your decisions?

JUSTINA BLAKENEY: I am just trying to follow the tingle. And I have this theory that if everybody in the world was able to follow their tingle to their most tingliest tingle, the world would be perfect. What's missing from the world is that not all people are allowed to just be who they are and follow their hearts.

—

When I was becoming a writer, I had to ask myself: *What matters more? That I write the great American novel or that I write a novel that I finish?* My dream is to write a book, and the only book I can possibly write is the one I write. I don't know if it's going to be great or good or bad or terrible, but that is none of my business.

My work here, the true thing that I need to do, is to let go of greatness. Don't let those wild ambitions get in the way of my wild intention, which is to write this story.

CHERYL STRAYED

I do these sabbaticals for myself, and the only practice is doing exactly what you want next. So I am like: *Okay, now what do I want to do? Oh, I want a bowl of cereal. Okay, now what do I want to do? I need to go put my feet on the dirt. Okay, then, now what do I want to do? It's time to write, an idea is coming.*

I find that if I clear the decks and just ask myself what I want to do, it always gets me to writing. That's how I know that that's my purpose. That's my thing I'm meant to do in the world. But it necessitates getting everything else out of the way.

The story of my life is "adrienne maree brown is a writer." Period. That's my main story. I found it, and I feel blessed that I found it as early in my life as I did.

People can go their whole lives without ever knowing what that sentence is for themselves. Even if you're living a very successful life, if you don't feel satisfied in it, it's probably because you haven't found that sentence yet. And that sentence can have commas. I'm also a daughter and an auntie. I'm the best auntie. But having that sentence for yourself is so important.

ADRIENNE MAREE BROWN

GLENNON: The fear of death is largely about fear of future regret. It's not just about the unknown of the afterlife; it's about the fear that we will arrive at our death not having done what we dreamed of doing in *this* life. Which is why all of your death work is really about life. The core question of your work is "What must I do to be at peace with myself so I may live presently and die gracefully?" No pressure, but can you just tell us: What must we do? What's the thing that we must do?

ALUA ARTHUR: Well, the question is mandatory. It's "What *must* I do?" Not "What are the things that would be really nice to do?" Yeah, I'd really like to go to Machu Picchu. But what *must* I do so that I may live presently and die gracefully? One of the fears we have about death is a fear of a life not fully lived. All the things that we didn't get to do, all the things that we wanted to do and maybe were too afraid or not worthy enough, or we thought we were too fat or too tall to do, all the lies that we tell ourselves. ⌇

⁓ ALUA: So stepping outside of those things: If I knew that tomorrow would be my last day, what choice would I make? Who would I be? Living like that would certainly make me more honest. I would tell people how I feel about them. I would make choices out of my purest authenticity. I'd eat a lot more cake, probably. I was so concerned with my weight before, but now I'm like: *Who cares?* The worms are going to have a field day when I die, they're going to be so happy I ate that cake.

So the question is:

What is your *must*?

For years, as I was working on *Briefly Perfectly Human*, finishing that book was my biggest *must*; until I finished it, it was *always* tickling at me.

GLENNON: Tickling at me. That's such a good clue. If something is tickling at you even when you're doing other things, that might be your *must*.

Glennon: I was walking along the beach, and I saw this little girl digging in the sand. I got a little close, so I could see. She'd written, "Melody is here." Melody is here. Not Melody *was* here but Melody *is* here. It was so beautiful. I thought: *That's what we're all doing every day, finding a million different ways to say:*

I'M HERE

Abby: Abby is here, Glennon is here. So beautiful.

One night, after we told the kids about my breast cancer diagnosis but before my surgery, Alice couldn't sleep. In the morning she told me how anxious she was about the one-mile run at school that day. She'd only been lamenting the one-mile run for three weeks, so I asked, "Baby, do you think that's part of why you couldn't sleep last night?" She was like, "Oh, maybe." She explained that they had to take a bus from the elementary school to the high school for the run and she was worried she would be so slow that the bus was going to leave before she was finished. I assured her that wouldn't happen, and she went off to school bravely, but a little shaky.

Later that morning, I was trying to push through a work project on deadline, and I couldn't stop thinking about her on that track. I had a sudden sense of total clarity. I ran to my car, drove to the high school, and ran like a fool until I saw her: one of just a few kids left to finish. There were some other parents there, and they were waving, trying to get my attention. I didn't even look over. *None of you will get an ounce of my energy. I just need to get to my girl.*

I ran to the fence around the track where she was just coming around the bend. When she looked up and saw me, a huge smile spread across her face. She gave me a thumbs-up and started running faster. I ran on the outside of the fence, in step with her as she ran. Eventually, she hollered, "This is my last lap!" I screamed back, "You can do it. You can do it. I'm so proud of you. You can do it." I just kept running, tracking with her on the outside, until she crossed the finish line. And then she was done with me. As I watched her celebrate with her friends, I realized: *I just want all the years of that. I know I'm not going to be able to really do anything for her, but I just want to be there to be a witness to her, to encourage her, to run beside her, to constantly tell her what a wonder she is to me. And then, when she's done with me and retreats to her people, to never stop celebrating her in my heart.*

A gift of this scary diagnosis was a bit of clarity. The clarity of pushing away from the desk and going to my girl. The clarity of not even making eye contact with anyone else, knowing: *That's my kid. I'm here for that one, and only that one.* The clarity of putting my energy—while I'm here—exactly, and only, where I most want it to go.

AMANDA

Life is messy. It's complicated. It doesn't happen neatly the way it does in books and movies. And yet when we give up the need to know how everything will work out, when we're willing to say, "I don't know," and step into the unknown, that's when we find the magic.

MELODY BEATTIE

I had this vision of myself as a little girl, and I was walking through a forest that was like another realm. It was so beautiful. I had a little notebook, as I always do. I was just observing and writing down all I saw and heard—just observing all the beauty. I was so happy. But then I stopped observing and starting thinking. It was like I'd switched my question from "What?" to "Why?" Suddenly I was trying to figure something out, and as a result, I lost all my joy. My eyes had been all wide—taking it all in—and now my head was down and my brow was furrowed. Finally, out of frustration, I just yelled into the air:

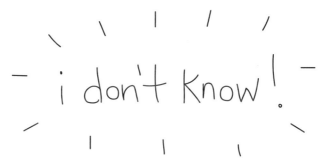

All around me, the forest exploded into a joyful celebration. The entire universe just became a party: Fireworks went off, flowers exploded. The realm was *delighted*. I was like: *What just happened?* Then I waited a few minutes and I said it again: "I don't know!" Another explosion of joy erupted.

The message of the vision was: Just notice and write what you see, Glennon. Just be awed by it all. You don't have to figure out a damn thing. That's above your pay grade.

The most beautiful gift you can give yourself and your people is to celebrate "I don't know" forever.

"I don't know" are magical, liberating words.

GLENNON

I work with these wonderful folks who are all older than seventy. I asked, "Guys, what adds up? You've had these lives. What benchmarks took you somewhere? Did you accomplish something? Were you at a kid's wedding? Did you become a certain kind of person? Just give me the math. I want to get there. Just give me the answers."

They just said, "Don't skip to the end."

There's no done. There's no formula. There's no enough—except those moments where you feel it, and you know it, and you're loved, and it feels like transcendence, and then the second it's gone, you feel like you're going to starve to death—because *that* is how the beautiful, good stuff is. Love makes us hungry. Beauty, it makes us hungry.

KATE BOWLER

Nothing matters.
And that's devastating.
But also: Nothing matters!
And that's freeing.
Take the risk.
Nothing matters!

TIG NOTARO

AMANDA: The masterpiece of our lives can never be finished, and it's never supposed to be finished.

GLENNON: The point is to just keep painting.

Part of being an author is responding to edits. When I sent the manuscript of my first book, my beloved editor sent back a million suggested edits and I accepted almost all of them. Now, four books later, my editor still sends a million edits and I almost always write the word STET over her suggestions. STET is a magical word in publishing—and now in my entire life—that means: Let It Stand. It means: *I hear your suggested change. But I meant what I said. I am who I am.* STET.

GLENNON

STET

The kick in the shorts about life is you never arrive.

I don't think any of us are where we thought we'd be. It doesn't matter how long I've been trekking up that mountain—of parenting, of marriage, of trying to cultivate some peace, fun, ease, or boundaries—when I feel like I'm making progress, I look up and I'm at the exact same place I started.

The reason I feel like I'm walking in circles is because I am. Because linear progress is a myth. We don't climb a mountain in a straight line from the base to the summit. We circle around and around, winding our way up. Sometimes, once in a blue moon, we'll be able to look up from our trek and see that it looks different from the place we were before. But mostly it looks the same. Mostly, as we slowly spiral up, we run into the same crap over and over. But that doesn't mean we're not moving. We're an inch higher than our last pass through here. ⁓

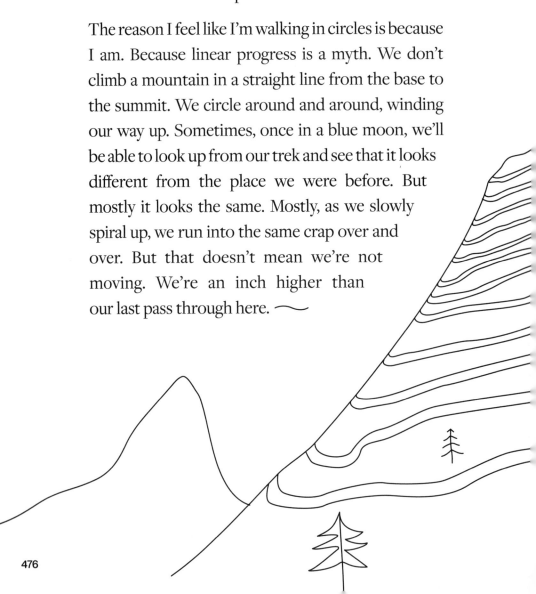

I heard Melody Beattie say that the changes she's made in her life all happened two years before anyone, including her, could see or feel the change. That's comforting to me, because all those micro-mental shifts, all those itty-bitty tweaks to how we speak to ourselves, all those baby steps in our boundaries—those will become the changes we see and feel eventually. We are coming round the mountain.

We'll be comin' round the mountain, we'll be comin' round the mountain, we'll be comin' round the mountain till we die. And that's not all bad. We could look at that trek up the mountain and think: *Ugh, it's interminable.*

Or, we could look at the path and think: *Hallelujah, it's interminable!* We've got all the time and space— we've got forever tries—to figure this out.

One step at a time. What a relief.

AMANDA

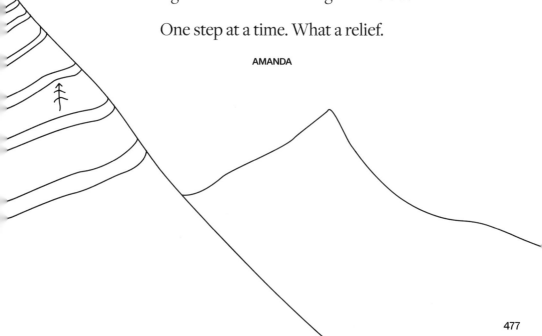

I spent so much of my life trying to figure myself out, trying to understand myself and how I fit into the world. My questions about why I'm here and what this is all about are *good*. These questions keep me alive and awake. Sometimes, though, they can take me out and make life unmanageable.

I need to know deep in my bones that I am good. While also remembering that "good" and "bad" are bullshit. And that I can't really know anything at all.

But that's okay, because I don't really need answers. Exploring the questions, exploring the world, is what I love to do most. Seeing things and doing things and experiencing things makes me *feel* the most. And isn't feeling the best?

Life isn't about nailing the answers. It's about dancing with the questions. ⌒

⁓ Can I trust that love exists and has been there with me from the beginning? It's here even when I doubt its existence. It's easier in some ways to agree that there is no magic, because if I don't believe in magic, I don't have to worry that it won't touch me, that it might leave me out. What if it's already here, though? What if I am the one hiding from love, not the other way around? What if it's already here—it's here for us all?

Love will never abandon you. You have never been abandoned. Love will never leave you. If you choose to jump, it will catch you. Those cracks on your heart that you think are unfixable, they healed a long, long time ago. It's just the story about them that you can't get over. And maybe this leap of faith into the arms of love could be the thing that helps you change that story. Love doesn't just live outside of you. It's everywhere. It's in everything. It's in everyone.

I understand how hard life can be. We can do hard things, right?

ABBY

My whole life, I've believed deeply that there was something wrong with me. I have treated life as a quest to solve that mystery so I can finally start living. It turns out that when you're looking for what's wrong, you can find a whole lot wrong.

What I'm working on now is: I want to stop working on things.

Recently I have wondered what life would be like if I stopped treating myself as a broken car and stopped treating life as an eternal trip to the mechanic. ⌒

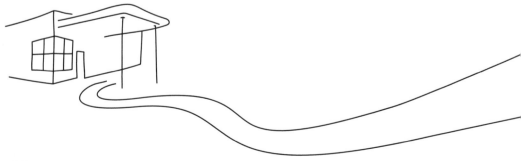

~ What's the point of even having a car if it's always in the shop? What if I quit fixing myself up and I just hit the road and drive— see things, hear things, eat, drink, be merry, soak it all up?

I want the rest of my life to be a little less backward and inward, a little more outward and onward.

Outward and onward!

GLENNON

I walked through fire
I came out the other side
I chased desire
I made sure I got what's mine
And I continued to believe
That I'm the one for me
And because I'm mine, I walk the line

Cause we're adventurers and heartbreak's our map
A final destination we lack
We stopped asking directions
To places they've never been
And to be loved, we need to be known
We'll finally find our way back home
And through the joy and pain that our lives bring
We can do hard things

I hit rock bottom, it felt like a brand-new start
I'm not the problem, sometimes things fall apart
And I continued to believe
The best people are free
And it took some time, but I'm finally fine

Cause we're adventurers and heartbreak's our map
A final destination we lack
We stopped asking directions
To places they've never been
And to be loved, we need to be known
We'll finally find our way back home
And through the joy and pain that our lives bring . . .

We can do hard things.

TISH MELTON

For More

The wisdom in this book is curated from conversations on the chart-topping *We Can Do Hard Things* podcast. You can listen to those full conversations, and hundreds more, on *We Can Do Hard Things* wherever you listen to podcasts. To discover more art that delights and heals, go to TreatMedia.com. We make art for humans who want to stay human.

About the Authors

Abby Wambach, Amanda Doyle, and Glennon Doyle, named among "The Most Powerful People in Podcasting" and "The Most Influential Podcasters," cohost the award-winning, critically acclaimed *We Can Do Hard Things* podcast. With more than half a billion plays since launching in 2021 as the #1 podcast on Apple, *We Can Do Hard Things* has been named one of Amazon's and Stitcher's Best Podcasts of the Year, and has earned two Webby Awards, a Gracie Award, and the iHeartPodcast Award for Best Advice/Inspirational Podcast.

ABBY WAMBACH is a two-time Olympic gold medalist, FIFA World Cup champion, and six-time winner of the U.S. Soccer Athlete of the Year award. An activist for equality, she was named one of *Time*'s Most Influential People, and is the author of the #1 *New York Times* bestseller *Wolfpack*. She is cofounder of Treat Media.

AMANDA DOYLE was a founder, vice president, and general counsel of Together Rising, a nonprofit that raised more than $55 million for women, families, and children in crisis. Prior to these roles, Amanda practiced at a global corporate law firm and as a Legal Fellow with International Justice Mission in Rwanda. She is cofounder of Treat Media.

GLENNON DOYLE is the author of the #1 *New York Times* bestseller *Untamed*, which has sold more than three million copies. She also authored the #1 *New York Times* bestseller *Love Warrior*, an Oprah's Book Club selection; the *New York Times* bestseller *Carry On, Warrior*; and *Get Untamed: The Journal*. She was founder and president of Together Rising. She is founder and CEO of Treat Media.

About the Wayfinders

ALOK is an internationally acclaimed poet, comedian, public speaker, and actor and the award-winning author of *Beyond the Gender Binary; Femme in Public;* and *Your Wound, My Garden.* Their dynamic presence has captivated audiences in over forty countries, and they are the subject of the docu-short *ALOK.*

ASHTON APPLEWHITE is an author and leading spokesperson for the emerging movement to raise awareness of ageism and to dismantle it. A cofounder of the Old School Anti-Ageism Clearinghouse, she has been recognized as an expert on ageism.

ALUA ARTHUR is a death doula, recovering attorney, the author of the *New York Times* bestseller *Briefly Perfectly Human,* and the founder of Going with Grace, a death doula training and end-of-life planning organization working to improve and redefine the end-of-life experience.

DR. GALIT ATLAS is a psychoanalyst and clinical supervisor on the faculty of New York University, and a leader in the field of relational psychoanalysis. Her book *Emotional Inheritance* is an international bestseller.

SARA BAREILLES is a Grammy Award–winning singer and songwriter and an actor nominated for a Tony Award and an Emmy Award. She composed music and lyrics for *Waitress* on Broadway, in which she was also the lead actor. Bareilles produced original music and executive produced the series *Little Voice.*

MELODY BEATTIE is the author of *Codependent No More,* a #1 *New York Times* bestseller, which has sold over 7 million copies. Her additional books include *The Language of Letting Go; Playing It by Heart; The Grief Club;* and *Beyond Codependency.*

DR. MARTHA BECK is a bestselling author, life coach, and speaker. In the words of NPR and *USA Today,* she is "the best-known life coach in America." Her books include the *New York Times* and international bestsellers *Beyond Anxiety; Finding Your Own North Star; Expecting Adam;* and *The Way of Integrity.*

JUSTINA BLAKENEY is a multidisciplinary artist, designer, entrepreneur, and a *New York Times* bestselling author. She is the founder and chief creative officer of Jungalow, a lifestyle brand based on her belief that good design increases the quality of life.

DR. YABA BLAY is the award-winning filmmaker of *The Whites of Our Eyes* and the bestselling author of *One Drop: Shifting the Lens on Race.* A scholar-activist and public voice in the service of Black liberation, her work centers global Black lived experiences, particularly those of Black women and girls.

KATE BOWLER, PHD, is a four-time *New York Times* bestselling author, award-winning host of *Everything Happens* podcast, and associate professor at Duke University. She studies the cultural stories we tell ourselves about success, suffering, and whether (or not) we're capable of change.

DR. LORI BROTTO is the author of *Better Sex Through Mindfulness*. She is also a professor in the UBC Department of Obstetrics and Gynaecology, where she holds a Canada Research Chair in Women's Sexual Health, and is the executive director of the Women's Health Research Institute.

ADRIENNE MAREE BROWN is an activist and writer who grows healing ideas through writing, music, and podcasts. Their work is informed by twenty-five years of social and environmental justice. She is the author/editor of texts including *Loving Corrections; Emergent Strategy; Grievers;* and *Maroons.*

DR. BRENÉ BROWN, a research professor at the University of Houston, has spent two decades studying courage, vulnerability, shame, and empathy. She is the author of six #1 *New York Times* bestsellers, including *Atlas of the Heart,* and hosts two award-winning podcasts, *Unlocking Us* and *Dare to Lead.*

DR. MARIEL BUQUÉ is a world-renowned trauma psychologist, the author of the instant national bestseller *Break the Cycle,* and founder of the therapy practice Break the Cycle Trauma Center, Inc. Her mission is to reduce the recurrence of Intergenerational Adverse Childhood Experiences within communities of color.

TARANA BURKE works at the intersection of sexual violence and racial justice. Her books, *Unbound* and *You Are Your Best Thing,* are *New York Times* bestsellers. She founded and led several campaigns to interrupt sexual violence and other systemic inequalities, including the "me too" movement.

SUSAN CAIN is the author of the #1 *New York Times* bestsellers *Quiet: The Power of Introverts in a World That Can't Stop Talking* and *Bittersweet: How Sorrow and Longing Make Us Whole,* an Oprah Book Club selection. To learn more about her and her Quiet Life community, please visit TheQuietLife.net.

BRANDI CARLILE is an eleven-time Grammy Award–winning singer, songwriter, and producer, a two-time Emmy Award–winning composer and lyricist, and a #1 *New York Times* bestselling author. She is the founder of the Looking Out Foundation, which has raised over $6 million for grassroots causes to date.

KELLY CLARKSON, a Grammy and Emmy Award winner, is one of the most popular artists of this era.

LILY COLLINS is a Golden Globe–nominated actress, philanthropist, cofounder of Case Study Films, and the author of the international bestseller *Unfiltered: No Shame, No Regrets, Just Me.* Her philanthropic endeavors include supporting vulnerable children around the world as an ambassador for the GO Campaign.

BRITTNEY COOPER is Professor of Women's, Gender, and Sexuality Studies and Africana Studies at Rutgers University and the author of the *New York Times* bestseller *Eloquent Rage*.

SLOANE CROSLEY is the *New York Times* bestselling author of the memoir *Grief Is for People*; the novels *Cult Classic* and *The Clasp*; and three essay collections: *Look Alive Out There*; *I Was Told There'd Be Cake*; and *How Did You Get This Number*.

BRITTANY PACKNETT CUNNINGHAM is an author, interdisciplinary activist and strategist, and principal and founder of the social impact agency Love & Power Works. An on-air political analyst, and host and executive producer of the *UNDISTRACTED* podcast, she has been a teacher, policy advisor, and Presidential appointee.

KAITLIN CURTICE is an award-winning poet, storyteller, and speaker. A citizen of the Potawatomi nation, she writes on the intersections of spirituality and identity and is a vital voice on decolonizing our bodies, faith, and families. She is the author of *Living Resistance*.

SARAH EDMONDSON is an actor, podcaster (*A Little Bit Culty*), cult-recovery advocate, and the author of the memoir *Scarred: The True Story of How I Escaped NXIVM*. HBO's *The Vow* documents her real-life saga escaping the personal and professional development cult NXIVM.

ALEX ELLE is the *New York Times* bestselling author of *How We Heal*, a certified breathwork coach, podcast host, and Restorative Writing teacher. Writing came into her life by way of therapy and the exploration of healing through journaling and mindfulness.

CAMERON ESPOSITO is a stand-up comic, actor, writer, and host. She has headlined tours and festivals nationwide and internationally. Their *Queery* podcast features some of the brightest luminaries in the LGBTQ+ community, and their book, *Save Yourself*, was an instant bestseller.

MEGAN FALLEY is a nationally ranked slam poet and the author of three poetry collections, most recently *Drive Here and Devastate Me*. Excerpts from her forthcoming memoir have won several national prizes. She runs an online writing workshop called Poems That Don't Suck.

JANE FONDA is an Academy Award–winning actor and producer of over forty-five films, as well as a #1 *New York Times* bestselling author. She is a lifelong activist for the rights of girls, women, and Indigenous peoples and a committed organizer for global peace and climate justice.

STEPHANIE FOO is a radio journalist and producer who has worked for *Snap Judgment* and *This American Life*. She is the author of the *New York Times* bestseller *What My Bones Know: A Memoir of Healing from Complex Trauma*. She has taught at Columbia University and is a sought-after speaker.

ASHLEY C. FORD is the author of the *New York Times* bestselling memoir *Somebody's Daughter,* published as An Oprah Book. She has taught creative nonfiction at the New School in Manhattan, served as Ball State University's Writer-in-Residence, and hosts the *Into the Mix* podcast.

DR. CHRISTINE BLASEY FORD is a Palo Alto University and Stanford professor and biostatistician. She testified before the Senate Judiciary Committee regarding her sexual assault in connection with the Committee's consideration of Judge Brett Kavanaugh's lifetime confirmation to the US Supreme Court.

DR. MARISA G. FRANCO is a professor, TED speaker, and the *New York Times* bestselling author of *Platonic: How the Science of Attachment Can Help You Make—and Keep— Friends.* She is known for digesting and communicating science in ways that resonate deeply enough with people to change their lives.

HANNAH GADSBY is an Australian comedian and writer whose groundbreaking special *Nanette* earned an Emmy and a Peabody, as well as awards in the United Kingdom and Australia. Hannah has since toured the globe, releasing two more specials, *Douglas* and *Something Special,* and the *New York Times* bestseller *Ten Steps to Nanette.*

INA GARTEN has published thirteen cookbooks, including eleven #1 *New York Times* bestsellers, and her memoir, *Be Ready When the Luck Happens.* She is host of the *Barefoot Contessa,* which has earned five Emmy Awards and a James Beard Award, as well as her interview series, *Be My Guest.*

ROXANE GAY is the author of several bestselling books, including the *New York Times* bestsellers *Bad Feminist* and *Hunger;* the national bestseller *Difficult Women;* and her most recent book, *Opinions.* She is a contributing opinion writer for *The New York Times* and authors *The Audacity* newsletter.

ANDREA GIBSON has changed the landscape of what it means to attend a "poetry show." Their poems center around LGBTQ issues, spirituality, feminism, mental health, and the dismantling of oppressive social systems. They are the author of seven books, most recently *You Better Be Lightning.*

LINDSAY C. GIBSON, PSYD, is a clinical psychologist and practicing psychotherapist. She is the *New York Times* bestselling author of several books, including *Adult Children of Emotionally Immature Parents* and *Disentangling from Emotionally Immature People.*

ELIZABETH GILBERT is the #1 *New York Times* bestselling author of *Eat Pray Love; Committed;* and *Big Magic,* and the novels *City of Girls; The Signature of All Things;* and *Stern Men.* She was a finalist for the National Book Award, the National Book Critics Circle Award, and the PEN/Hemingway Award.

AUBREY GORDON is a cohost of the *Maintenance Phase* podcast. She is the author of the *New York Times* bestseller *"You Just Need to Lose Weight" and 19 Other Myths About Fat People,* as well as *What We Don't Talk About When We Talk About Fat.*

DR. ORNA GURALNIK is a psychologist, psychoanalyst, and writer focused on the intersection of psychoanalysis, dissociation, and cultural studies. She has filmed six seasons of *Couples Therapy,* a docu-series airing on Showtime.

CHELSEA HANDLER is a comedian, television host, author, and advocate whose humor and candor have established her as one of the most celebrated voices in entertainment. She has written six #1 *New York Times* bestsellers, earned a Grammy nomination, and won a People's Choice Award.

FORMER VICE PRESIDENT OF THE UNITED STATES KAMALA HARRIS is the highest-ranking elected woman in US history, the first South Asian American Senator, and the first woman or Black American to be California's Attorney General. She is a stalwart champion for freedom and justice, including leading the fight for the freedom of women to make decisions about their own bodies.

JEN HATMAKER is the author of multiple *New York Times* bestsellers, host of the award-winning *For the Love* podcast, and curator of the Jen Hatmaker Book Club. She cofounded Legacy Collective, granting millions of dollars toward sustainable projects around the world.

TOBIN HEATH, regarded as one of the most gifted soccer players of her generation, had thirty-six goals and forty-one assists for the US Women's National Team and won two World Cup championships and two Olympic Gold medals. She cofounded RE—INC, which reimagines the way women are seen and experienced in sports.

ALEX HEDISON is an acclaimed photographer, artist, director, and actor. She has exhibited in galleries in the United States and abroad. Her acting career spans numerous television roles, including a pivotal character in the cultural phenomenon *The L Word.* She directed the short documentary film *ALOK.*

PRENTIS HEMPHILL is an embodiment facilitator, political organizer, and therapist. They are the founder and director of the Embodiment Institute and the Black Embodiment Initiative and the host of the *Becoming the People Podcast.* Their book, *What It Takes to Heal,* is a national bestseller.

LAURIE HERNANDEZ is an Olympic medalist, with both Gold and Silver medals in gymnastics, and the *New York Times* bestselling author of *I Got This.* A fierce advocate for the importance of mental health, she travels broadly speaking to the next generation about following their dreams.

TRICIA HERSEY is a multidisciplinary artist, theologian, community organizer, and the *New York Times* bestselling author of *Rest Is Resistance* as well as *We Will Rest!* She is the founder of The Nap Ministry, which curates spaces for community rest as a form of resistance and reparations.

SAMANTHA IRBY writes the *Bitches Gotta Eat* blog and is the *New York Times* bestselling author of *Quietly Hostile; Wow, No Thank You; We Are Never Meeting in Real Life;* and *Meaty*. She has written and produced TV shows including *And Just Like That, Work in Progress, Shrill,* and *Tuca & Bertie*.

JUSTICE KETANJI BROWN JACKSON earned her undergraduate and law degrees from Harvard University. She served as a judge on the US District Court for the District of Columbia and on the US Court of Appeals for the DC Circuit. She made history in 2022, becoming the first Black woman to ever serve on the Supreme Court of the United States.

ABBI JACOBSON is an actor, writer, director, producer, and *New York Times* bestselling author and illustrator. She is best known for her work cocreating and starring in the critically acclaimed television shows *A League of Their Own* and *Broad City*.

SULEIKA JAOUAD is the *New York Times* bestselling author of *Between Two Kingdoms* and *The Book of Alchemy: A Creative Practice for an Inspired Life*. An Emmy Award–winning journalist, she wrote the *New York Times* column "Life, Interrupted" and writes the weekly newsletter *The Isolation Journals*.

CHLOÉ COOPER JONES is a professor, journalist, and the author of *Easy Beauty*, which was named a best book of 2022 by *The New York Times, Los Angeles Times, The Washington Post,* and *Time* magazine and was a finalist for the 2023 Pulitzer Prize. She was also a Pulitzer Prize finalist in Feature Writing in 2020.

LUVVIE AJAYI JONES is the author of four *New York Times* bestsellers, including *Professional Troublemaker: The Fear-Fighter Manual*. She is a sought-after speaker and book marketing coach who thrives at the intersection of culture, business, and leadership.

ALEGRA KASTENS is a licensed therapist, OCD specialist, writer, and the founder of the Center for OCD, Anxiety, and Eating Disorders in New York City. Fueled by lived experience with a lesser-known manifestation of OCD, education and advocacy about OCD are at the forefront of her career.

DR. BECKY KENNEDY, recognized as "the Millennial Parenting Whisperer" by *Time* magazine, is a clinical psychologist, mother of three, and #1 *New York Times* bestselling author. She is also the founder of the Good Inside, a company with an innovative mobile app that serves as a "24/7 parenting coach."

BILLIE JEAN KING is a pioneer, tennis champion, social activist, author of the *New York Times* bestseller *All In*, and a recipient of the Presidential Medal of Freedom. In her legendary tennis career, she captured thirty-nine Grand Slam titles, including a record twenty Wimbledon championships.

ALI KRIEGER is an Olympian, two-time World Cup champion, and two-time SheBelieves Cup champion. In her final season before her retirement, she won the 2023 National Women's Soccer League championship with Gotham FC and was recently ranked #7 of the Most Marketable Athletes in the World.

POOJA LAKSHMIN, MD, is a board-certified psychiatrist and *New York Times* contributor. Her bestselling book *Real Self Care* was an NPR Best Book of 2023. She serves as a clinical assistant professor of psychiatry at George Washington University School of Medicine and maintains a private practice.

JENNY LAWSON, an award-winning humorist known for her irreverent candor in sharing her struggle with mental illness, is the author of four *New York Times* bestsellers and proprietor of Nowhere Bookshop, an independent bookstore and bar in San Antonio.

MARISA RENEE LEE is a grief advocate, entrepreneur, and the author of *Grief Is Love.* She uses research-based advice and wisdom to help others navigate the complicated and challenging emotions of experiencing loss, offering unique insights for women and Black communities.

DANIEL LEVY is a multi-hyphenate Emmy Award–winning creator. He's best known for his work on the beloved show *Schitt's Creek,* which he cocreated with his father, Eugene Levy. His other credits include his feature directorial debut, *Good Grief,* and *The Big Brunch,* a series he created and hosted.

DR. KATE MANGINO is the author of *Equal Partners: Improving Gender Equality at Home* and a gender expert who has worked in international development for more than twenty years. She has written and delivered curricula in over twenty countries on issues such as women's empowerment, healthy masculinity, and HIV prevention.

VANESSA MARIN is a licensed psychotherapist with two decades of experience in the sex therapy field. She is the author of the instant *New York Times* bestseller *Sex Talks: The Five Conversations That Will Transform Your Love Life,* cowritten with her husband, Xander Marin.

MAE MARTIN is an award-winning comedian, actor, screenwriter, and producer. They cocreated, cowrote, and starred in the comedy series *Feel Good.* They are a cohost of the *Handsome* podcast and the author of *Can Everyone Please Calm Down?: A Guide to 21st Century Sexuality.*

KATHERINE MAY is the author of multiple international bestsellers, including *Wintering; Enchantment;* and *The Electricity of Every Living Thing,* her memoir of a midlife autism diagnosis. She hosts a top-rated podcast, *How We Live Now,* and is the creator of the newsletter and community *The Clearing.*

DR. HILLARY MCBRIDE is a psychologist, researcher, podcaster, author, and speaker. She has clinical expertise in the areas of trauma, embodiment, eating disorders, and the intersection of spirituality and mental health. Her books include *Mothers, Daughters, and Body Image* and *The Wisdom of Your Body.*

MELISSA MCCARTHY is a screenwriter, producer, and actor who has won two Emmy Awards and a People's Choice Award, as well as Academy Award and Golden Globe Award nominations. *The New York Times* ranked her among the 25 Greatest Actors of the 21st Century.

LAURA MCKOWEN is the bestselling author of *We Are the Luckiest: The Surprising Magic of a Sober Life* and *Push Off from Here: Nine Essential Truths to Get You Through Life (and Everything Else).* She is a speaker and founder of The Luckiest Club, a global sobriety support community.

TISH MELTON is a singer, songwriter, and multi-instrumentalist. On her debut EP, *When We're Older,* she teamed up with eleven-time Grammy Award winner Brandi Carlile. Her work has received praise from *Variety, V Magazine, FLOOD Magazine,* and *Magnet Magazine.*

RESMAA MENAKEM is a therapist and licensed clinical worker specializing in racialized trauma and communal healing. He is the founder of Justice Leadership Solutions and the Cultural Somatics Institute, and author of several books including the *New York Times* bestseller *My Grandmother's Hands.*

CHANEL MILLER is a writer and artist. Her critically acclaimed memoir, *Know My Name,* was a *New York Times* bestseller, a National Book Critics Circle Award winner, and was named a best book of 2019 by *Time, The Washington Post,* and NPR.

ALEX MORGAN is an entrepreneur, author, marketing icon, two-time FIFA Women's World Cup champion, Olympic Gold medalist, UEFA Women's Champions League champion, and NWSL champion. She is the leading founder of TOGETHXR, a company with a focus on youth and equality storytelling.

ALANIS MORISSETTE is an artist, an activist, and a seven-time Grammy Award–winning singer/songwriter/musician. She has sold over 75 million albums worldwide. Her podcast, *Conversation with Alanis Morissette,* covers psychosocial topics with a special focus on a return to wholeness.

EMILY NAGOSKI, PHD, is the award-winning author of the *New York Times* bestsellers *Come As You Are; Burnout;* and *Come Together.* She combines sex education and stress education to teach women to live with confidence and joy inside their bodies.

DR. KRISTIN NEFF earned her PhD at UC Berkeley and is now an Associate Professor in Human Development at the University of Texas at Austin. The author of the book *Self-Compassion,* she also developed an eight-week program teaching self-compassion skills called Mindful Self-Compassion.

CELESTE NG is the #1 *New York Times* bestselling author of *Everything I Never Told You* and *Little Fires Everywhere,* as well as the *New York Times* bestseller *Our Missing Hearts.* She is the recipient of fellowships from the National Endowment for the Arts and the Guggenheim Foundation.

CHANI NICHOLAS is the *New York Times* bestselling author of *You Were Born for This.* A counseling astrologer for over twenty years and founder of the viral app CHANI, she guides her community of more than 2 million monthly readers to discover and live out their life's purpose.

MORGAN HARPER NICHOLS is an artist, poet, musician, and the author of *Peace Is a Practice; All Along You Were Blooming;* and *You Are Only Just Beginning.* She has performed as a vocalist on several Grammy Award–nominated projects and written for various artists.

TIG NOTARO, named by *Rolling Stone* as one of the 50 Best Stand-Up Comics of All Time, has been nominated for Emmy, Grammy, and Screen Actors Guild awards. She cohosts the *Handsome* podcast, starred in the TV series *One Mississippi* and the documentary *Tig,* and codirected, with her wife, Stephanie Allynne, the film *Am I OK?*

FORMER FIRST LADY OF THE UNITED STATES MICHELLE OBAMA is a graduate of Princeton University and Harvard Law School. She worked in the Chicago mayor's office, at the University of Chicago, and at the University of Chicago Medical Center. She is the author of the #1 global bestseller *Becoming.*

JENNY ODELL is a multidisciplinary artist, former teacher of digital art at Stanford University, and the author of the *New York Times* bestsellers *How to Do Nothing: Resisting the Attention Economy* and *Saving Time: Discovering a Life Beyond the Clock.*

SARAH PAULSON is a film, Broadway, and television actor and director with lead roles in productions including *12 Years a Slave, Ocean's 8, American Horror Story, The People v. O. J. Simpson, Appropriate,* and *Hold Your Breath.* She has earned an Emmy Award, a Golden Globe Award, and a Tony Award.

ESTHER PEREL is a psychotherapist, *New York Times* bestselling author, and one of today's most insightful voices on modern relationships. She is a consultant for Fortune 500 companies, host of the podcast *Where Should We Begin?,* and creator of a collection of conversation prompts by the same name.

AI-JEN POO is the President of the National Domestic Workers Alliance, the Executive Director of Caring Across Generations, a Senior Advisor to Care in Action, a cofounder of SuperMajority, and a trustee of the Ford Foundation. She is an expert on caregiving, and is the author of *The Age of Dignity.*

NATALIE PORTMAN is a director, author, and actress who has won an Academy Award for Best Actress as well as two Golden Globe Awards. She is a cofounder of Angel City Football Club and an activist in support of women and girls.

CHRISTEN PRESS is a two-time World Cup champion, two-time Olympic Gold medalist, and an equal-pay pioneer. She is one of the all-time top ten goal scorers on the US Women's National Team and cofounder and co-CEO of RE—INC, which reimagines the way women are seen and experienced in sports.

CATHERINE PRICE is the author of books including *The Power of Fun* and *How to Break Up with Your Phone*. She is an award-winning health and science journalist and founder of Screen/Life Balance. She writes the *How to Feel Alive* Substack newsletter, and her TED Talk has been viewed more than five million times.

DEVON PRICE, PHD, is a social psychologist, clinical associate professor at Loyola University Chicago's School of Continuing and Professional Studies, and proud Autistic person. His books include *Unmasking Autism; Unmasking for Life; Laziness Does Not Exist;* and *Unlearning Shame.*

MEGAN RAPINOE is a two-time World Cup champion, Olympic Gold medalist, and *New York Times* bestselling author. A vocal leader on and off the pitch, she was named one of *Time*'s Most Influential People and was awarded the Presidential Medal of Freedom.

AMY RAY started the Indigo Girls with Emily Saliers, and together they have recorded sixteen albums and sold over 15 million records. They cofounded Honor the Earth, a nonprofit dedicated to the survival of sustainable Native communities, Indigenous environmental justice, and green energy solutions.

COLE ARTHUR RILEY is a writer and poet. She is the author of the *New York Times* bestsellers *This Here Flesh* and *Black Liturgies*. She is the creator of and writer of Black Liturgies, a project that integrates spiritual practice with Black emotion, Black literature, and The Black body.

AMANDA RIPLEY is an investigative journalist and cofounder of Good Conflict, a training and media company. Her book *High Conflict* chronicles how people get trapped by conflict—and how they get out. Her other books are *The Unthinkable* and *The Smartest Kids in the World,* a *New York Times* bestseller.

TRACEE ELLIS ROSS is an award-winning actress and producer and director. She has won a Golden Globe Award and nine NAACP Image Awards and was nominated for five Emmy Awards and two Critics Choice Awards. She is the founder and CEO of the haircare brand PATTERN Beauty.

ALLISON RUSSELL is a singer-songwriter and activist. In addition to eight Grammy Award nominations and a 2023 win, she has earned numerous Americana Award nominations, and won Album of the Year, as well as multiple International Folk Music and Juno awards. She made her Broadway debut as Persephone in *Hadestown*.

RABBI DANYA RUTTENBERG is an award-winning author of eight books, including *On Repentance and Repair*, which won the National Jewish Book Award and was an American Library Association Sophie Brody Honor Medal Winner. She now makes her primary writing home at LifeIsASacredText.com.

BOZOMA SAINT JOHN is a marketing executive and the author of *The Urgent Life*. She has held roles including Global CMO of Netflix, CMO of Endeavor, CBO of Uber, Head of Marketing of Apple Music & iTunes, and Head of Music and Entertainment Marketing at PepsiCo.

EMILY SALIERS started the Indigo Girls with Amy Ray, and together they have recorded sixteen albums and sold over 15 million records. They cofounded Honor the Earth, a nonprofit dedicated to the survival of sustainable Native communities, Indigenous environmental justice, and green energy solutions.

DR. LAURIE SANTOS is the Chandrika and Ranjan Tandon Professor of Psychology at Yale and former Head of Silliman College. She is an expert on the science of happiness. Her podcast, *The Happiness Lab,* launched in 2019 and has over 150 million downloads.

RICHARD C. SCHWARTZ, PHD, is the creator of the Internal Family Systems therapeutic model. His IFS Institute offers training for professionals and the general public. He is currently on the faculty of Harvard Medical School and has published five books, including *No Bad Parts*.

BRIANA SCURRY has led the US Women's National Team to two Olympic Gold medals as goalkeeper. She also carried the United States to victory in the 1999 FIFA World Cup championship and was selected to the US Women's National Team's All-Time Best XI. Scurry's bestselling memoir is *My Greatest Save.*

MAGGIE SMITH is the *New York Times* bestselling author of eight books of poetry and prose, including *You Could Make This Place Beautiful; Good Bones; Goldenrod; Keep Moving;* and *Dear Writer: Pep Talks & Practical Advice for the Creative Life.*

DR. ALEXANDRA SOLOMON is a licensed clinical psychologist with twenty-five years of experience and the founder of the Institute for Relational Self-Awareness. She teaches at Northwestern University, hosts the *Reimagining Love* podcast, and is the bestselling author of three books including *Love Every Day.*

SARAH SPAIN is a sports journalist who has earned two Emmy Awards and a Peabody Award for her more than two decades of work in the field, including as a radio and podcast host, writer, and television analyst with ESPN. She is host of the podcast *Good Game with Sarah Spain* and the author of *Runs in the Family*.

GLORIA STEINEM is a feminist writer and political activist. An organizer for peace and justice, she is focused on the shared origins of sex and race caste systems, gender roles, and child abuse as roots of violence; nonviolent conflict resolution; and cultures of Indigenous Peoples.

CHERYL STRAYED is the author of the #1 *New York Times* bestselling memoir *Wild*, which was made into an Oscar-nominated film, as well as *Tiny Beautiful Things*, which was adapted for a Hulu television show and a nationwide play. She also wrote *Brave Enough* and *Torch*, and hosted two hit podcasts.

MORI TAHERIPOUR is a faculty member at the Wharton School of UPenn, where she teaches Negotiations and Dispute Resolution. She is a cofounder of the Wharton Sports Business Initiative and the author of *Bring Yourself: How to Harness the Power of Connection to Negotiate Fearlessly*.

NEDRA GLOVER TAWWAB, MSW, LCSW, is the author of multiple *New York Times* bestsellers, including *Set Boundaries, Find Peace; Drama Free;* and *Consider This.* She is a licensed therapist, sought-after relationship expert, and founder of the group therapy practice Kaleidoscope Counseling.

SONYA RENEE TAYLOR is a *New York Times* bestselling author, world-renowned activist, award-winning artist, and founder of The Body Is Not an Apology, a global movement exploring the intersections of identity, healing, and social justice through the framework of radical self-love.

REBECCA TRAISTER is a writer-at-large for *New York* magazine and a National Magazine Award winner. She is the author of the *New York Times* bestsellers *Good and Mad* and *All the Single Ladies,* as well as the award-winning *Big Girls Don't Cry.*

EVELYN TRIBOLE, MS, RDN, is the author of ten books and a coauthor of the bestseller *Intuitive Eating,* a mind-body self-care eating framework, which has given rise to over two hundred studies to date.

CARSON TUELLER is a coach, speaker, and writer whose transformational work explores notions of freedom, identity, and self-discovery. Identifying as queer and disabled, his work began when the trajectory of his life changed—when at twenty-three years old, in the same year he came out, he was paralyzed from the chest down.

GABRIELLE UNION is an actress, executive producer, activist, entrepreneur, and the author of multiple *New York Times* bestsellers, including the Shady Baby children's series, *You Got Anything Stronger?,* and *We're Going to Need More Wine.*

OCEAN VUONG, author of the critically acclaimed poetry collection *Night Sky with Exit Wounds* and the *New York Times* bestselling novel *On Earth We're Briefly Gorgeous,* is a recipient of the 2019 MacArthur "Genius" Grant and the winner of the Whiting Award as well as the T. S. Eliot Prize.

RUBY WARRINGTON is an author, editor, and book coach, and the creator of the term "sober curious." Her *Sober Curious* book and podcast have sparked a global movement to reevaluate how we use alcohol. Her other books are *Women Without Kids; The Sober Curious Reset;* and *Material Girl, Mystical World.*

KERRY WASHINGTON is an Emmy Award–winning, SAG Award–winning, and Golden Globe–nominated actor, director, producer, and organizer. She is the *New York Times* bestselling author of *Thicker than Water,* and as Olivia Pope in *Scandal,* she became the first Black woman since 1974 to headline a network television drama.

REESE WITHERSPOON is an actress, entrepreneur, and producer. She has earned an Academy Award, an Emmy Award, and two Golden Globe Awards. She is a #1 *New York Times* bestselling author and the founder of Reese's Book Club and the media brand and content company Hello Sunshine.

JESSICA YELLIN is the founder of the Webby Award–winning independent digital media brand News Not Noise and former chief White House correspondent for CNN. She earned Emmy, Peabody, and Gracie Awards as a political correspondent for ABC, MSNBC, and CNN.

ACKNOWLEDGMENTS

Allison Schott

Liz Book

Valerie Gnaedig

Audrey Bernstein

Annie Lenon

Rachel Hochhauser

Dynna Cabana

Lauren LoGrasso and Bill Schultz

Whitney Frick and The Dial Press

Margaret Riley King

Uncle Keith

The Worldwide Pod Squad

I keep serving the tiny pretzels. I stop trying to make everything make sense. I trust that there is enough time.